Readings in
Developmental Psychology
Today

Contributing editor, Phebe Cramer

RESEARCH ASSOCIATE, INSTITUTE OF HUMAN LEARNING,
UNIVERSITY OF CALIFORNIA AT BERKELEY

Dr. Cramer chose and organized the articles appearing in this
book and wrote the overview introducing each article

Readings in
Developmental Psychology
Today

CRM BOOKS
Del Mar, California

Copyright © 1967, 1968, 1969, 1970 by
Communications/Research/Machines, Inc.

Library of Congress Catalog Card Number: 78–91136
Standard Book Number: 87665–103–1

Manufactured in the United States of America
First Printing

BF
721
.R34

Contents

Contents

V Children with Handicaps

Introduction

The focus of developmental psychology is the child—how he grows, cognitively, emotionally, morally, artistically. Several methods of studying development are represented in this collection. Some points of view conflict with others presented here, but all are recent studies by psychologists who are in the forefront of their fields.

The psychoanalytic viewpoint is presented in articles like Matthew Besdine's, while the opposite end of the psychological spectrum is represented by Israel Goldiamond's behavioristic study of moral development. Besdine draws from the psychoanalytical theory of the Oedipal conflict, and Goldiamond draws from the school of B. F. Skinner, seeing conditions of reward and punishment as keys in the growth and change of behavior. The application of behavioral principles in real life situations is recorded in articles like James Lent's. At Mimosa Cottage, an institution housing retarded girls (measured IQs 25 to 55), a token system of reinforcement (reward) was developed to train the girls in personal hygiene and other tasks aimed at allowing them to return to the community. Dr. Lent records the successes and failures of the system.

The role of education in development has also been studied across cultures—the Coles' examination of Russian nursery schools—and through the results of experiments in education—A. S. Neill's controversial theories of education as practiced at his Summerhill School and Emmanuel Bernstein's interviews of the school's alumni. On an even broader front of interests, Robert Hess dissects the development of children's political attitudes, and Rhoda Kellogg tells how children's art, usually misinterpreted by adults, shows a regular pattern of aesthetic development.

Scientific laboratory experiments on growth and change in human development are related in articles like Jerome Kagan's ("The Many Faces of Response"). He discusses a skill crucial for cognitive development—attention—in infants as young as four months. Some aspects of growth, however, cannot be studied using human subjects; animal experiments, like the continuing ones of the Harlows with primates ("The Young Monkeys") have implications for human emotional development.

Abnormal development is a vital subject for psychological investigation because of its hopeful therapeutic possibilities. Todd Risley talks about methods for improving the development of children from deprived socioeconomic backgrounds; Sidney Bijou discusses the training of the mentally retarded; and C. B. Ferster shows how autistic children can be brought back into contact with the world through the proper application of a behavioral technology.

Although the primary focus of developmental psychology is the small child, these children grow to become youths, and this generation of the nation's youth is currently the center of much attention. Richard Flacks investigated the family backgrounds of student activists and suggests that these students are not in revolt—rather, they reflect in a normal way their parents' belief that self-expression is to be preferred to self-control. Robert Kavanaugh takes another view of campus life today.

The wide-ranging, sometimes divergent, points of view in this collection have this in common: a scientific dedication to gaining understanding of man's growth in order to make human life better.

I
The Development of Cognitive Abilities in Early Childhood

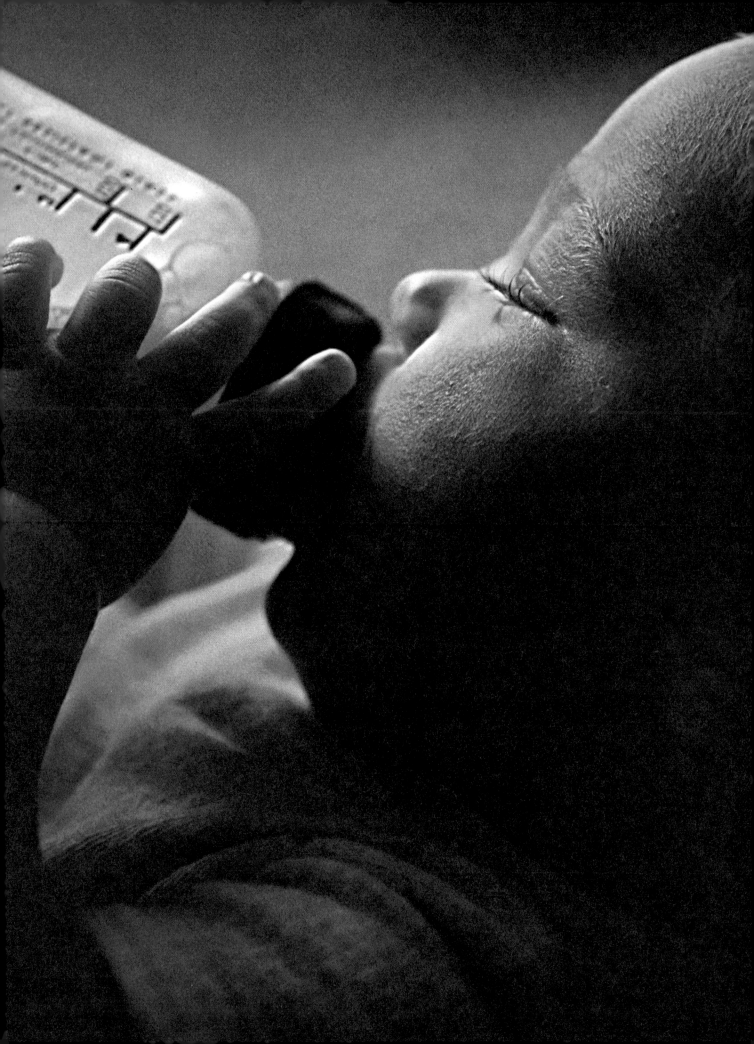

Up from Helplessness

Jerome Bruner

Rather than being a jumble of awkward, meaningless flailings, the early, seemingly simple behaviors of sucking and looking, reaching and grasping, and prelinguistic communication are bases for the development of capacities that are uniquely human and critically tied to the development of culture. In fact, the author describes the development of the infant as a crucial link between biological evolution and the creation of a human culture.

A series of observations and experimental studies shows certain consistencies across different modes of behavior. For example, the infant finds it difficult to coordinate looking with a second activity, whether sucking or grasping. Similarly, certain forms of later behavior seem to be an outgrowth of earlier reflexes. However, the author warns against automatically assuming a continuity of development between the earlier forms, like reflexive grasping or crying, and later forms, like voluntary grasping and speech. It is possible that the later forms are, in fact, quite distinct from the earlier reflexive behaviors. In an intriguing original hypothesis, Professor Bruner points out an underlying analogy in the later development of such disparate areas as motor skills, paying attention, and the use of language.

It is a working premise of mine that infant development cannot be understood without considering what it proceeds from and what it moves toward. The human infant has behind him a long process of primate evolution, which has endowed him with certain biological capacities. In front of him, in adulthood, lie not only the behavior man shares with other primates but the use of a culture that is uniquely human. Human culture, as Claude Lévi-Strauss pointed out, is based on three types of exchange, carried out through language, kinship arrangements, and economies. They are used by all men and by men alone.

From his evolutionary inheritance, then, the newborn child develops the capacity to use a culture that is exclusively human. This is not to say that evolution or culture *causes* infants to develop as they do, but merely to point out the central position that the infant in fact occupies.

It may seem that this view of infant development places a large burden on a very small pair of shoulders. The equipment and the actions at a child's disposal when he begins his enormous task look, at first glance, rudimentary. To illustrate, the research I am about to describe focuses on sucking and looking, reaching and grasping, and prelinguistic communication—little acorns indeed.

Through these activities, however, the infant develops four abilities that are crucial to the use of human culture. He develops, first, voluntary control of his behavior, a highly complex matter that requires the anticipation of an outcome, the choice of a means to achieve it, and the ability to start and sustain a chosen series of acts. Second, he gains internal control of his attention, so that he can direct it toward solutions to problems instead of following the dictates of external stimuli. Third, he learns to carry out several lines of action simultaneously. Fourth, he establishes reciprocal codes that pave the way for speech and other forms of human exchange.

Before I discuss how these abilities develop, I should point out that there are certain inequities in the young child's situation. For example, the infant's sensory equipment provides him with more information than his motor system can use: he can look at a toy well before he can reach out his hand to take it. Similarly, his motor system has more slack, more degrees of freedom for movement, than he can control. He begins to learn by cutting down drastically on his available neuromuscular freedom, developing that form of clumsiness so characteristic of human infancy. Initial learning, then, may be learning to reduce the complexity of response in order to gain control.

Sucking and Looking

The human infant is notorious for his helplessness, but one thing he can do from birth is suck. Sucking begins as a reflex action, and the infant uses it for several functions apparently preordained by evolution: nutrition, discomfort reduction, and exploration. Even on the first day of life, however, the child has some control over his sucking and can adapt it to changes in the environment. If milk is delivered to a day-old child in response to only a little pressure on the nipple, the baby will almost immediately reduce the amount of pressure he exerts.

Another thing the child can do almost as soon as he is born is look, but he cannot look and suck at the same time. The newborn infant sucks with his eyes tight shut. If he begins to look at something, he stops sucking. By two or three months of age, when a burst-and-pause sucking pattern has become established, the baby will suck in bursts and look during the pauses between. At four months, he seems able to suck and look simultaneously, but this turns out to be not quite true. Though suctioning stops when the baby looks, a mouthing of the nipple continues. This phenomenon is called place-holding. By maintaining one feature of an ongoing activity, the infant seems to remind himself to resume that activity after he has carried out a different one. His ability to suck-(look)-suck is probably part of a general decrease in the extent to which one activity preempts all others.

One way to test an infant's voluntary control is to see whether he will use an action as a means to some new end. Infants as young as one or two months old show considerable ability to use sucking for a novel purpose. They can learn to suck on pacifiers in order to bring about visual clarity—to increase the illumination of a picture in a darkened room (as in E. R. Siqueland's experiment at Brown University)—or to bring the picture into focus (as in one by Kalnins in our laboratory at Harvard).

Watching infants do this has taught us something about how they learn to coordinate the two ordinarily independent activities, sucking and looking. A six-week-old baby will suck the picture into focus, but then he starts looking and stops sucking, so that the picture drifts back out of focus again. He may try to resolve this dilemma by sucking without looking until the picture is in focus and then looking and sucking together for a brief period. As soon as he stops sucking, and the picture starts to blur, he averts his gaze. Gradually, the amount of time he can spend both sucking and looking increases. What the child seems to be learning here is not so much a specific response as a sequentially organized, adaptive *strategy* of responses.

Reaching and Grasping

Grasping, like sucking, is one of the infant's very early reflexes. By the time he is four weeks old, he automatically catches and holds an object that touches his hand. What role this reflex plays in the development of *voluntary* grasping is a matter of considerable controversy. Some psychologists see a very close relation between the two: they say that voluntary grasping develops from reflexive grasping through a purely internal process of maturational unfolding. Others see little or no relation; they say that a voluntary grasp develops only through interaction with the environment.

In my opinion, both views are false. The existence of prepared reflex machinery clearly facilitates the acquisition of voluntary motor control. For one thing, as T. E. Twitchell of Tufts Medical School has observed, voluntary control often starts with the self-evocation of a reflex, much as in the recovery pattern of hemiplegics. But to leave the matter at that ignores one crucial aspect of voluntary control: intention. Much of the infant's earliest voluntary activity is characterized by the *absence* of aid from prepared reflex mechanisms. Instead, it begins with diffuse activity that bears less resemblance to organized reflex responses than to athetoid behavior (the wormlike movements of fingers, toes, hands, and feet seen in certain brain-damaged children). Even when a reflex pattern does precede voluntary control, there is a period of diffuse, athetoid activity before voluntary control begins.

Once it has begun, how does it proceed? As I mentioned earlier, the infant has much more freedom of movement than he can control. His strategy for increasing his control is to impose severe restrictions on his freedom—to keep his elbow locked as he reaches for something, for instance—and to reduce the restrictions as he consolidates his skill within them.

The child uses this strategy as he learns to reach. If an object crosses the visual field of a month-old child, he will move his head in pursuit. As the object approaches him, he changes his level of activity, becoming quieter if he was active or more active if quiet before. Tension in the child's trunk increases. In a six-week-old, this tension takes the form of an attempt to lift the shoulders and arms, even though the child has had no experience reaching for or retrieving objects. By ten or twelve weeks, the approach of the object makes the infant pump his arms, shoulders, and head, staring at the object and working his mouth at the same time. From this position, he may launch swiping movements toward the object, keeping his hand clenched in a fist. I have seen babies blink in surprise as they execute the

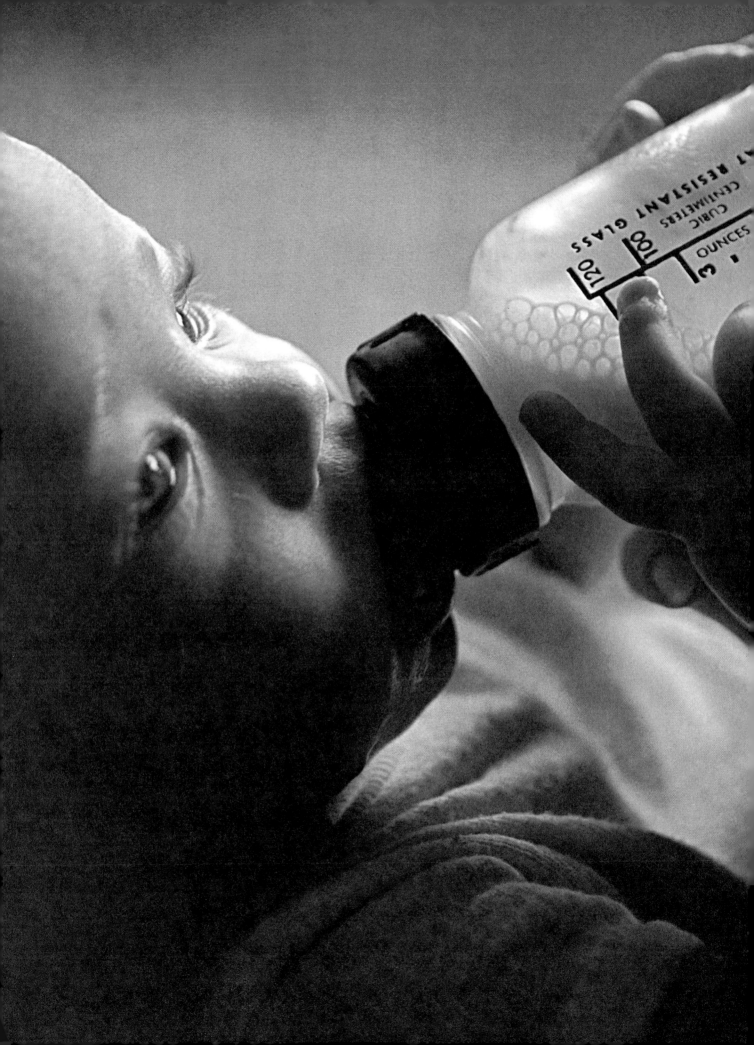

swipe, as if the "connection" between intention and act were unexpected, that is, as if a "reafference copy" of the act had not been widely distributed to supporting sensory and motor systems.

At about four months, the child has enough control to execute a less explosive, slow reach. He extends his arm toward the object, hand wide open now. His mouth and tongue are working, and his intention is clearly to put the object in his mouth. Indeed, a slow reach always follows the same sequence: activation, reach, capture, retrieval to the mouth, and mouthing. If you insert a finger for him to close on, you will stop the action.

The open mouth and wide-open hand serve a place-holding function similar to that of the rhythmic mouthing of the nipple, which reminded the younger infant to resume sucking when he had finished looking. The open mouth keeps the terminus of the act in evidence during the execution of its components; the rigidly opened hand, which is a step forward from the more primitive closed fist, maintains in exaggerated form an intention whose fulfillment has been delayed. As with so much early development, processes that later become internal, such as intention and attention, have external motor representations at first.

A word here about reaching and looking. A seven-month-old may begin a reach with visual guidance, but he is likely to execute the reach without it. When one of our seven-month-olds, Kathy, is in the midst of reaching for a cup, her eyes are closed. If a reach involves some conflict between the line of vision and the course the hand must follow (detour-reaching), the child is especially likely to look away or close his eyes as he reaches. Also, when Kathy tries to get both hands around a cup already held with one hand, she reduces degrees of freedom drastically by the simple expedient of shutting her eyes.

The Use of Tools

Kathy and her cup can show us a little about how the infant begins to develop an ability to use tools. When a seven-month-old starts to use a cup, he has no appreciation of the problem of holding the cup level as he lifts it to his mouth. By fourteen months, he solves this problem by making four to six jerky adjustments of his hands and arms as he raises the cup. By twenty-seven months, the choppiness is gone, and the child keeps the rim of the cup horizontal in a smooth movement all the way up.

This is "tool use" of a sort, but it is quite crude. Several preliminary skills are still missing. An experiment with two-year-olds, performed at Harvard by A. R. Jonckheere, suggests what they might be. We wanted to see whether two-year-olds would use strings as tools to get prizes, a task that required them to pull toward them strings with prizes at the ends in preference to other unbaited strings. They would not. They either

pulled in all the strings, or just the one closest to them.

Three things seemed to make it difficult for the children to maintain problem-solving behavior long enough to retrieve their prizes. First, they tended to play with the strings, the edge of the playpen, and so forth: they altered their goals to suit the means at hand instead of altering means to meet the requirements of a fixed goal, as problem-solving requires. The situation reminded us of the lobotomized cook who could never get to the center of the city to shop because of all the tempting things she encountered en route. Second, the children preferred to use adults as "tools" instead of the strings. They would plead for help, stretching their arms toward the prizes and crying, rather than pull in the strings by themselves. Third, the problem seemed to include too many features for the children to handle. They would look at the prizes, the strings, the bars of the playpen, and seem to be overwhelmed.

Before a child can learn to use tools, then, he must be able to adapt means to ends instead of ends to means; he must do this in preference to asking for help; and he must have enough control of his attention to keep a goal in mind while he decides how to reach it and carries through his plan. We are now at work on several studies dealing with these capacities and will be ready to report on them soon.

Codes and Language

We come now to the acquisition of codes that precede the rules of syntax. There is a sharp distinction, in the first year or so of life, between "doing" behavior and "communicating" behavior—between behavior addressed to things and behavior addressed to persons. For instance, eye contact, which is a major link between parent and child, has no counterpart in "doing" behavior, and neither do smiling, crying, and vocalization.

Either the infant has an innate predisposition to expect reciprocation of some kind to these gestures, or he acquires that expectation very quickly. When the expectation is fulfilled by an adult's response to the child's initiative, that seems to convert the child's behavior into a signal, and he proceeds to conventionalize it by stripping it down to its essential elements. For example, the quality of his crying changes, becoming less intense, once it has started to serve as an effective signal.

It is easy to fool one's self into seeing a connection between prelinguistic and linguistic behavior. What an infant does before he can speak may be quite different from what he does when he begins to speak, even within the category of verbalization itself. When a baby starts to babble, for example, he acquires front vowels and back consonants first, and back vowels and front consonants last. But when he learns to speak, the reverse is true. In speech, vowels come in from back to front, starting with /a/, and consonants from front to back, starting with /p/. As David McNeill has said, the baby completes his vocabulary of phonemes by filling in the space between the two.

It is almost surely true, however, that early interaction codes are the basis for some aspects of later communication and language. The channel for any kind of signal system, prelinguistic or linguistic, must derive from the enrichment of these interaction codes.

But the *form* the signal system takes must come from elsewhere. I believe that it constitutes a refinement of human sensorimotor skill. Indeed, the growth of phonology itself requires the refinement of a neuromuscular skill: the ability to delineate the sounds produced by the mouth as a funnel opened outward (the voiced /a/) and as a funnel opened inward (the unvoiced /p/).

I would even suggest that the modularization present in phonology, which can be described as the formation of binary oppositions, can be seen in cruder form in the development of other human skills. The way the infant moves his hands progresses from the "babble" of athetoid movement of the fingers to the sharply contrasting tight-fisted and then wide-open hand during reaching. Also, the infant's early attempts to combine syntactic structures are reminiscent of the choppy movements of his arm and hand as he first tries to keep his cup level. In both cases, there is a division of part acts into roughly equal time segments, and then the coordination of part acts into a smooth sequence.

It is even possible to conceive of a nonlinguistic origin for so essential a rule of language as predication. All languages, without exception, employ this principle, which involves dividing an event into a topic and a comment. For instance, in the statement "John is a boy," John is the topic and his boyhood is the comment on the topic.

There are two homologues in human nonlinguistic behavior that might predispose us toward language that uses predication. One of them concerns information processing; the other has to do with manipulative skill. Many cognitive theorists distinguish between focal attention and a more diffuse sort of sensing. They postulate that we organize events by synthesizing successive focal attendings. Each instance of focal attention requires the extraction of one or a few features from a more general sensory input and is, therefore, a "comment" on a "topic." Other theorists say that when we direct our attention toward something, we do so because we have noted a deviation from a "neural model" of some steady state. When deviation reaches some critical level, we attend or orient. The deviation, then, is a "comment" on the neurally represented steady state, or "topic."

The parallel between predication and the use of the hands is based on the distinction between a power or holding grip and a precision or operating grip. Many primates have no precision grip at all, though it is well developed in the great apes. But only man is predisposed to use one hand (usually the right) for the precision grip and the other for the power grip. Once specialization has begun, which is not until the infant is about a year old, the child works out many routines for holding an object with one hand and working on it with the other. This is a predicative procedure, and it probably has a profound effect on tool use and tool making.

Let me risk the speculation that the differentiation between holding and operating on what is held may follow the same rule as the differentiation between focal and diffuse attention, and that both may presage the use of topic and comment in language. The same rule may also undergird the other two systems of exchange that are unique with man, kinship and economy.

This examination of infant development has shown, I hope, that the infant's behavior is intelligent, adaptive, and flexible from the outset. The degrees of freedom the child can control at first may be few, but the strategies he devises for working within his limitations are typical of a species that plainly is different from other primates. Infancy may be a limited enterprise, but it already has within it the pattern that makes possible man's growth as a user of culture.

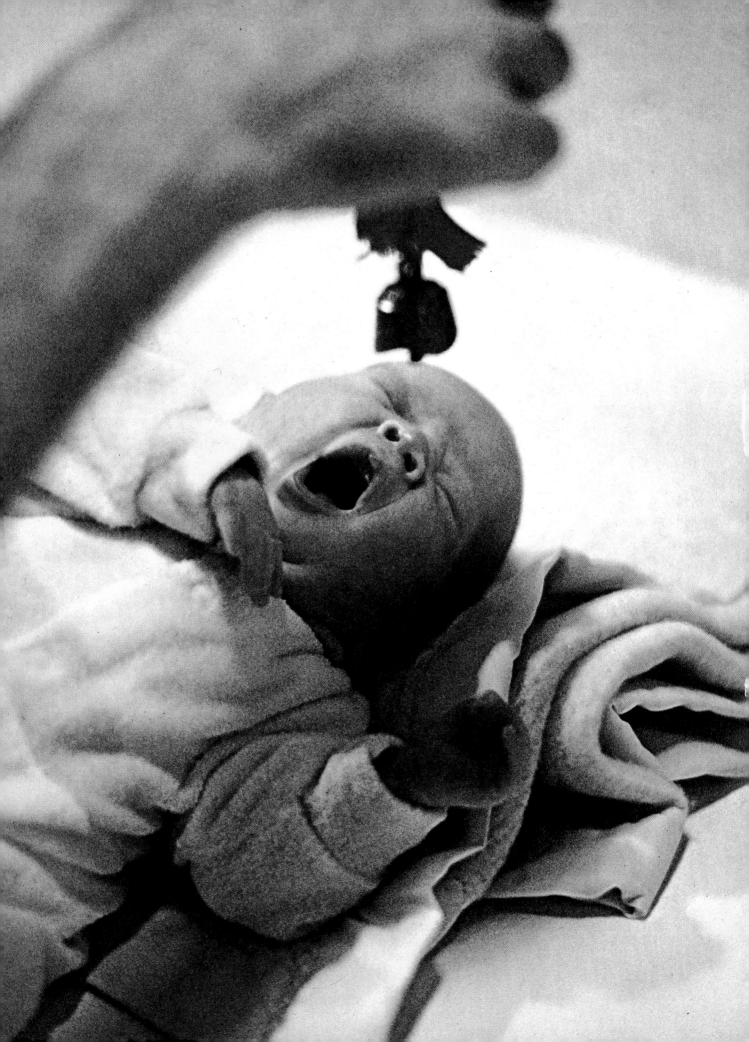

The Many Faces of Response

Jerome Kagan

How early in the infant's life is it possible to detect differences that appear to be related to his subsequent developmental level? Professor Kagan's investigations deal with perceptual attention—the ability to look at, or pay attention to, an object in the environment—a crucial building stone for later intellectual development.

He designed a series of ingenious experiments to determine exactly what the infant is looking at and why—the infant, of course, cannot tell you. The experiment results showed that perceptual attention is determined by different factors at different stages of development. During the first two months of life, infants pay attention to objects that move and that show much figure-ground contrast. During the third or fourth month, these factors become less important, and attention depends more on novelty—a slight discrepancy between a perceptual image that the infant has stored in memory and the object actually presented to him. At two years of age, this factor becomes less important, and attention is determined more by richness of associative memory.

The results show that even at four months, when perceptual attention is determined by novelty, there are clear differences among infants related to social class. Professor Kagan discusses the possible reasons and implications of these and other findings and suggests steps that might be taken to modify this class-related handicap that appears so early in life.

Each generation of psychologists seems to discover a fresh set of phenomena and a sparkling new object to study. The favorite of the academic psychologist during the opening years of this century was the adult trained to report sensations of color, light, and weight. Then, as psychology decided that learned habits and biological drives were more critical than feelings and sensations—and easier to objectify—the white rat captured the stage. The current star is the human infant, and the theme centers on his emerging mental life.

The human child has become a favorite subject for many reasons. Historical explanation always has been basic to American psychology. The belief that early learning governs later behavior stems in part from our recently strong commitment to behaviorism, and from our hope that bad habits learned early in life can be unlearned, or at least that good habits can be taught to the next generation.

The work of Harry Harlow and his colleagues with monkeys and terry-cloth mothers has intensified psychologists' concern with the effects of early experience on later behavior, as has the heavy stress that psychoanalytic theory places on the first five years of life.

Interest in the young child clearly rests on more than one base. But a major catalyst for experimentation with the infant was the work of Robert Fantz of Western Reserve University, which showed that by remarkably simple methods one could determine what a baby was looking at. To everyone's surprise, the infant turned out not to be perceptually innocent. The hope that we might be able to determine what a baby perceives led us to believe that we might begin to probe his mind.

Moreover, some psychologists believe that the infant provides a simple prototype of adult processes. After all, important discoveries about heredity in man were made by biologists who studied generations of fruit flies. The maxim that the easiest way to discover basic principles is through the study of simple forms has become a part of scientific catechism. Thus, many hope that the infant will yield some of nature's basic truths about psychological functioning.

Three primary questions currently motivate infant watching. Observation of the baby may lead to a better understanding of the laws of perceptual processing and the principles of learning. In addition, the belief—which derives from the overwhelming differences among day-old babies—that variations among young infants preview the psychological structure and behavior in the older child requires validation.

Finally, there is the "early learning" hypothesis. How

early during the first year of a child's life do different experiences begin to influence later behavior? This question was the main impetus for the research project that I shall describe.

Social Class and Attention

There are many possible approaches to the problem. The one we chose was to study infants of divergent social classes in order to determine how early and in what form the lower-class child begins to behave differently from the middle-class child, and perhaps to detect the experiences that produced the differences. It already is known that by the time children are five years old, differences from class to class are enormous.

Membership in a social class stands for a varied and complex set of experiences. One of its most predictable consequences is difference in the quality of mental performance. The lower-class child is likely to differ from the middle-class child in many aspects of intellectual functioning. If the specific areas of retardation could be diagnosed, remedial procedures could be suggested.

| OUTLINE OF THE STUDY | Our research group at Harvard has been attacking this problem through a longitudinal study of infants from lower-middle-, middle-, and upper-middle-class families. The major focus of the study was mental development. Specifically, the study was directed at differences in the rate and quality of the development of schema. (A schema can be defined as a kind of mental image or memory of an event. It is not a photographic copy but a caricature of an event—a partial representation. It is somewhat like a diagram that represents only the essential aspects of an object.)

We presented the infants in our study with facsimiles of human faces and human forms. Then we recorded how long they looked, how much they babbled, how frequently they smiled, and how their hearts reacted to these stimuli. In essence, the focus of inquiry was the attentional behavior of the infant.

Several forces control the duration of an infant's attention to a visual event, and the relative importance of each force changes during the first two years of life. For the first six to nine weeks, the infant maintains long spans of attention to stimuli that move and to stimuli that contain a high degree of physical or black-and-white contrast. Newborn infants tend to focus their eyes on the apex of a black triangle against a white background rather than on the center; that is, they focus on the border between the black triangle and the white background, which is where the physical contrast between light and dark is greatest.

The infant's initial study of the environment is directed by an unlearned preference, but this force soon gives way to a second that is dependent upon learning. Before the infant is four months old, the length of time he watches an object is governed by the degree to which what he is watching differs from an internal schema that he has now acquired.

Stimuli that resemble or are not very different from the infant's schema will attract and maintain his attention with the greatest intensity. Stimuli that are almost identical to or ones that have no relation to his schema will hold his attention for a much shorter time. It is not clear why this is true, but it may be that the sustained attention reflects the infant's attempt to match the somewhat novel event to his schema—an effort to assimilate or to understand it.

A third principle that governs early attention involves the nests of associations to particular objects and events built up during the child's first two years. During this period, he learns collections of reactions to objects. A two-year-old often labels and describes familiar objects in his environment. "Look at the cat," he says. "Look at the doggie eating," or "Baby is crawling out the door."

The child's attention often remains riveted on an event while a chain of associations is expressed. Since the child does not learn complex nests of symbolic associations until the second year, this factor would not be expected to exert a strong influence on attention until that time.

Each of these three processes—physical contrast, discrepancy between event and schema, and rehearsal of acquired associations—emerges at different times in the child's development, but each is always operative at least to some extent. It is reasonable to assume that these factors join together to affect attention. An event that presents high physical contrast, that differs somewhat from the infant's schema, and that elicits long nests of associations will hold his attention longest. Perhaps this is why the television commercial can capture the child's attention so effectively.

The data from our study lend support to this assumption. We studied 160 first-born Caucasian infants, from families with different social-class backgrounds. In the lower-middle-class group, one or both parents had failed to finish high school, and the fathers were employed as unskilled laborers. In the middle-class families both parents had finished high school and some had attended college; the fathers were either white-collar workers or skilled laborers. In the upper-middle-class group, both parents were college graduates and some had graduate training; the fathers were employed in professional or executive jobs.

We observed the infants in the laboratory at 4, 8, 13, and 27 months of age. To date, all of them have been studied at 4, 8, and 13 months. Half have been assessed at 27 months. Mothers and children also were observed at home when the children were 4 and 27 months old.

Each time the infants came to the laboratory, we showed them a set of three-dimensional, flesh-colored clay faces (see Figure 1). The 4-month-old infants were placed on their backs in cribs, and the masks were

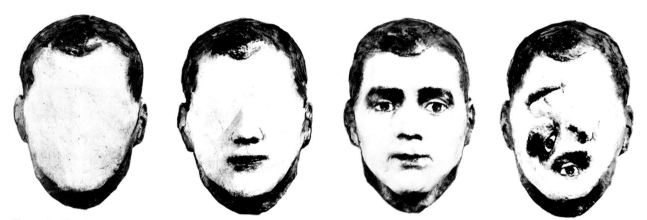

Figure 1. Clay faces used to test attention of infants from 4 to 27 months old.

presented above them. The older babies sat in high-chairs that faced a screen, while their mothers sat beside them. Each face was displayed on the screen for 30 seconds at a time; then the field was blank for 15 seconds before the next face appeared. The child saw each mask on four separate occasions, and the four masks were presented in random order. During each episode we recorded the length of the child's fixation on the face, his vocalizations, smiling, fretting or crying, and changes in his heart rate.

| DURATION OF FIXATION | One index of attention is the duration of an infant's fixation on the mask. The fixation times were highest at 4 months, dropped dramatically at 8 and 13 months, and then began to rise again at 27 months, a pattern consistent with the varying influences on early attention already discussed. Contrast is the major factor governing attention at 4 months, and discrepancy is most important for 8-month-olds. At 4 months, the masks are very different from the child's schema of a human face, while at 8 months and 13 months his schema of a face is so well formed that discrepancy is not so great.

Two of the masks had eyes. Since the eyes provided physical contrast, 4-month-old infants watched these masks longer than they did the two masks without eyes. But contrast is subordinate to discrepancy at 8 and 13 months of age. Thus the presence of eyes becomes less important at the older ages; by the time the child is 13 months old, the presence of eyes has no effect at all.

The richness of associations affects the length of time a child will study objects when he is 27 months old, but its effect is weaker at the younger ages. At 27 months, fixations were longest to the disarranged face; the richness of associations acted together with schema discrepancy to lengthen the attentional span.

Support for this conclusion comes from a related investigation. Gordon Finley, now at the University of British Columbia, has shown chromatic paintings of facial stimuli to 1-, 2-, and 3-year-old middle-class children in Cambridge and to peasant Mayan Indian children living in the Yucatan Peninsula of southeastern Mexico (see Figure 2). At all three ages, the American children showed longer fixation times than the Mayan children, and at 2 and 3 years of age the disarranged face elicited longer fixation times for both groups of children than did the regular faces (see Figure 3).

At both 2 and 3 years of age the American children vocalized much more to the masks than the Mayan children did. The American 3-year-olds talked to the faces for an average of 10 seconds; the Mayan children talked for only 3 seconds. This suggests that the longer fixation times of the American children were accompanied by rehearsal of associations to the faces.

Social-class differences in attentiveness emerge clearly during the first year of life, but the time at which they appear depends on the particular response studied. With infants of 4, 8, and 13 months, the association between social class and fixation times became stronger with age, and it was always higher for girls than for boys (see Figure 4). One group of infants was tested at 4, 8, and 13 months. The stimuli seen first at 4 and 8 months were four human faces. At 13 months, the first stimuli seen were four human forms (see Figure 5). The relation to social class was low at 4 months, moderate at 8 months for girls but low for boys, and high for both sexes at 13 months but higher for girls than for boys.

Social Class and Gender Differences

The stronger association between social class and duration of fixation for girls has two possible interpretations. Perhaps girls are biologically more homogeneous at birth than boys are, and perhaps this means that differential experience in the world is more faithfully reflected in the behavior of girls. That is, if girls differ from each other less than boys at birth, we might expect

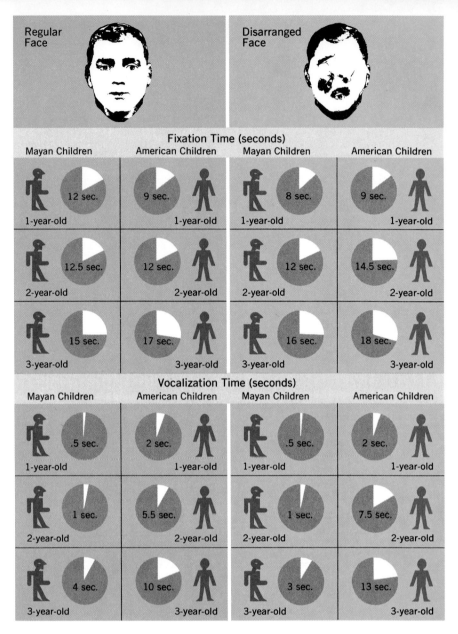

Figure 2. Differences between Mayan and American children's responses to paintings of regular and disarranged human faces.

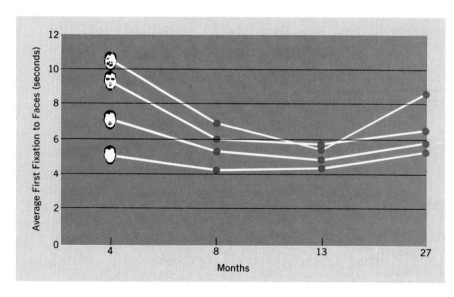

Figure 3. Changes in length of fixation time with infants' age. The different spans correspond to known influences on early attention.

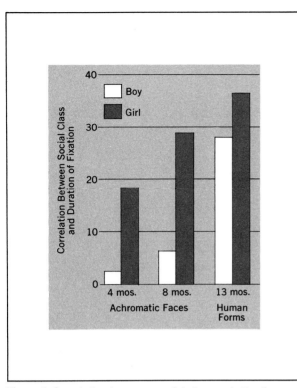

Figure 4. Correlation between social class and attentiveness for girls and boys.

Figure 5. The natural and disarranged human forms used to test the attention of 13-month-olds of different social-class backgrounds.

a more consistent relation in girls between specific experiences that are presumed to promote attention and subsequent attentive behavior.

Consider the following analogy: Two hands are placed separately on two pieces of clay, each piece of clay representing an infant. One piece of clay is of uniform softness and pliability; the other is lumpy, and varies in pliability. If the two hands come down on the two pieces of clay with the same force, each makes a different impression. The homogeneous clay reflects more faithfully the force that was imposed on it than does the clay with variable pliability.

An alternative interpretation is not inconsistent with the first, but it requires no biological assumptions. It assumes instead that social class has a stronger influence on the way mothers treat their daughters than on the way they treat their sons. Observation of some of our 4-month-old children in their homes supports this idea. Middle-class mothers talked substantially more to their daughters than lower-class mothers did; this difference was not present between lower- and middle-class mothers of sons. The longer fixation times at 8 and 13 months by the daughters of well-educated mothers may be a function, in part, of the greater face-to-face stimulation that the child may receive. Longer face-to-face contact may cause the child to show longer fixation times not only to interesting facial stimuli but perhaps to all classes of interesting events.

A study by Judith Rubenstein, of the National Insti-

tute of Mental Health, supports this argument. On two occasions she visited the homes of 44 Caucasian babies 5 months old and observed the behavior of their mothers. The mothers were classified as high-attentive, medium-attentive, or low-attentive, depending upon the number of times they looked at, touched, held, or talked to their babies.

The babies with highly attentive mothers spent longer times studying and manipulating a novel stimulus than did babies of least attentive mothers. It was as if the close reciprocal play experienced by the babies with highly attentive mothers established their interest in long explorations of interesting events.

Attention and Heart Deceleration

The use of a decrease in heart rate to assess processes related to attention has a short but interesting history. One reason cardiac deceleration was not used earlier to measure attentional reactions can be traced to general arousal theory. This theory implies that when an organism is "tense" about anything—fear, sexual passion, or intense attention—it will show autonomic reaction patterns that reflect internal arousal. That is, among other things, it should show an *increase* in heart rate. Thus investigators did not search for *decreases* in heart rate in response to episodes that involved attention, and they often did not know how to interpret them when such did appear.

Then John and Beatrice Lacey of the Fels Research Institute demonstrated clearly that cardiac deceleration was a dominant reaction when an organism attended to external events. Once a relation between cardiac deceleration and attention to external events had been established in adults, it became useful with young children, who cannot tell you what they perceive.

In a recent study, Robert McCall of the University of North Carolina and I showed that an infant was likely to show a cardiac deceleration when the stimulus was moderately discrepant from an existing schema—when the event surprised the child, but not too much.

Bearing this hypothesis in mind, let us turn to the social-class differences noted in our study. The differences in cardiac deceleration between the lower- and upper-middle-class children in response to the clay faces were largest at 4 months, and statistically significant. The differences were smaller at 8 months and minimal at 13 months (see Figure 6). Thus the relation between social class and an attentive reaction to the faces increased with age for fixation time, but it diminished with age for cardiac deceleration.

The relatively large difference between classes on cardiac deceleration at 4 months is to be expected if we view cardiac deceleration as most likely to occur when the infant is surprised by a stimulus that is a bit discrepant from his schema. If the lower-class child had a poorer schema for a human face, then these three-dimensional clay faces, particularly the blank faces, would bear minimal resemblance to his schema. A related point here is that, at 4 months of age, not one lower-class boy smiled at the blank face, whereas 22 percent of the middle-class boys did. The smiles can be interpreted as signs of recognition, indicating some perception of similarity between the blank face and the child's schema for a face.

The absence of large cardiac decelerations at 13 months suggests that the faces were not surprising to these infants. However, neither large decelerations nor class differences in deceleration should be expected at that age. The long fixation times shown by upper-middle-class children at 13 months are a result of rich nests of associations. The less rich associations of the lower-class child lead to shorter fixation times.

Social Class and Play Behavior

Class differences in infant behavior show up not only in the laboratory but in the playroom as well. At 8 and 13 months, the children were brought with mothers into a small room containing a variety of toys—a brightly colored wooden bug, a red plastic dog, a pail, a set of wooden blocks, a wooden mallet, a pegboard, a shaft of plastic quoits, a toy lawn mower, and a furry dog.

We recorded the number of changes of activities that each child made within the free-play period—that is, the number of times the child changed his active attention from one toy to another. The number of changes decreased in lower-class children between 8 and 13 months, but it increased in middle- and upper-middle-class infants (see Figure 7).

These differences are interpreted to mean that the upper-middle-class children had a richer response repertoire at 13 months and thus did not tire of the toys as quickly as the lower-middle-class children did. This interpretation is congruent with the longer fixation times displayed in the laboratory by upper-middle-class children at 13 months. As with fixation time, the increase in the number of activity changes during play between 8 and 13 months was more striking for girls than for boys, paralleling the greater effect of social class on fixation time for girls.

Differences in the behavior of infants from divergent

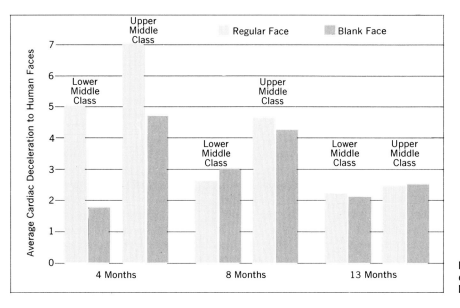

Figure 6. Differences in heart-deceleration reaction to stimuli by age and social class.

classes appear to emerge as early as the first year of life and in an expected direction. By the time the child is three years old, the differences are even more obvious. Lower-class children have a limited vocabulary, they speak less intelligibly, and they seem to be less involved in problem solving.

Our data suggest that these later differences may have their roots in the first-year period. It seems reasonable to begin educational procedures with lower-class mothers at this time in order to persuade them that the child learns schema for his environment from the first weeks on. The effect of educating mothers at a time when their children are experiencing rapid mental growth might help the infant, and it also might increase the emotional involvement of the mother with her child. Ultimately, it might facilitate the child's formation of those motives and standards during the preschool years that have such an important bearing on later development.

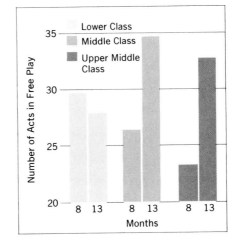

Figure 7. Differences in free-play activities by age and social class.

The Mystery of the Prelogical Child

Joachim F. Wohlwill

How a child comes to develop the rational mode of reasoning we associate with adult thinking has been a subject of controversy since the pioneering work of Jean Piaget. Piaget studied how children develop conservation—the idea that such basic attributes as the amount or weight or volume of an object do not change simply because the location or position of the object is changed. The young child does not have this capacity for conservation. He is misled by appearances and makes errors because he pays attention only to the more salient cues, ignoring the less dominant but compensatory perceptual factors. When the child attains conservation, he is ready to enter a qualitatively new stage of mental development, which Piaget terms the stage of "concrete operations." Piaget's postulation that the emergence of this new mental stage occurs spontaneously, relatively uninfluenced by teaching or experience, has been hotly debated by other investigators; however, efforts to demonstrate that conservation can be taught directly have been largely unsuccessful.

Professor Wohlwill suggests an alternative way in which experience may be important in developing conservation. He hypothesizes that through experience the child develops a conceptual attitude—for example, regarding weight—that enables him, when asked a conservation question, to ignore the misleading perceptual cues and to focus on the relevant conceptual features. He expresses considerable optimism that appropriate experiences during the primary-school years can enhance the development of logical thinking in children.

A five-year-old girl, Mary, has been taken out of her kindergarten class to participate in a psychological experiment. She is seated in front of a table on which two brightly colored necklaces lie side by side; they are of equal length, and their ends are neatly aligned. "Let's pretend that the blue one is yours," the psychologist tells her, "and the red one is mine. Who do you think has the longer necklace, you or me?" Mary, slightly puzzled, replies with conviction, "We both do!"—her way of asserting that the two lengths are equal. "That's right, but watch carefully," says the experimenter as she picks up her own necklace and forms a circle out of it. "Now tell me, Mary, whose necklace is longer, or is mine still just as long as yours?" Mary stretches out her arms to illustrate length and beams: "Mine is longest! You made yours into a ring, and mine is all *this* long."

In schools, psychological laboratories, and child-study centers across the country and throughout the world, children are participating in such experiments in our attempts to answer one of the most difficult and puzzling questions about child development: How does the uniquely human capacity for logical thought develop? How does the child's thinking evolve from a prelogical stage to one defined by the rules of adult logic? Children are being asked questions about lengths, weights, amounts, and numbers, and about space, time, and probability to see if they use a type of reasoning qualitatively different from that used by adults, or if children —naive realists that they are—place undue trust in appearances.

By the time she is six or seven, Mary will know that the length of a string of beads is conserved—that is, that its length will not change even if its longness disappears when both ends are joined in a circle. How does she gain the concept of length as a dimension so that she ignores the perceptual cues presented by changes in shape? Does understanding of dimension, class, probability, and the like come from a natural process of maturation or from extensive teaching and experience? A generation ago the child mind was pictured either as an empty shell that gradually fills with knowledge picked up piece by piece from the environment, or as an adult-mind-in-miniature that grows to its full size as the child develops. Today, many psychologists believe that neither view is correct. Instead, they see a structured mind, internally consistent yet externally illogical—a kind of Alice-in-Wonderland world where lengths, weights, and distances have as much constancy as the shape of Silly Putty.

This new picture has aroused widespread and vigorous debate not only among child psychologists but also among educators because it raises a host of questions about our understanding of mental processes in general and about child development in particular. Do we develop in specific stages on our way to adult reasoning? Is this development "preset," as is a child's physical growth, or can it be speeded up by teaching and experience? If so, by what methods of teaching and by what kinds of experiences? Since what we call intelligence involves to a large extent conceptual thinking, our inquiry holds important implications for our understanding of this much-debated subject.

Jean Piaget—Explorer of a New World

The current concern with the conceptual world of childhood and with the child's mode of reasoning has been inspired very largely by the work of Jean Piaget at the Institut Jean-Jacques Rousseau in Geneva, Switzerland. During the past thirty years, Piaget and his collaborators have mapped out, step by step and book by book, the dimensions of the curious and fascinating world that exists in the child's mind.

Let us sit in on one of Piaget's experiments. On the table in front of Johnny, a typical five-year-old, are two glasses identical in size and shape. Piaget's glass is half full of orange soda and Johnny's glass is half full of lemonade. Piaget puts a tall, thin glass on the table and

pours Johnny's lemonade into it. "Now who has more to drink, you or me?" the famous experimenter asks the five-year-old. "I have," Johnny says. "There's more lemonade in mine because it's higher in the glass." The five-year-old is convinced that he has more lemonade in his new glass even when he is asked: "Are you sure it just doesn't look as though there is more?" Piaget points out that his own glass is wider than Johnny's new glass, but the child replies, "Yes, but this one goes way up to *here*, so there's more." Pointing to the original lemonade container, the experimenter then asks: "Suppose we pour your lemonade back into the glass it came from—then what?" Johnny remains firm: "There would still be more lemonade."

The responses of Lonny, a typical six-year-old, are interestingly different. When the lemonade is poured into the taller, narrower glass and Piaget asks, "Do we both have the same amount to drink?" Lonny, on thinking it over, says, "Well, no." Asked to explain why, he says, "Your glass is bigger." But he becomes confused when the experimenter points out that the new glass is taller: "I guess there's more lemonade in the tall glass." Piaget asks, "Suppose we poured your lemonade back into the glass it came from?" Shades of Alice in Wonderland, the answer is, "Then we'd have the same amount to drink."

But now here is Ronny, a year older than Lonny. When the lemonade is poured into the narrow glass, Ronny is sure that there is still the same amount of lemonade as there was before. The conversation goes this way:

"How do you know it is still the same?"
"Well, it was the same before."
"But isn't this new glass higher?"
"Yes, but the old glass is wider."

What do these three tests tell us? Five-year-old Johnny's insistence that there is more to drink in the tall, narrow glass comes from his preoccupation with the most salient fact about the liquids—the difference in their heights. He blithely ignores the difference in the widths of the two glasses. Six-year-old Lonny shows some confusion. He seems to recognize that both the height of the liquid and the width of the glasses must be taken into account, but he can focus only on one aspect of the situation at a time. He recognizes, however, that if the lemonade is poured back into its original container, equality will be restored. But seven-year-old Ronny has no doubts. He *knows* the amount of liquid remains the same because he understands the compensatory relationship between height and width; he understands the concept of conservation of amount.

The Idea of Logical Necessity

Ronny's *understanding* is the critical point for Piaget. It is not merely that Ronny, at seven, can simultaneously perceive both the height and the width of the con-

tainers, but also that he can understand the inverse relationship between the two dimensions and can thus recognize that conservation of amount is a logical necessity. Some children may express this recognition without referring to dimensions at all: "You only poured my lemonade into that glass; it's still just as much." Or, "Well, it's the same as it was before; you haven't given me any more lemonade."

The conservation of amount—which Ronny understands at seven—is but one of a set of dimensions for which children acquire the concept of conservation at different ages. The more important of the "conservations" and the ages at which children, on the average, first show understanding of them, are the following:

Conservation of number (6–7 years): The number of elements in a collection remains unchanged, regardless of how the elements are displaced or spatially rearranged.

Conservation of substance (7–8 years): The amount of a deformable substance such as dough, soft clay, or liquid remains unchanged, regardless of how its shape is altered (as in transforming a ball of clay into a long, narrow snake).

Conservation of length (7–8 years): The length of a line or an object remains unchanged, regardless of how it is displaced in space or how its shape is altered.

Conservation of area (8–9 years): The total amount of surface covered by a set of plane figures (such as small squares) remains unchanged, in spite of rearranging positions of the figures.

Conservation of weight (9–10 years): The weight of an object remains unchanged, regardless of how its shape is altered.

Conservation of volume (14–15 years): The volume of an object (in terms of the water it displaces) remains unchanged, regardless of changes in its shape.

It must be emphasized that the ages given above are only gross averages: first, because children vary considerably in the rate at which their thinking develops, and second, because their recognition of the concept depends to a certain extent on the way the problem is presented. For example, children may recognize that the number of checkers in a row remains unchanged when the length of the row is expanded but fail to recognize it when the checkers are stacked in a pile.

The Stage of Concrete Operations

The responses of young children to tests such as those I have described give us a fascinating glimpse into processes that we, as adults, take so much for granted that they scarcely seem to involve thinking at all. But what is the significance of the conservation problem for an understanding of mental development? Piaget holds that the attainment of conservation points to the formation of a new stage in the child's mental development, the stage of concrete operations. This stage is manifested by conservation, and in a variety of other ways that attest to a new mode of reasoning.

For example, if children who have not yet reached the stage of concrete operations are presented with a set of pictures comprised of seven dogs and three horses and are asked, "How many animals are there?" they will readily answer, "Ten." They are quite able to recognize that both the subsets—dogs and horses—are part of a total set—animals. But if asked, "Are there more dogs or more animals?" these "preoperational" children will maintain there are more dogs. They translate the question into one involving a comparison of majority to minority subsets and have difficulty in comparing the elements of a single subset with those of the total set.

For Piaget this indicates that these children as yet lack mental structure corresponding to the logical operation of adding classes—or to use modern jargon, they are not "programmed" to carry out this operation.

The various manifestations of the stage of concrete operations do not necessarily appear at the same time. As we saw, concepts of conservation are attained for various dimensions at different age levels, and one concept may consistently lag behind another closely related concept. Suppose we present a child with two balls of modeling clay, identical in appearance and weight. Let us flatten one of the balls and roll it out into the form of a sausage. Now we will ask the conservation question for two different dimensions, *substance*—"Is there still as much clay in the ball as in the sausage?"—and *weight*—"Does the ball still weigh as much as the sausage?" The same child often will give opposite answers to these questions, and in such cases the child almost invariably asserts conservation for substance while denying it for weight. Thus it appears that the mode of reasoning involved in recognizing conservation of substance precedes that for weight.

The Young Child: Prelogical or Merely Naive?

Piaget holds, first, that these phenomena represent qualitative developmental changes in the child's mode of thinking, and second, that they are largely spontaneous and occur independently of teaching or of specific experiences. His views have aroused controversy as vigorous and at times as heated as did the views of Freud. Piaget's descriptions of the phenomena themselves—the diverse ways in which children respond to conceptual tasks—have been on the whole verified and accepted as essentially correct. The controversy rages over the explanation for them. Can the young child's lack of conservation be explained as resulting from a qualitatively different mode of reasoning, characteristic of the preoperational stage? Or is it merely the result of a naive trust in perceptual cues, combined with a strong tendency to respond to the most obvious, or perceptually salient, aspect of a situation?

For example, the sight of liquid rising in a narrow glass to a height well above that of the shorter, wider glass from which it came conveys a compelling impression of difference in quantity. It is easy to lose sight of the compensating difference in the width of the two glasses. Moreover, in the child's everyday life, glasses tend to be fairly similar in size; thus the height of liquid in a glass is a reasonably reliable index to its amount. There is indeed some evidence to support naiveté as an explanation. Studies carried out at Harvard suggest that children who initially lack the notion of conservation can recognize it if the misleading perceptual cues are screened out—that is, if the child cannot see the level of liquid as it is poured into the new container. It must be said, however, that other investigators who replicated this experiment did not obtain similar results.

Martin Braine of Walter Reed Medical Center conducted experiments using the ring-segmented illusion (see Figure 1) that showed that children can learn to resist perceptual cues when they are induced to differentiate between appearance and fact. Two shapes, A and B, are first superimposed so that the child can see that B is bigger. A is then placed above B; the child now will assert that A both looks bigger and really is bigger. As a result of a series of such problems in which the experimenter corrects all erroneous responses, the child will learn to pick B as really bigger than A, in the face of the contrary evidence of the senses.

Figure 1. The ring-segmented illusion.

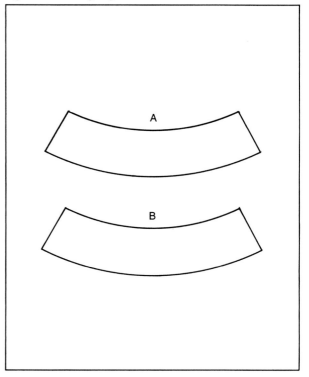

These experiments suggest that the child is inclined to respond naively to perceptual clues, but is this really the whole truth? In collaboration with a student, Michael Katz, I recently carried out the following experiment on the class-inclusion (set-subset) problem described earlier. Instead of presenting pictures of animals, we asked five- and six-year-old children, "Suppose that on a farm there are seven dogs and three horses. Are there more dogs or more animals?" Lo and behold, when the problem was presented in purely verbal form, avoiding perceptual cues, many of the children did consistently better than they did when asked to solve the problem on the basis of pictures.

On the face of it, this finding is the reverse of what might be expected. It is generally considered that at this age children's thinking is highly concrete, making it difficult for them to deal with purely hypothetical situations. However, it may be that the children did better when the problem was presented verbally because the pictures offered perceptual cues that strongly impelled the children to compare the two subsets. This explanation is in line with the view that children have difficulty with such tasks not because their reasoning is faulty but simply because they focus on the compelling aspects of appearance.

Nevertheless, further data uncovered in our studies seem to show that the interpretation is at best a gross oversimplification of the situation. When we tabulated the results for each child and compared scores on the verbal and the picture tests, we found the following: Among the large number of children who did not give any correct answers at all on the picture test, almost half also failed to give any correct answers in the verbal test. But of those who did give at least one correct answer to the picture test, 90 percent scored higher on the verbal test.

Eliminating the perceptual factor did *not* guarantee that a child could relate the subsets to the total set. These children seemed quite incapable of recognizing that an object can belong to two classes at once. Improved performance on the verbal test seems to indicate that there is an intermediary phase in the establishment of the class-inclusion concept. During this phase the perceptual cues are still dominant enough to bias the child's recognition of the concept.

Moreover, it is difficult to interpret the results of Piaget's experiment with the two balls of clay on the basis of perceptual cues alone. Why should the change in shape from sphere to sausage, with length becoming salient, bias the child toward thinking that the *weight* has changed and yet not bias the same child with respect to the *amount of substance?* The question becomes even more significant when we ask ourselves why one concept precedes another.

If we assume that conservation concepts are acquired primarily through experience, we would be led to the conclusion that weight conservation should be acquired first. The weight of an object, or more particularly the difference in weight between two objects, can be verified directly by weighing an object in one's hand; experiencing differences in the weight of objects begins in infancy. On the other hand, how does one *know* that amount of substance is conserved with change in shape? Yet the child recognizes that this "unexperienced" abstraction, amount of clay, is conserved and recognizes it well before he agrees that the readily defined, often-experienced entity, *weight*, is conserved.

Conceptual Development—Taught or Spontaneous?

The problems just discussed raise a more general question. Let us return to the types of reasoning displayed by Johnny, Lonny, and Ronny. I did not choose these names just to create a nursery-rhyme effect; I intended to suggest that the three boys could very well have been the same child at five, six, and seven years old. For, in the normal course of events, we expect Johnny to come to think as Lonny did, and Lonny, as he matures, to reason as Ronny did. Yet these changes usually occur spontaneously. In the course of play activities and everyday experience, children pour liquid from one container to another, roll balls of modeling clay into snakes, form rings with strings of beads. But five- and six-year-olds rarely ask themselves questions—or are asked questions by others—that lead them to ponder about things like the conservation of length. They are even less likely to be given direct information about questions involving conservation.

Somehow, therefore, these logical notions must be acquired indirectly, by the back door, as it were. The question is, where *is* the back door? If we assume that these seemingly spontaneous changes in mode of thinking do not occur in a vacuum, what sorts of experiences or activities can we postulate that may mediate them? What facets of his experience play a role in the child's acquisition of logical principles? It is this question that has been the subject of a great deal of concentrated discussion and research the world over.

Can such rules be taught before the child has discovered them for himself? A great deal of ingenuity has been expended to devise approaches aimed at teaching children "the logical facts of life," especially the conservations. Many such attempts have met with indifferent success, although recent studies have been more encouraging. Nevertheless, even where the zealous psychologist has succeeded in demonstrating the beneficial effect of this or that type of training, the results have been quite limited. That is, the learning has rarely been shown to have much transfer, even to similar concepts or tasks.

There is a real question, then, whether such restricted, short-term training offers sufficient conditions for establishing the basic rules of thought, which, according to Piaget, are "of the essence" in the child's mental development. At least equally important, however, is the question—do such experiences represent *necessary* conditions for the development of logical thought?

If we look at what children actually do during the years in which changes in their mode of thinking take place, the answers to our questions may not be quite so difficult to find. For example, children do gain considerable experience in counting objects, and so it does not seem unreasonable to suggest that the child comes to realize—quite implicitly—that *number* is a dimension totally independent of the perceptual aspects of a situation. But doesn't this directly contradict the suggestion that such concepts are not established through knowledge gained from experience? What I am suggesting is this: Through his experience in measuring, counting, and the like, the child may develop a *conceptual attitude* toward dimension in general. Then, confronted with a conservation-type question, he is able to ignore the perceptual cues that had previously been predominant and can respond to those aspects that, as a result of his experience, have now become dominant. Thus for Johnny, at five, the situation was dominated by a single perceptual cue—height of liquid in the glass. By the time he is seven, Ronny has, one might say, become an operationist; his concept of quantity is determined by the criteria he utilizes in measuring—for instance, as with the number of glasses of equal size that could be filled with the contents of a jar.

Ronny has developed a concept of quantity, furthermore, that may be of sufficient generality to encompass related dimensions that cannot be directly measured. This is particularly true if the dimension that is difficult to measure—for example, amount of substance—is assimilated to one that is easily measured—for example, quantity of liquid. Indeed, conservation for substance and liquid do appear at about the same time! It is interesting to note that the conservation-promoting attitude can go astray by dint of overgeneralization—a square and a circle made from the same piece of string do not have the same areas, counter to what even many adults assume.

Counting, Measuring, Ordering, Classifying

This interpretation of the way young children form logical concepts suggests that we may better understand their development by looking at activities such as counting, measuring, and ordering or seriating, for these are clearly relevant to concepts of quantitative attributes like weight, length, area, and the like. In a similar vein, classifying or sorting are relevant to understanding class and subclass relationships.

Counting, measuring, sorting, and the like are usually part of children's spontaneous, unprogrammed, everyday experience along with the more formal instruction they may receive in school. In research currently underway at Clark University, we are focusing on an intensive study of these activities and on their possible relationships to concepts like conservation and class-inclusion.

For instance, we want to see the extent to which children will arrange spontaneously a set of stimuli according to some plan or order. Children are offered a set of nine blocks with different pictures on each face, representing six classes of pictured objects—houses, birds, flowers, vehicles, stars, and dolls. Each class is subdivided according to size, color, and type; for example, there are three kinds of flowers, each pictured in one of three colors. The child is given a board divided into nine compartments in a three-by-three layout, into which he can place the blocks in whatever way he thinks they should go, though he is asked to do so in successively different ways.

We are interested in seeing how many categories the child constructs and how much internal order is displayed in each arrangement. In addition, we want to see how actively and systematically he handles the blocks (for example, in searching for a particular face). Not surprisingly, there is a close relationship between the two aspects of a child's performance: Children who receive high scores for recognition of categories and internal order generally go about their task in a much more systematic manner and manipulate the blocks more actively than the low scorers.

A perfectly consistent arrangement, showing three rows and three columns filled with pictures belonging to the same category, would earn a score of six. The five- to seven-year-olds we have studied thus far tend to be relatively unsystematic in their handling of the blocks, and lacking in consistency and order. On any one trial the median number of rows or columns filled with pictures in the same category is only 0.6. In one study carried out with a group of lower-class children from a day-care center, we found, however, that their scores could be substantially raised by intensive experience in responding to dimensions of order and to relationships of identity and difference in a set of stimuli.

Thus far, we have not found an unequivocal correlation between these measures of block-sorting behavior and conservation. However, we did find that of those children who were very poor in ordering the blocks, only 25 percent showed number conservation, whereas among the children who did somewhat better at ordering the blocks, 64 percent did show number conservation. The relation between block-sorting scores and performance on the class-inclusion task is much closer, as would be expected, since the two tasks are similar.

In other experiments we looked at children's approach to comparing and measuring lengths, heights, and distances. In general, almost no kindergartners and few first-graders showed awareness of the function of a unit of distance or a reference object. They failed to make use of a plastic ruler to measure distance. In many instances they did not even think of placing two objects side by side to see which was longer. In other words, since they had as yet no real understanding of length as a dimension, it is not surprising that many lacked conservation.

Other interesting insights were provided by experiments with the dowel board. When children are given a set of red dowels of different lengths and asked to put them any way they like into the holes of the accompanying wooden base, a majority come up with an ordered series. They are then given an identical set of blue dowels, but the holes in the accompanying base vary in depth, matching the variations in the lengths of the dowels. Thus, if they like, the children can arrange the blue dowels in a series identical to that of the red dowels or, by matching the lengths of the dowels with the depth of the holes, they can produce a series of equal height. Many children find this "problem" highly puzzling. Their behavior often becomes so disorganized and erratic that they produce no sort of order whatsoever. Of the thirty-five children we tested, twenty-five were unsuccessful. Again, comparing this kind of ordering ability with conservation-of-number ability, we found that, of the twenty-five unsuccessful children,

sixteen lacked number conservation, whereas among the ten successful children, only two lacked conservation of number.

Though our research is still in its early stages, the results thus far obtained encourage us to believe that our approach may help solve the mystery of the prelogical child and tell us something about how the conservations and other concepts manifested in the stage of concrete operations come into existence.

Our finding that children's scores could be raised by intensive experience suggests a profitable focus for instruction in the primary grades, where little attention is generally given to cultivating the child's measuring and classifying skills. Our guess is that concerted efforts to encourage and guide children's activities in this area might well pay handsome dividends. Beyond merely speeding the development of the skills themselves, an imaginative approach should provide children with a sounder, more broadly based foundation on which subsequent learning of mathematical and scientific concepts can be built.

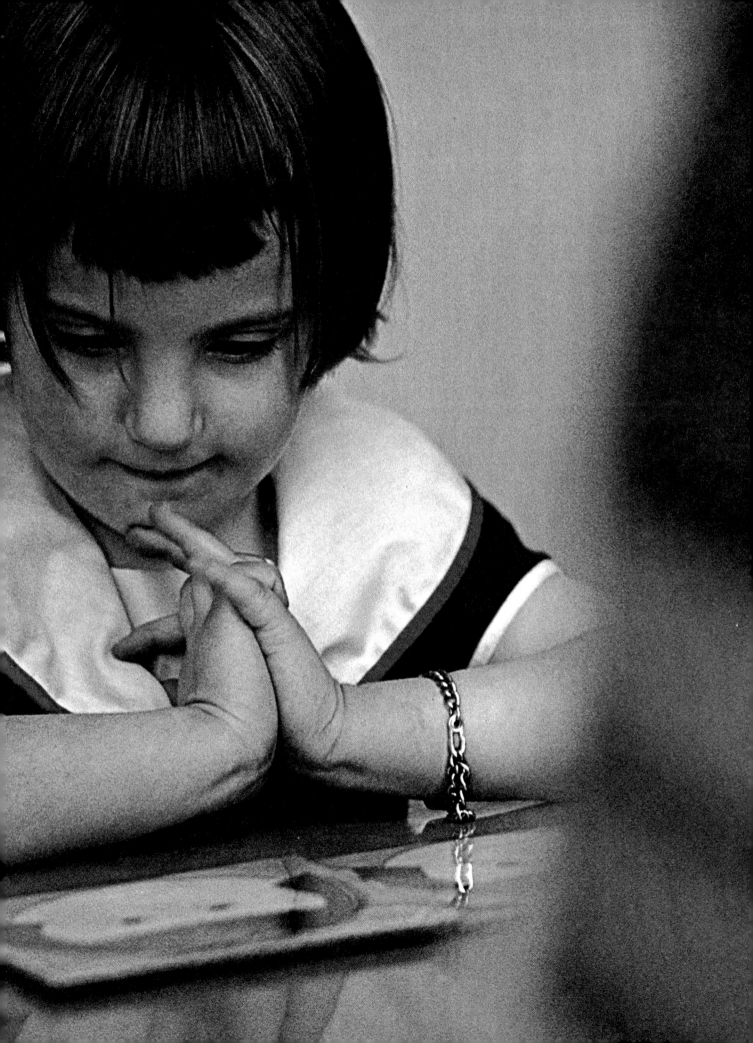

Pay Attention

Tom Trabasso

To study the processes involved in children's concept learning, experimental psychologists presented a child with two stimuli, only one of which was the correct, payoff, one. The child had to learn to discriminate between them. Careful analysis of the data gathered from these experiments revealed that there were two phases involved in this type of learning: paying attention to the relevant features of the stimulus, and associating these features with the correct response. In other words, the child must first be able to identify what it is he should respond to before he can learn to make the correct response when that stimulus appears.

Experiments have shown that the length of the attentional phase (1) is closely related to speed and capacity for learning, while there is relatively little difference among children in the time required to form the correct associations, and (2) can be modified by changing the learning situation so that the child's attention is directed to the relevant features of the discrimination problem. Professor Trabasso shows how this line of reasoning can be applied in training children to solve conservation problems.

People have been saying that everyone knows what attention is, at least since William James brought out his *Principles of Psychology*. In James' time, "attention" was generally understood to mean the process or act of admitting into the conscious mind a mere dribble of the oceans of stimuli around us—the focusing on some event, idea, or object and the simultaneous exclusion of millions of others. Attention is so understood in our own time as well, although some of us probably would be happier with a term like "stimulus selection" or something of the sort.

Although attention was a thing or concept accorded textbook status in the late nineteenth century, it was excluded as a subject of study or even comment by all the major schools that followed. For some thirty years, the dominant (behaviorist) theories of learning had nothing at all to say about attention because "everybody knows what it is."

We are now, however, witnessing a revival of interest in the operation of attentional processes in learning, a revival generated by pressures both from within and from outside of learning research. (This in itself is a fascinating tale of the *Zeitgeist*.)

Rosslyn G. Suchman (now at the University of Cali-

fornia at Berkeley) and I tested nursery-school children for their "preference" for color and form as attention-getting stimuli. Then we had the children learn to sort cards into bins on the basis of color and form. If we made color the relevant stimulus feature (the one that led to the right answer), those children who preferred color as a stimulus learned very rapidly; if color was of no use in solving, learning was very slow. That is, the ease or difficulty of learning seemed to depend on the probability that a child would attend to and use the relevant stimulus feature.

In another series of experiments, Gordon Bower (of Stanford University) and I presented college students with a problem in which they had to learn to sort out red triangles and blue circles. Color and form both were relevant; either one or the other, or both, could be used to solve. After the students had (speedily) solved the problem, we tested them for what they had learned. Clear evidence of selective attention was found. Many students had not learned triangles versus circles, or red triangles versus blue circles, but only redness versus blueness.

Thus we can say that one's preference for or attentional interest in form versus color stimuli sometimes can block or impede learning. One practical upshot of this is a warning not to use distracting colors with letters in the teaching of reading. Another is that there is some danger in enriching a learning environment— perhaps we might do better as teachers to impoverish the environment by displaying only those objects, words, or relationships that are to be learned.

From Stimulus to Concept

It has been commonly assumed that learning consists fundamentally of the association between stimulus and response. But in order for such associations to occur, it is necessary for the learner to detect a stimulus and to discriminate it from other stimuli. It is also essential that he be able to deal with similar stimuli in some generalized way. Differences and similarities among environmental events may be conveniently described in terms of simple stimulus dimensions or attributes like form (round or square) and color (red or blue). When similarities are perceived and generalized in terms of more abstract attributes, we speak of a concept—roundness, squareness, redness, and so on.

The learning of elementary concepts may be conveniently studied. A child is given a simple two-choice problem in which he is asked to find a trinket or a piece of candy under round as opposed to square objects. In such a problem, we have made form relevant; if the child is successful in making rewarded choices all the time, we say that he has demonstrated a grasp of the concept of form. To complicate matters, we can color each form red or green, producing four patterns: a red ball, a green ball, a red square, and a green square. If we make the color uncorrelated with reward, we say that color is irrelevant: the child cannot use it to solve the problem and therefore must disregard it in making his choices.

When performance on such discrimination tasks is analyzed, the data are usually reported in terms of learning curves that represent the average performance of a group of children. The typical group learning curve is a smooth arc and is negatively accelerated; that is, gains in learning become smaller as the number of trials or amount of time spent learning increases (see Figure 1a). Most investigators have tended to interpret this group curve as characteristic of the individual learner.

But Betty House and David Zeaman, of the University of Connecticut, conducted analyses that were more sensitive to the character of the *individual* learning process, and thus were among the first researchers to show the importance of attentional factors in learning. They took a group of retarded children and segregated them in terms of which day the children reached a learning goal. This amounted to separating the children into divisions of fast, moderate, and slow learners (see Figure 1b). *Backward* learning curves were then constructed for each of these groups.

A backward learning curve begins with the trial on which each child makes his last error. In Figure 1c each child thus "starts" his criterion of learning in the upper right-hand corner. His proportion of successes on trials approaching the criterion is then plotted downward to the left. The result is therefore a curve that may be read backward to examine the rate at which subjects in a relatively homogeneous grouping approach the criterion of learning, in this case zero errors.

In the analysis of the backward and grouped curves for fast, moderate, and slow learners an interesting picture emerged. All of the backward curves showed two distinct portions: an initial phase that was quite flat with performance near a chance level of success, and a second phase that showed a sharp rise from chance responding to nearly perfect performance. These phases of chance successes and a sudden shift to perfect learning were identified as two subprocesses: an *attention* phase, where the learner is viewed as searching among several possible features of the stimulus patterns until he attends to those features that are relevant, and an *association* phase, where the learner attaches correct responses to those features he has selected as relevant.

The main difference between the fast and slow learners was in the length of the initial attention phase; the association phases for both fast and slow learners were approximately the same, as is indicated by nearly identical slopes in the backward curves.

House and Zeaman's identification of two phases of learning implied that deficits in learning by children, normal or otherwise, might lie not in their intellectual inability to form associations or to solve problems but in their inability to attend to the critical features of the task. This conjecture was supported by further analyses of backward learning curves for bright and dull children, both normal and retarded. Those children in each group with higher mental age scores showed faster overall learning, but their initial phases of chance responding were short; those children of lower mental age showed considerably longer initial phases. The slopes of the association sectors of the curves, however, were virtually identical for all groups and were steep-rising.

Cues and Learning Rates

In subsequent studies, it was found that the attention phase of the learning curves (but *not* the association phase) could be shortened by many stimulus factors that are known to affect the salience of a cue.

A clear demonstration of the relationship between stimulus salience and learning speed was made by Brian Shepp of Brown University, in collaboration with Zeaman. These investigators picked, as the relevant stimulus feature in a learning problem, a difference in the size of two blocks. For one group of learners, the size difference was small; for another it was very large. When the larger size difference was used, the overall learning rate was found to be very much faster and the initial (attention) portion of the backward curve much

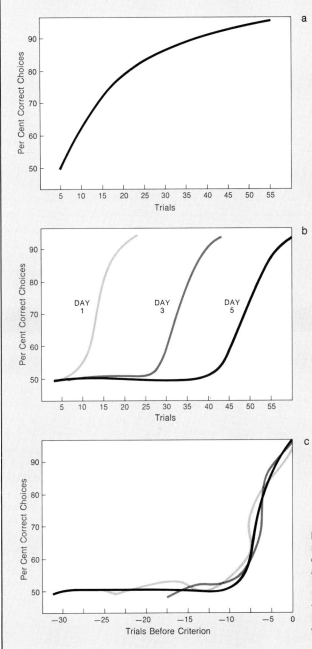

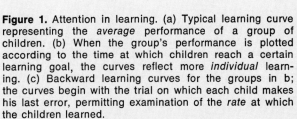

Figure 1. Attention in learning. (a) Typical learning curve representing the *average* performance of a group of children. (b) When the group's performance is plotted according to the time at which children reach a certain learning goal, the curves reflect more *individual* learning. (c) Backward learning curves for the groups in b; the curves begin with the trial on which each child makes his last error, permitting examination of the *rate* at which the children learned.

shorter. However, the slope of the association phase was not materially affected by changes in the saliency of the size difference.

Gordon Bower and I have obtained similar results with college students who learn simple classification problems involving geometric patterns. In two-choice concept-identification tasks, where the subject must learn to base his responses on a single attribute such as the color of the patterns, we have frequently found evidence for one-trial learning. The backward learning curves show long, flat initial phases at the chance level

of responding while the association phase occurs in one trial.

The reason for one-trial learning is that the associations required are trivial from the point of view of an adult; all that is needed is a single association such as: "Red patterns are alphas." Most of the "learning" in these tasks appears to consist of a search process whereby the subject selects and tries hypotheses based upon different stimulus attributes until he finally hits upon the relevant one and then solves immediately.

The overall learning rate of these problems seems to

depend upon the ease with which the subject comes to attend to and use whatever attribute the experimenter has chosen to be relevant. We can directly influence the length of the attention phase by manipulating the obviousness of the relevant features or cues. For example, we have facilitated learning by using markers, arrows, or underlined letters that direct the learners' attention to attributes; we have also slowed discovery by embedding the relevant features among several varying and irrelevant attributes.

The role that attention plays in the conceptual development of the child has been dramatically demonstrated in a recent doctoral thesis by Rochel Gelman at the University of California at Los Angeles (now at the University of Pennsylvania). Gelman was particularly interested in the development of certain abstract and logical concepts known as "conservation." To understand conservation means that one can appreciate the fact that a substance preserves certain kinds of identity despite some transformation.

We may illustrate a standard test for conservation with the familiar water-beaker problem. Here a child is first shown two beakers of water that are identical in all respects: they are of the same height and width and are filled with water to identical levels. The child is asked: "Do the jars contain the same amount of water?" After the age of three or so, the typical answer is "Yes." Then the experimenter pours the water from one jar into another jar that is taller and narrower than the first and again asks if the jars hold the same amount of water. If the child says "Yes" and gives a reasonable explanation such as, "You just changed the jars but the water is the same," then he is judged to have the concept of conservation of volume. If, however, he answers, "No, they are different because one is taller," then he "fails" to conserve. The child who does not conserve is said not to appreciate that the amount of water is invariant despite changes in the shapes of the containers. Most children under age seven fail this test and therefore do not seem to demonstrate true conservation behavior. Their erroneous explanations are typically based upon the salient perceptual changes in the jars' height and width.

Does a failure to pass these tests mean that the child is at that point incapable of understanding the concept of conservation? Do we wish to conclude, like the great Jean Piaget, for instance, that conceptual development is dependent upon a number of stages, that each stage is related to the next, and that the child must pass through each stage in turn before he shows true conservation? Piaget has insisted that the child must possess certain cognitive structures or schemata before he is able to perform the formal, logical operations involved in conservation behavior.

In analyzing the tasks used to test conservation, Gelman reasoned that perhaps children who do not conserve by these tests fail as a result of some perceptual fixation—not because they cannot understand. Perhaps

when children err, they do so because their attention—and hence their resulting decisions—are based upon perceptual changes in the width, height, or thickness of the beaker. Could one devise a procedure that would train the child to ignore irrelevant changes and to pay attention to quantities that do not change?

Gelman's experimental design was quite simple. A number of children were first given standard conservation tests on length, number, mass, and volume. All children *who failed all tests* were then given training in one or two main conditions. In an experimental group, the child learned a series of short "oddity" discriminations, where he was shown three objects, two of which were identical; his task was to choose either two that were the same or two that were different. After each choice, the child was told whether or not his choices were correct. This "reinforcement" informed the child that certain attributes of the stimuli were relevant (for example, quantity) and others (such as changes in color, size, and shape) were irrelevant. Over a two-day period, the children in the experimental group learned thirty-two six-trial problems; half of these problems involved *length* as the relevant concept and the other half involved *number*. Features like size, shape, color, proximity, arrangement, and the like were varied so that they could not be consistently used as a solution for any of the problems.

A control group underwent exactly the same training experience with one exception: no feedback as to the correctness of their responses was given. Thus the only difference between the groups was in terms of an opportunity to learn which features of the stimuli were actually relevant to the problems. After training was completed, both groups of children were given identical tests. Half the tests were for specific transfer on standard conservation tests of length and number, while the other half tested for generalization on mass and volume. It will be noted that the mass and volume concepts were not involved in the training session. Recall that before training, similar tests had shown *no* correct responding by any of the children.

After training, the children in the experimental group responded correctly to 94 percent of the length and number conservation tests while the control subjects gave 25 percent correct answers. Of greater significance was the finding that the experimental group answered correctly 62 percent of the conservation tests on mass and volume. The control group showed about 7 percent generalization to these tests. Retention tests two weeks later gave nearly identical results.

On the basis of these impressive findings, one is forced to reconsider what is meant when one says that a child lacks the metaphysical underpinnings for a certain concept, or for that matter, what one means by learning per se. In the case of conservation concepts, the usual testing procedures seem to hide or baffle rather than demonstrate a cognitive ability, and one has merely to offset perceptual interference in order to show what ability the child actually has.

The Learning Environment

A final word or two about attention and the learning environment. A series of experiments similar to those I mentioned at the beginning of this article have shown that you can pare down the initial, or attention, phase and hence speed up the overall learning rate by increasing (1) the *number* and (2) the *vividness* or saliency of relevant stimulus cues. These same experiments have shown, however, that this accelerated learning can be inefficient or eccentric. If more stimulus patterns or cues are provided than are needed to solve, they will not all be used or learned. Furthermore, what *is* learned may be learned in odd, sometimes undesirable ways. A child who distinguishes Ts from Fs because "Ts are purple," has really only learned an unfortunate association, which sooner or later will impede his reading progress.

Thus it appears that more efficient engineering of the learning environment will require the seemingly para-doxical effort to impoverish the environment by eliminating potentially distracting and irrelevant material, while at the same time enriching it by using attention-getting cues having maximum vividness and interest. As early as 1912, Montessori advocated the use of three-dimensional cutouts in the teaching of form-and-number discriminations, a technique whose efficacy has only been recognized experimentally since World War II. On the other hand, brain-injured children seem to learn to read better and faster when, for instance, the windows of their room are covered, and when the children sit before a blank wall and are exposed to a small portion of reading material through a small opening in a screen—poverty of stimuli with almost a vengeance, it would seem.

It appears certain that many of the keys to successful teaching or training will be found in the close study of the attention planes or phases of the learning process. Such study may enable us to build a more productive learning environment and perhaps allow us finally to deal more cleverly with hoary old classroom menaces like the "slow" reader.

Understanding Children's Art

Rhoda Kellogg

An analysis of an extensive number of children's scribblings has led the author to conclude that there is a meaningful consistency to be found among the "basic scribbles" of children's self-taught art—the kind they produce before they come under the influence of adults or other children. As postulated in preceding articles, there appear to be definite stages in development—in this case, of children's art. These stages are identified as reflecting concern for placement, for shape, for design, and finally for the pictorial. The child's initial concern is not with accurately representing reality but rather with creating a pleasing, esthetically balanced design. Contrary to the belief of many adults, children do not arrive at the pictorial stage by learning to copy forms that appear in nature. Rather, they learn that some of their spontaneously produced abstract designs are in fact similar to certain objects found in the world, and that adults attach names to these designs. The emphasis of adults on representation is seen as interfering with the child's further artistic development. Some additional ways in which children's art has been misunderstood are discussed.

During the last hundred years, there has been increasing interest in children's drawings and paintings. Adults flock to gallery or museum shows of children's art, delighting in its freshness and originality and in the glimpse it offers of the child's world. Moreover, ever since Freud drew attention to the ways by which repressed psychological material is overtly expressed, psychologists have used children's drawings as a means of understanding child development in general, and the problems of individual disturbed children. And for many years the ability of the child to copy simple forms or to "draw a man" has been widely used as a test of intelligence for preschool children.

My study of children's art began more than twenty years ago, primarily out of a desire to understand very young children, my favorite people. I had already read many books on psychoanalysis, among them the works of Carl Jung, who believed that mandalas, or designs based on a crossed circle, were of great human and psychological significance. When I first noticed that three-year-olds were drawing crossed circles, my interest in child art was intensified and I wanted to know what kinds of drawings preceded the crossed circle, and what kinds followed it. Thereafter, no scribblings made in the nursery schools operated by the Golden Gate Kindergarten Association in San Francisco landed in the wastebasket. Each child's dated drawings were filed, and

I began to sort a few hundred scribblings into look-alike groups.

Since then, I have seen more than a million pieces of children's art, half produced by children below the age of six and the rest by grade-school children. About a third of these works are now housed as the Rhoda Kellogg Child Art Collection at the Phoebe A. Hearst Preschool Learning Center in San Francisco, and the rest are still in storage elsewhere. More works by some 300 children between the ages of two and twelve who attend the nursery school, or the child art classes at the Center, are being collected.

To most people, "child art" calls to mind the stick figures that children draw as representations of people. Contrary to popular belief, however, the stick man is not a spontaneous product of child art. It is a figure children learn after the age of five from adults or from other children. Because there are such important differences between the work done by preschoolers and that done later, I call the former *self-taught child art*. This article will emphasize the early art, which children under six teach themselves before adults start showing them "how to draw."

For generations, adults have viewed children's scribblings as no more than the natural products of random motor activity. Most adults rate a child's drawing according to how well it represents a person or a familiar

Figure 1. Child's painting of a human figure.

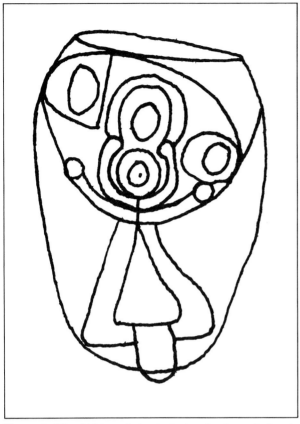

Figure 2. The hidden abstract design in the painting in Figure 1.

object. This representational approach has prevented adults from appreciating the wealth of structured, non-pictorial work that children teach themselves to produce before they begin to pictorialize.

Because most adults consider the ability to draw representationally to be an exceptional talent possessed by only a few individuals, and because almost every child possesses the capacity for scribbling, it is very difficult for us as adults to see that early scribblings can be valuable documents for understanding the origins of art. Some parents may save their children's pictorial drawings, but few save their children's scribblings. From my recent analysis of these nonpictorial, early works produced before age three, I have concluded that early scribblings are essential to understanding all forms of graphic art as well as child art.

As I studied the self-taught art work of children from all over the world, the main sequential stages of child development in art became evident. In 1955 I reported my findings for the work of three- and four-year-olds in a book, *What Children Scribble and Why*. Not until 1965, however, did I understand the work of two-year-olds; therefore the *why* of scribbling is much better explained in my new book, *Analyzing Children's Art*, published in 1969.

At this point you may ask: By what criteria can the term "art" be applied to the scribblings of two-year-olds? I answer that graphic art of whatever kind is produced by the human hand moving over a surface with a marking instrument. Any number of descriptive labels can be applied to these markings—scribblings, designs, gestalts, motifs, charts, symbols, signs, compositions, abstractions, representations, or pictures. The label depends upon who does the labeling and in what context the work is viewed.

Basic Scribbles

Every form of graphic art, no matter how complex, contains the lines found in children's work, which I call the *twenty basic scribbles*: vertical, horizontal, diagonal, circular, curving, waving or zig-zag lines, and dots (see Figure 3a). Basic scribbles can be made whether or not the eye controls the movement of the hand, for scribbles are the product of a variety of directional muscular movements that human beings make even before the age of two. Basic scribbles are not learned from adults—they are spontaneous human "events" that take place when a finger or marking instrument moves over a surface and leaves a record of the movement. Not until I had studied child art for many years did I realize that though these early scribblings are visually meaningless to adults, they are visually significant to the child who makes them.

The basic scribbles are the building blocks out of which all graphic art, pictorial and nonpictorial, is constructed. And when the child looks at his scribblings, he sees them as visual wholes or entities.

Before young children can draw the figures called a "man," a "horse," a "dog," and so forth, they will not only have scribbled, but will have constructed many abstract components and designs. I now know that children's first pictorial drawings are not early attempts to draw specific objects as the sight of those objects registers in the mind. Instead, children gradually realize that certain objects resemble their own designs and observe that adults call some of these designs "houses," "boats," "people," "flowers." Thus children learn which drawings are pictorial and which are not. Drawing "from life" comes at a much later time. All children spontaneously scribble and make designs, but adults must teach them how to "copy nature."

It is difficult for adults to appreciate and understand self-taught art because the minds of children and of adults are so different. Through years of living, adults have accumulated a store of rich associations, which children have yet to acquire. For example, when a child looks at an O he has drawn, he sees only a round form, or gestalt, but the adult may see this as a scribble, a letter, a circle, an ornament, a symbol, a sign, a wheel, a ring. . . . The famous psychologist Arnold Gesell once said that our knowledge of the child is about as reliable as a fifteenth-century map of the world. The scribblings of children can help adults gain a more reliable map.

Sequential Development in Self-taught Art

As children progress from scribbling to picture making, they go through four distinguishable stages: the Placement Stage, the Shape Stage, the Design Stage, and the Pictorial Stage.

| PLACEMENT STAGE | Even the very earliest scribblings are not placed on the paper by happenstance. Instead, most of them are spontaneously drawn on the paper in *placement patterns*, that is, with an awareness of figure and ground relationships. I have detected seventeen different placement patterns. The Spaced Border Pattern is shown below, left, and six others are shown in Figure 3b. The seventeen patterns appear by the age of two, and once developed are never lost.

| SHAPE STAGE | Placement patterns produce overall gestalts, or forms, which result from the location of the scribblings on the page. These gestalts contain implicit shapes. For example, the spaced border pattern below, right, usually implies a rectangular shape:

By age three, most children can draw these implied shapes as single-line outline forms, called *diagrams*, and have reached the Shape Stage. There are six diagrams: circles (and ovals), squares (and rectangles), triangles, crosses, Xs, and odd forms.

| DESIGN STAGE | As soon as children can draw diagrams, they almost immediately proceed to the Design Stage, in which they put these simple forms together to make structured designs. When two diagrams are united, the resulting design is called a *combine*:

and when three or more are united, the design is called an *aggregate*:

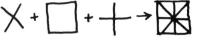

| PICTORIAL STAGE | Between the ages of four and five, most children arrive at the Pictorial Stage, in which their structured designs begin to look like objects that adults can recognize. The Pictorial Stage can be divided into two phases: the first contains *early pictorial* drawings, and the second contains *later pictorial* drawings.

The early pictorial drawings differ from the gestalts of the Design Stage in that they are suggestive of "human figures," "houses," "animals," "trees," and the like. The later pictorial drawings are more clearly defined and are easily recognized as familiar objects by adults. The later pictorial drawings do not necessarily represent a more advanced stage of artistic develop-ment; they are merely those pictorial drawings that adults recognize and approve of.

In his pictorial drawings, the child is not necessarily trying to draw representationally but is more concerned with creating esthetically satisfying structures. For example, a multiple-loop scribble (smoke) might appear more pleasing to him if it circles around a square aggregate (a house). Logical consistency does not become his concern until adults restrict his expression along lines considered to be "proper."

From Humans to Rockets

The child's first drawings of the human figure look very odd to adults; the figure is round like a ball and the arms come out of the head. The reason for this lack of likeness is that the child is not drawing persons as seen, but is modifying the mandalas and suns of the late Design Stage in order to give his familiar gestalts a new look.

Mandala is a Sanskrit word denoting a "magic circle," though crossed squares and concentric circles or squares are also mandalas. The distinguishing characteristic of a mandala is its perfect balance, and mandala balance is dominant in self-taught art. The child's mandalas are prominent in the combines and aggre-

Figure 3. The lines found in children's art. (a) The twenty basic scribbles; (b) Placement patterns; (c) Diagrams; (d) Combines; (e) Aggregates; (f) Early and late pictorial.

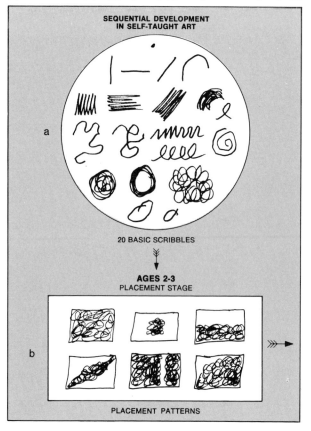

gates, and are a departure point for proceeding to draw suns, radials, and human figures. The mandala gestalt (1) suggests the sun gestalt (2), and the two of them evolve into the first human figure (3). In the first drawings of humans, the arms are attached to the head and there are markings on top to balance the legs. Later the child omits arms from his drawings, perhaps in the effort to relieve the monotony of mandala balance. But

actually almost all drawings of humans that children create before age six do fit nicely into an implied circular or oval shape, no matter what distortions of anatomy are required. This leads me to conclude that the child is not at all concerned with trying to draw his "humans" so that they look like people; he is striving for variety within a set of esthetic formulas.

Drawings of human figures are followed by drawings of animals that are only modified gestalts of humans. For example, when the ears are on top of the head, the human becomes what adults call an animal (compare drawings in top row of Figure 4).

In the same way, the "buildings" that children spontaneously draw are not attempts to depict real houses. Instead, these gestalts are interesting variations on designs made up of squares and rectangles. This applies to drawings of boats, cars, trees, airplanes, and rockets.

Before age five there are no differences between art gestalts produced by boys and girls. From then on, however, cultural influences lead them to draw different subject matter.

Is Picasso Right About Child Art?

The child's production of art gestalts collides head-on with the conception of art that adults have learned after age six and have passed on from one generation to another, according to the approved formulas of the local culture. Adults who coach children to draw real-life objects are not really being helpful; they may even be causing harm. The child's purpose is not that of drawing what he sees around him; rather, he is probably a very experienced master of self-taught art, concerned primarily with the production of esthetic combinations that are often the envy of adult artists. In fact, Picasso

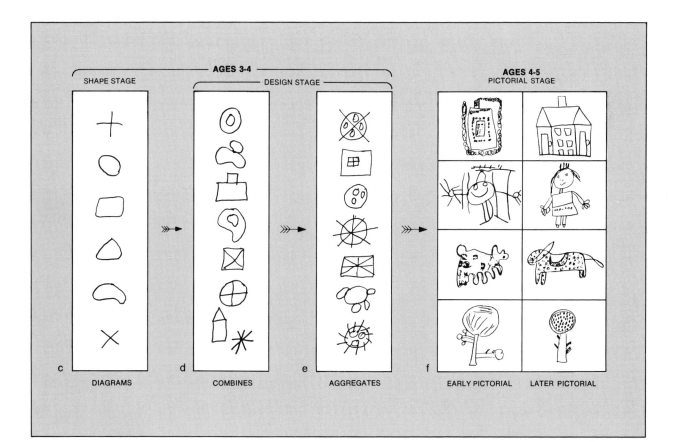

says that adults should not teach children to draw but should learn from them.

It is very difficult to convince adults that art is not essentially a matter of portraying reality. A deep appreciation of art derives from an appreciation of both the explicit and the hidden esthetic gestalts present in all art; the pictorial aspect of art is important, but it is not the ingredient that separates mundane art from great art.

Children left alone to draw what they like, without the interference of adult "guidance," usually develop a store of gestalts that enables them to reach the culminating stage of self-taught art. From there, if they are especially gifted, they may develop into great artists, unspoiled by the stenciled minds of well-meaning

adults. Few children, however, are given this opportunity, and most relinquish art after the first few years in school.

Child Art and Learning to Read

Failure to allow self-taught art to take its natural course of development after age six causes confusion in the child mind and misunderstandings between children and adults, both of which interfere with learning and discipline in school. The child whose ability to create art gestalts has been developed usually learns to read quickly and well. Since neither parents nor educators know the value of scribbling, they fail to provide a place, under proper supervision, for the very young to scribble. This is unfortunate, because scribbling and

Figure 4. Progressive changes of mandalas from scribbles to representation.

drawing develop the child's ability to perceive abstract gestalts, an ability so necessary for learning to read. The teaching of reading and writing has never been based on any awareness of the child's interest in abstract expression. Children who have been free to experiment with and produce abstract esthetic forms have already developed the mental set required for learning symbolic language.

As the child learns to read, he is expected to comprehend difficult systems of gestalt-making, each with its own order and rules: (1) the written and printed language system of the culture; (2) the simple art gestalts that teachers and parents make and that the child is supposed to copy; (3) adult art used as illustrations in books; (4) gestalts as they appear in photographs, movies, and television; and (5) gestalts as they appear in charts, graphs, diagrams, and maps.

Reading and writing primarily involve visual skills, yet prevalent teaching methods emphasize association of the spoken word with the graphic symbols for those words. I believe that teaching the alphabet and stressing phonetics may be the wrong approach. Reading can better be taught by recognizing the importance of the child's inherent gestalt-making system as it is developed in self-taught art, and then by building upon it. Allowing a child to draw what he likes for at least thirty minutes every day in school might very well free him to continue developing his capacity to perceive abstract gestalts. This would lay the groundwork for improving his reading and would improve his writing ability also, because scribbling and drawing develop the fine muscle skills required for making precise markings on paper.

Using Child Art to Test Intelligence

In our country today, drawing is widely used as the basis for measuring general intelligence in young children. These "intelligence" tests can be categorized according to the kinds of drawing abilities that they emphasize. In the Goodenough test, the child is rated by his ability to draw a man; in the Bender test, he is rated by his proficiency in copying visual gestalts; and in the Lantz test, his spontaneous art is subjectively judged by an "expert." Because we fail to understand the nature of child art, these tests are imperfect instruments of measurement.

For example, the Goodenough Draw-a-Man test, devised in 1926 and recently revised by Dale Harris, is based on such erroneous conceptions of the child mind and of child art that its use today is pure psychological ritual with no scientific validity. Scientific statistical treatment has been given to data so meager and so highly selected as to be absurd, but the human mind finds ritual comforting where knowledge is lacking. For the last forty years the intelligence of many American four-year-olds has been measured by the Goodenough test, which is "standardized" on only 119 drawings of children of that age. The test itself was devised on the basis of but 2,306 drawings, made for the most part by children of various ages who lived on the wrong side of the tracks in Perth Amboy, New Jersey. In revising the test, Harris standardized 3,000 more drawings, but his conceptions of how children should draw the parts of the body—that is, the 71 features to be scored—resemble neither anatomy nor natural child art. The use Goodenough and Harris made of child art cannot be justified on rational grounds because both of them refused to consider the esthetic components of children's drawings as being relevant.

Before a child can learn to draw from the stimulus of an adult's drawing—that is, learn to copy—he must have developed certain skills of hand-eye-brain coordination. Gesell found that few three-year-olds could copy perfect circles and squares, and he claimed that children could not draw the mandala below, left, until the age of seven. (Yet five-year-olds will commonly draw this mandala in non-test situations.) The Bender Motor Gestalt test consists of a set of tricky gestalts that the child is asked to copy but that no one would ever draw outside of a test situation. Few children or adults can complete the test perfectly. The Bender test is not a good test because it fails to take into consideration the natural development of child art. The gestalt below, center, would look wrong to any child, for the figure below, right, is the natural way to combine a square and a circle. Another gestalt might look to a child somewhat

like an awkward diagonal cross, for which a substituted graceful cross is a "failure."

Still another test based on art is the Lantz Easel Age Scale, which is standardized on 3,000 paintings of such subject matter as houses and boats—because drawings of the human figure are too complicated to rate. The test is "satisfactorily correlated" with the Goodenough test and has been given the usual statistical treatment so that it looks scientific. The ratings on the test are based on an Easel Age Score, which is said not only to measure intelligence but to measure it quantitatively. I do not see how this is possible when even adults, whose intelligence has been proved by their functioning, are not able to "draw a man," make paintings of houses, or copy designs perfectly in the Bender test. Another flaw in the test arises from the fact that children who persist in painting abstract works, called "Q" paintings, are said to be in need of help of a special psychological or medical nature. This discourages the natural development of artistic expression and may send perfectly healthy children into unnecessary clinical treatment.

A Proposed Child Art Test

I am not sure that we need more tests for children, but if we must have them they should be as accurate and as harmless as possible. A child's artistic creations could be used as the basis for assessing more general mental functioning if the usual drawbacks associated with the testing situation were eliminated. Since any child's file of drawings shows that he can waver between scribbles and suns from one day to the next (see Figure 5), it is unreasonable to suppose that the child's "intelligence" can be assessed on the basis of his performance during a short test period. Spontaneous drawings done over a period of several weeks should be examined for the presence or absence of certain gestalts considered to be "normal" at certain age levels.

In order to set up the standard against which the child's performance would be evaluated, a large number of children's works would have to be studied to determine the age range for the first appearance of particular gestalts. A frequency distribution of selected aggregates, mandalas, suns, and human figures could then be plotted as a function of age level. Any child's stage of artistic development could then be compared with the norm to determine his relative performance.

This test would be particularly useful for diagnosing mental retardation—and pseudoretardation. Often I

have been able to convince the parents of a supposedly retarded child that their child was perfectly normal in his art development and hence probably perfectly normal in intelligence.

Universals and Universities

Parents, educators, and psychologists are not the only adults who fail to understand the significance of the origins of art in childhood. Art historians, anthropologists, and archeologists, who encounter the motifs of self-taught art in their studies of primitive and past cultures, usually view these gestalts as products of the adult mind, rich in symbolic meaning and characteristic of local cultures. For example, Giedion, the noted art

Figure 5. Each pair of drawings compares one child's "best" and "poorest" representations of a human, both done within the same week.

historian, interprets triangular diagrams as vulvas and fertility symbols; and Margaret Mead believes that "art comes from art"—that each generation teaches its favorite gestalts to the next generation. A better understanding of these ancient gestalts could be achieved through a greater knowledge of the universal nature of self-taught child art.

Human beings throughout the world, from Paleolithic times to the present, have used some of these basic motifs of child art. Pictorial drawings made by children in many lands are remarkably similar because they are the outgrowths of earlier scribblings and designs (see Figure 6). Since this early art is so uniform in expression from country to country, culture to culture, past to present, I conclude that the child's early abstractions (as well as later, derivative, pictorial drawings) are the products of innate patterns of neurological growth and human development.

Indeed, Max Knoll has discovered that the phosphenes, or light patterns that adults experience when the cortex is electrically stimulated, are similar to children's scribblings. This suggests that there are some inherent neurological mechanisms that enable us to produce and to perceive the basic line gestalts out of which art forms are produced. Several studies have shown that infants only a few weeks old can respond with movement of their eye muscles to the stimulus of abstract patterns, and it is now generally agreed that the mind at birth is not a blank, nor is it a "blooming buzzing confusion," as William James suggested.

Live Art Scribbles

Children's scribblings and drawings contain a voluminous written message, a message that has not yet been completely deciphered. It may turn out that "live art scribbles" are as important as the Dead Sea Scrolls.

I believe that the hidden message in child art, when properly understood, will free us to recapture the un-*adult*erated esthetic vision of the child. Perhaps the day will come when adult and child can enjoy self-taught art together, not as "cute" or "remarkable" products of the childish mind but as the groundwork of all art. Then adults will not make stencils for children to fill in, nor will they patronizingly laugh at what they do not understand.

Children are happy when they can draw objects to fit into implied esthetic shapes. What the great artist struggles to achieve, the child creates naturally.

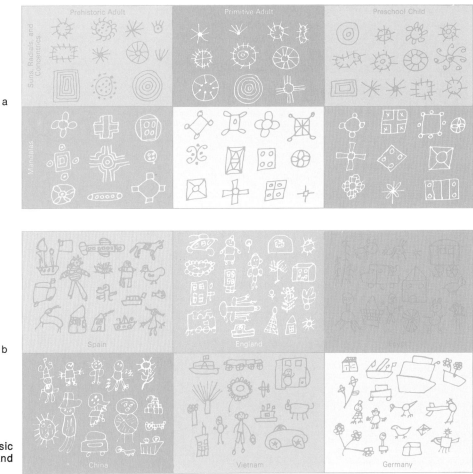

Figure 6. Universality of basic art motifs (a) across time and (b) across cultures.

II
Education and the Development of the Child

Self-fulfilling Prophecy

Robert Rosenthal

A behavioral scientist can, in all innocence, influence the outcome of his studies. He may be biased in his perception and/or interpretation of the event being studied, or some bias may occur as a result of his interaction with the subject being studied. Such factors as the age, sex, or race of the investigator, conveyed through visual or auditory cues, may determine the outcome of otherwise carefully controlled experiments. Professor Rosenthal cites several experiments that clearly show these effects.

Just as the expectations of research investigators may lead to biased results, so the expectations of teachers may influence whether their pupils learn or not. The author reports a series of studies on the effects of teacher expectations that bear out this hypothesis. When teachers are led to believe that certain students will perform better than others, they not only see the selected children as having more positive personality traits but they also teach them more and better, as reflected in the students' improved performance on standard tests—this, when the children who were pointed out as superior were in fact equal in ability with the rest!

Much of our scientific knowledge is based upon careful observation and recording of events. That the observer himself may have a biasing effect on his observations has long been recognized. There are two basic types of experimenter effects. The first operates without affecting the event or subject being studied. It occurs in the eye, the hand, and the brain of the researcher. The second type is the result of the *interaction* between the experimenter and the subject of the experiment. And when the research deals with humans and animals, as it does in the behavioral sciences, this interaction actually can alter the responses or data that are obtained.

Quite unconsciously, a psychologist interacts in subtle ways with the people he is studying so that he may get the response he expects to get. This happens even when the person cannot see the researcher. And, even more surprisingly, it occurs when the subject is not human but a rat.

If rats became brighter when expected to by their researcher, isn't it possible that children become brighter when their teachers expect them to be brighter?

Lenore Jacobson, of the South San Francisco Unified School District, and I set out to see if this is so. Every child in an elementary school was given an intelligence test, a test described by us as one that would predict "intellectual blooming."

The school was in a lower socioeconomic neighborhood on the West Coast. There were three classrooms for each grade—one for children of above average ability, one for average ability, and one for below average ability. About 20 percent of the children in each classroom were chosen at random to form the experimental group. The teachers were given the names of this group and told that these children had scored high on the test for intellectual blooming and would show remarkable gains in intellectual development during the next eight months.

In reality, the only difference between these children and their classmates was *in the minds* of their teachers.

At the end of the school year, all the children were again given the same IQ test. In the school as a whole, the children who had been designated as "bloomers" showed only a slightly greater gain in verbal IQ (two points) than their classmates. However, *in total* IQ, the experimental group gained four points more on the average than their counterparts did, and in reasoning IQ, the average gain was seven points more.

Usually, when educational theorists talk of improving scholastic achievement by improving teacher expectations, they are referring to children at the lower levels of achievement. It was interesting to find that teacher expectations affected children at the highest level of achievement as much as it did children at the lowest level.

At the end of the school year, we asked the teachers

to describe the classroom behavior of all their pupils. The children in the group designated as the bloomers were seen as more interesting, more curious, and happier. The teachers also found "blooming" children slightly more appealing, better adjusted, and more affectionate, and with less need for social approval.

Many of the other children in the classes also gained in IQ during the year, but teachers reacted negatively to *unexpected* improvement. The more the undesignated children gained in IQ points, the more they were regarded as *less* well adjusted, *less* interesting, and *less* affectionate. It appears that there may be hazards to unpredicted intellectual growth—at least in the eyes of the teacher. This is particularly true of children in the low-ability groups.

The effects of teacher expectation were most evident in reasoning IQ gains. But only the girls in the group designated as "bloomers" showed greater gains than the rest of the class. The boys designated as bloomers actually gained less than their classmates. Partly to check this finding, Judy Evans and I repeated the experiment with schoolchildren in a small Midwestern town. The children here were from substantial middle-class families.

Again we found that teacher expectations affected reasoning IQ gains in pupils. However, this time it was the boys who tended to show greater gains than girls. These results underline the effects of teacher expectations, but they also indicate the complexity of these effects as a function of the pupil's sex, social status, and very likely other variables as well.

In another study, conducted by Lane K. Conn, Carl N. Edwards, Douglas Crowne, and me, we selected an East Coast school with upper-middle-class pupils. This time we also measured the children's accuracy in judging the emotion conveyed in tone of voice. The children who were more accurate in judging the emotional tone of an adult female's voice benefited most from favorable teacher expectations. And in this school, both the boys and girls who were expected to bloom intellectually showed greater reasoning IQ gains than their classmates.

W. Victor Beez of Indiana University conducted an experiment in 1967 that sheds some light on the phenomenon of teacher expectancy. His pupils were sixty preschoolers from a summer Head-Start program. Each child had one teacher who taught him the meaning of a series of symbols. Half of the teachers were led to expect good symbol learning, and the other half were led to expect poor learning.

Nearly 77 percent of the children designated as good intellectual prospects learned five or more symbols. Only 13 percent of the children designated as poor prospects learned five or more symbols. A researcher from the outside who did not know what the teachers had been told about the children's intellectual prospects assessed the children's actual performance.

What happened in this study was that the teachers with favorable expectations tried to teach more symbols to their pupils than did teachers who had unfavorable expectations. This indicates that the teacher's expectations may not only be translated into subtle vocal and visual nuances but also may cause dramatic alterations in teaching style. Surprisingly, however, even when the amount of teaching was held constant, the children who were expected to learn more did learn more.

Teacher expectancy effects are not limited to the teaching of intellectual tasks. Recent research reported by J. Randolph Burnham and Donald M. Hartsough of Purdue University indicates that the teaching of motor skills also may be affected by teacher expectations. At a camp for underprivileged children from the Philadelphia area, Burnham administered a test to nonswimmers that ostensibly would predict psychological readiness to swim. He then randomly selected children from various age groups and gave their names to the waterfront counselors as those who were "ready" to swim. He found that the children designated as "ready" tended to pass more of the tests in the Red Cross beginning swimmer's course than the average for their peer group.

If the expectancy effect occurs in the laboratory and in the classroom, then it is not surprising to find it occurring in everyday life. Your expectation of how another person will behave often may become a self-fulfilling prophecy. We know that nonverbal and unintentional communication between people does take place. What we don't know is *how* such communication occurs. Further research on the interaction of the experimenter and the subject may eventually teach us more about dyadic interactions in general.

The interaction of experimenter and his subject is a major source of knowledge in the behavioral sciences. Until recently, however, this interaction has been an uncontrolled variable in psychological research. The demonstration of experimenter effects does not necessarily invalidate a great deal of behavioral research. It does mean, however, that we must take extra precautions to reduce "expectancy" and other unintended effects of the experimenter.

Just what does a behavioral scientist unintentionally do in gathering his data so that he unwittingly influences his subjects' responses? This question must be answered satisfactorily if we want to have dependable knowledge in the behavioral sciences.

In our research, we have distinguished five categories of interactional effects between the experimenter and his subjects: biosocial, psychosocial, situational, modeling, and expectancy effects.

Biosocial Effects

The sex, age, and race of investigators all have been found to affect the results of their research. It is tempting to assume that the subjects simply are responding to the biosocial attributes of the investigator. But the investigator himself, because of sex, age, or race, may respond differently to male or female, young or old, white or Negro subjects. And even a slight change in behavior alters the experimental situation.

Our evidence suggests, for example, that male and female experimenters conduct the same experiment quite differently. The different results they obtain are not due to any error as such, but may well be due to the fact that they have unintentionally conducted different experiments.

In one study of the effect of the characteristics of subjects on the experimenter, the interaction between experimenters and subjects was recorded on sound film. Only 12 percent of the investigators smiled even a little at male subjects, but 70 percent smiled at female subjects. These smiles may well have affected the results of the experiment. It may be a heartening finding to know that chivalry is not dead, but as far as methodology is concerned, it is a disconcerting finding. In general, the experimenter treated his male subjects and female subjects differently, so that, in a sense, men and women really were not in the same experiment at all.

Moreover, when we consider the sex of both the experimenter and the subject, other interaction effects emerge. In the study recorded on film, we found that the experimenters took more time to collect some of their data from subjects of the opposite sex than from subjects of the same sex.

The age of the investigator may also affect the subject's response. Studies suggest that young subjects are less likely to say "unacceptable" things to much older investigators, indicating that an age barrier may exist in at least some behavioral studies.

The skin color of the investigator also may affect response, even when the response is physiological.

A number of studies have found that Negroes tend to control their hostility more when contacted by a white rather than a Negro experimenter and give more "proper" responses to white than to black interviewers.

Psychosocial Effects

Experimenters are people, and so they differ in anxiety, in their need for approval, in personal hostility, authoritarianism, status, and in personal warmth. Experimenters with different personalities tend to get different responses from their experimental subjects. For example, researchers higher in status—a professor as compared to a graduate student, or a captain as compared to a corporal—tend to obtain more responses that *conform* to the investigator's suggestions. And investigators who are warmer toward people tend to obtain more *pleasant* responses.

Situational Effects

Investigators experienced in conducting a given experiment usually obtain responses different from those of less experienced investigators. This may be because they behave differently. Also, experimenters who are acquainted with the people in the experimental group get results that differ from those obtained by researchers who have never met their subjects before.

What happens to the experimenter during the course of his experiment can influence his behavior, and changes in his behavior may lead to changes in the subjects' responses.

For instance, if the first few subjects respond as expected (that is, confirming the experimenter's hypothesis), the behavior of the researcher alters, and he influences subsequent subjects to respond in a way that supports his hypothesis.

Modeling Effects

Sometimes, before an experimenter conducts a study, he first tries out the task he will have his research subjects perform. For example, if the task is to rate a series of ten photos of faces according to how successful or unsuccessful the persons pictured appear to be, the experimenters may decide to rate the photos themselves before contacting their subjects. Though evidence is not yet definite, it appears that at least sometimes the investigator's own ratings become a factor in the performance of his subjects. In particular, when the experimental stimuli, such as photos, are ambiguous, the subjects' interpretation may agree too often with the investigator's interpretation, even though the latter remains unspoken.

Some expectation of how the research might turn out is virtually a constant factor in all scientific experiments. In the behavioral sciences, this expectancy can lead the investigator to act unconsciously in such a way that he affects the responses of his subjects. When the investigator's expectancy influences the responses in the direction of what he expects to happen, we can appropriately regard his hypothesis as a *self-fulfilling prophecy*. One prophesies an event, and the expectation of the event then changes the behavior of the prophet in such a way as to make the prophesied event more likely.

In the history of psychology, the case of Clever Hans is a classic example of this phenomenon. Hans was a horse owned by a German mathematics instructor named Von Osten. Hans could perform difficult mathematical calculations, spell, read, and solve problems of musical harmony by tapping his foot.

A panel of distinguished scientists and experts on animal behavior ruled that no fraud was involved. The horse was given no cues to tell him when to start or when to stop tapping his foot.

But, of course, there *were* cues. In a series of brilliant experiments reported in 1911, Oskar Pfungst showed that Hans could answer questions only when the questioner himself knew the answers and when the horse could see the questioner. Finally, Pfungst learned that a tiny forward movement of the experimenter's head was the signal for Hans to start tapping. A slight upward movement of the head, or even a raised eyebrow, was the signal for the horse to stop tapping.

Hans' questioners expected him to give the right answers, and their expectation was reflected in their unwitting signals to start and stop tapping. The horse had good eyesight, and he *was* a smart horse.

Self-fulfilling Prophecies

To demonstrate experimenter effects in behavioral research, we must have at least two groups of experimenters with different expectations. One approach is to take a survey of investigators in a certain area of research and ask those with opposite expectancies to conduct a standard experiment. But the differences in the results could be due to factors other than expectancy, and so a better strategy is required.

Rather than trying to find two groups of experimenters with different expectations, we could *create* such groups. In one experiment, we selected ten advanced undergraduate and graduate students of psychology as our researchers. All were experienced in conducting research. Each was assigned a group of twenty participating students as his subjects. The experiment consisted of showing ten photographs of people's faces, one at a time, to each subject. The participant was to rate the degree of success or failure reflected in the facial expression of the person in the photo. Each of the faces could be rated from −10 (extreme failure) to +10 (extreme success). The faces in the photos were actually quite neutral, and on the average the total ratings should have produced a numerical score of zero.

All ten experimenters had identical instructions to read to their subjects, and they also had identical instructions on how to conduct the experiment. They were specifically cautioned not to deviate from these instructions.

Finally, we informed our researchers that the purpose of the experiment was to see how well they could duplicate results that were already well established. We told half of the experimenters that the "well-established" finding was that people rated the faces in the photos as successful (+5). And we told the other half that people rated the faces in the photos as unsuccessful (−5). Thus informed, they began their research.

The results were clear-cut. Every researcher who was led to expect that the photographed people were successful obtained a higher average rating of success from his group than did any experimenter who expected low-success ratings.

We repeated this experiment twice with different groups with the same results. Research in other laboratories has shown much the same thing. Although not every experiment showed a significant effect, the probability that results of all these experiments occurred by chance is less than one in a thousand billion.

Having found that what the experimenter expects to happen can affect the outcome of his research, we then began to look for some clues as to *how* the experimenter unwittingly communicates his expectancy to his subjects.

Through the use of accomplices who acted as subjects in an experiment, we learned how the responses of the first few subjects affected the experimenter's behavior to subsequent subjects. If the responses of the first few subjects confirmed the experimenter's hypothesis, his behavior to subsequent participants somehow influenced them also to confirm his hypothesis. But when the "planted" accomplices contradicted the expectations of the experimenter, the following subjects were affected by the experimenter's behavior so that they, too, tended to controvert his hypothesis. It seems, then, that the early returns of data in behavioral research can affect and possibly shape the final results.

Reverse Effects

In some of our experiments, when we offered too-obvious incentives or too-large rewards to investigators to bring in "good" data, the expectancy effect was reduced, and in some cases even reversed. Both the autonomy and the honesty of the researchers may have been challenged by the excessive rewards offered. It speaks well for the integrity of our student researchers that they would not be bribed. In fact, they tended to bend over backward to avoid the biasing effect of their expectation. But they often bent so far backward that the results of their experiments sometimes were the opposite of what they had been told to expect.

The process by which an experimenter unintentionally and covertly communicates instructions to his subjects is very subtle. For six years we have studied sound films of research interviews in an attempt to discover the cues that the experimenter unwittingly gives to the subject, and for six years we have failed, at least partly.

We know, however, that visual cues *are* important. Placing a screen between the investigator and the person he is interviewing reduces the investigator's influence on the results. But the expectancy effect is not eliminated completely, indicating that auditory cues are also important.

This was dramatically demonstrated by John G. Adair and Joyce Epstein of the University of Manitoba in their tape-recording experiment. They first duplicated the expectation effects study in which ten photographs of people's faces are rated successful or unsuccessful. Half the investigators were told to expect a success response and half a failure response. Adair and Epstein tape-recorded each of the sessions. The results matched those of the original studies.

Next, with a new group of subjects a second experiment was conducted. Instead of having live investigators, the subjects listened to the tape-recording of an investigator reading the standard instructions to the previous group. Again the results were much the same. Self-fulfilling prophecies, it seems, can come about as a result of the prophet's voice alone. Since in the experiment all prophets read standard instructions, self-fulfillment of prophecies may be brought about by the tone in which the prophet prophesies.

Early in our research on self-fulfilling prophecies, we thought that some form of operant conditioning might be the explanation. It could be that when the investigator obtained a response consistent with his expectations, he would look more pleasant, or smile, or glance at the subject approvingly. The investigator could be entirely unaware of these reinforcing responses. We analyzed many experiments to see if this type of operant conditioning was present. If indeed it was, then the subject's responses should gradually become more like those expected by the investigator—there would be a "learning curve" for subjects.

But no learning curve was found. On the contrary, it turned out that the first responses of the subject were about as much affected by the investigator's expectations as the last responses.

Further analysis revealed that while there was no learning curve for the subjects, there seemed to be a learning curve for the investigators. As the investigator interviewed more and more subjects, the expectancy effect grew stronger. It appeared possible that the subject's response was the reinforcing event. The subjects, then, may quite unintentionally shape the investigator's behavior. So, not only does the experimenter influence his subjects to respond in the expected manner, but the subjects may well influence the experimenter to behave in a way that leads to fulfillment of his prophecies.

Perhaps the most significant implication of this research is that human beings can engage in highly effective and influential unintended communication with one another—even under controlled laboratory conditions.

But do expectancy effects occur when the experimental subjects are not human? We designed a study to find out. Twelve experimenters were each given five rats that were to be taught to run a maze with the aid of visual cues. Six of the experimenters were told that their rats had been specially bred for maze brightness; the other six were told that their rats had been bred for maze dullness. Actually, there was no difference between the rats.

At the end of the experiment, researchers with maze-bright rats found superior learning in their rats compared to the researchers with maze-dull rats.

A second experiment made use of the special training setup designed by B. F. Skinner of Harvard. Half the researchers were led to believe that their rats were "Skinner box bright" and half were told that their rats were "Skinner box dull." Initially, there were not really such differences in the rats, but at the end of the experiment the allegedly brighter animals *were* really brighter, and the alleged dullards *really* duller.

How can we reduce the expectancy effect in behavioral research?

One way is to design procedures that enable us to assess whether the expectancy effects have altered the results of an experiment. In addition, the experimenter could employ investigators who have not been told the purpose of the study, or automated data-collection systems could be used.

Perhaps a new profession of full-time experimenters could be developed who would perform others' experiments without becoming involved in setting up a hypothesis or interpreting the results. Precedents for such professionals are found in both medical research and public-opinion surveys.

Dependable Knowledge

Because of the general nature of expectancy and other experimenter effects, it would be desirable to use more experimenters for each study than we presently use. Having a larger number of returns, we could assess the extent to which different experimenters obtained different results, and in any area of psychological research this is worth knowing.

Scientists have long employed control groups in their experiments. Usually the experimental group receives some kind of treatment while the control group receives no treatment. To determine the extent of the expectancy effect, we could add two special "expectancy control" groups to the experiment. In one of these special groups, the investigator would be told that the group's subjects had received some treatment, when in fact they had not. The experimenter in the other group would be told the subjects had not received treatment when in fact they had. Such a research design would permit us to assess the magnitude of the effect of experimenters' expectancy.

To the extent that we hope for dependable knowledge in the behavioral sciences, we must have dependable knowledge about the psychological experiment and the interaction of experimenter and subject. We can no more hope to acquire accurate information for our disciplines without understanding the experimenter effect than astronomers or zoologists could hope to acquire accurate information without understanding the effects of their telescopes and microscopes. And behavioral scientists, being as scientifically self-conscious a group as they are, may one day produce a psychology of those psychologists who study psychologists.

Then, in the laboratory, in the classrooms, in every sector of our lives we will come closer to understanding the effect of a smile.

Russian Nursery Schools
Michael and Sheila Cole

The state-controlled program for preschool children in the Soviet Union is uniform nationwide. The official philosophy regarding children is that they are an important natural resource, the development of which is a responsibility of the state. However, despite the centralized programming, the teachers in these schools show ample recognition of individual differences among children in both temperament and capacity, and this attitude toward individuality is part of official policy. Also part of standard policy is the attitude toward reward and punishment: verbal praise is given when the child acts in a desirable way, and punishment, which is used very sparingly, only takes the form of withdrawal of praise or affection; there is general disapproval of physical punishment.

The nursery school program emphasizes the beginnings of spelling, grammar, and comprehension, as well as physical constructions and activity. The general orientation is one of practicality. Even activities like story telling and drawing are taken seriously; each has an attached lesson to be learned. This emphasis in the Soviet program on training rather than on creativity and self-discovery differs from some of the attitudes expressed in the first section of this book and from the philosophy of most American nursery schools. The Russians place particular emphasis on what they call sensory training. By this, they mean training children to recognize the various attributes and function of objects. In this way, the children are taught how to form concepts—initially on a concrete level—with the belief that there will be a practical carry-over to later learning of more abstract concepts.

It was free-play period at Preschool 67 in the northwest suburbs of Moscow, and it was early summer. Two three-year-old boys were building a castle in the sandbox, occasionally getting in the way of a little girl who was tunneling. A red-faced youngster was hard at work hauling pails of water for the boys from a nearby pond. In a far corner of the yard, two little girls were playing with dolls. Sitting under an arbor in another corner, alone, was a three-year-old girl with short dark hair, singing softly to herself.

We had seen the girl spend the play period that way for several days, and we mentioned her to the teacher, a young woman who had been trained at one of the Soviet Union's pedagogical institutes. "Oh, that's Irichka," she replied. "Irichka is happy to be alone. She's that kind of child—quiet and able to amuse herself."

To us, it seemed odd that a woman who was supposed to be raising children in a collective should show such an easy acceptance of individualism. But the more we learned about Soviet nursery schools, the more

apparent it became that we had brought with us from the United States a full bag of misconceptions.

We spent the summer of 1966 in the Soviet Union, chiefly to help with preparations for the Eighteenth International Congress of Psychologists. In the United States at the time, Head Start programs were springing up all over, and the newspapers were full of heartwarming accounts of children listening to stories and receiving medical checkups for the first time in their lives. A heated debate was also underway among teachers and psychologists about what kinds of programs would best prepare these children for the public schools, whose task in turn would be to make them productive and socially useful members of our society.

Especially because of this situation at home, we were eager to find out all we could about Soviet nursery schools. We spent almost a week at Preschool 67, talking to the children, teachers, and principal. Later, we visited the Institute of Preschool Education in Moscow and interviewed its director, A. V. Zaporozhets. The Institute is responsible for recommending a nursery-school program to the Soviet Union's Ministry of Education, and its psychologists perform the research on which the recommendations are based. Once the program has been adopted by the Ministry, it is used throughout the country.

Nursery schools have been part of the system of universal education in the Soviet Union since the time of the Bolshevik Revolution. Although they are not compulsory, preschools are the first link in the Soviet educational system. The Communist Party assigns to nursery schools the task of ensuring the normal development of all children—preparing them for school and teaching them proper work habits, so that they, like their American counterparts, will grow into productive and socially useful members of their society.

Preschool 67 is just like thousands of nursery schools in the Soviet Union. Its drab two-story building comes from a blueprint used throughout the country for almost ten years, and its educational program and goals are also identical to those in effect elsewhere.

The pupils range in age from two to seven; there are 150 of them, all from homes in the neighborhood of the school. One group of 25 lives in the school's small dormitory, going home only on weekends and holidays. The others arrive between eight and nine in the morning and leave between four and six in the afternoon.

There is a long waiting list at Preschool 67, as there is at most nursery schools, and admission is based on need. Priority is given to children who have two working parents and no grandmother or other baby-sitter, to orphans, and to children from very large families or from homes where there is sickness or some other problem. Payment, which is determined by the parents' income, ranges from $2.20 to $13.00 a month.

"Work" Training

When we arrived at Preschool 67, the children were eating breakfast on one side of a large, airy, toy-cluttered room. The older children used cloth napkins and sat at tables covered with white cloths. These amenities, we were told by Sofia Shvedova, the warm, grandmotherly director of the preschool, were both a reward for good table manners and an incentive to improve. "We ask the children to see how clean they can keep the tablecloth," she said. "But we never shame them when they have an accident."

"We know that some children eat less than others, but we give them all the same amount anyway," Mrs. Shvedova went on. "We let them eat as much as they can. We occasionally feed the little ones. But we don't force a child to love all food. We try to teach him little by little."

At nursery school, the children receive three substantial meals a day—they are not supposed to eat at home on school days except for an occasional snack—and they take their naps there as well.

In other words, the nursery school is responsible for the health and physical development of the child. This lessens the burden on the working mother, and it also reflects the Soviets' very different view from ours of the relation between children and society. The Soviets believe that children are a natural resource, perhaps the most valuable resource a society has. Although the raising of the child is entrusted to the family, the ultimate responsibility for the child's development belongs to the state.

As the children finished their breakfast, they wiped their mouths on their napkins, asked the nanny if they could be excused, thanked her, and went to the other side of the room to play. A few children stayed behind; it was their turn to help clear the table.

Teaching the children to take care of their own needs, and to help with the chores and with the younger children, is an important part of the "work training" portion of the nursery-school program. The children do not receive concrete rewards for their "work," but they are profusely praised when they do a good job.

"They should all work well," Mrs. Shvedova said. "But we know that there are individual differences and that one child is not as capable as another. We try to measure them all against their own achievement. We can't give a child a gold star when he breaks a plate, but we can say, 'Tolia did a very good job today. He tried very hard. He broke a dish, but he did it because he was trying so hard.'"

Surprising as it might seem to many Americans, Mrs. Shvedova's insistence on acknowledging individual differences and on judging the child against his own abilities is based on official ideology. The government-distributed manual for preschool teachers says that nursery schools should teach friendship and cooperation and also form individuality: the school's program of physical, intellectual, moral, work, and esthetic training should take into account the age and individual characteristics of each child.

Language Training

Later in the morning, a teacher took Preschool 67's three- and four-year-olds aside to read them a story. The children listened intently. When the teacher had finished, she asked them to retell parts of the story and to answer questions about it, gently correcting their mistakes and insisting on answers that were complete, grammatical sentences. One little girl was overeager: she shouted the right answer before a slower and shyer child could finish. The teacher restrained her gently and then encouraged the other child to answer by himself.

Teaching the children to speak Russian correctly and to express themselves fully is one of the major aims of the preschool program. Language training is a continuous process, carried on throughout the day by means of books, stories, and direct contact with adults.

In another room, the older children followed their teacher's story in books of their own. Before the teacher began to read, she asked the children several questions about books and how they are used. During the story, she stopped often to ask what letter or sound a word began or ended with. Later, she requested summaries of the plot and descriptions of the characters.

For five- and six-year-olds, who will soon start school, there is great emphasis on skills like these. The preschool is in close touch with the grade schools that the children will attend, and it teaches them the work habits and procedures that are used there. Reading and writing as such are not formally taught in nursery school, but reading and writing readiness are. The children learn to analyze the sounds they hear in the spoken language and to write the elements used in the letters of the Russian alphabet.

Elementary mathematical concepts are introduced gradually, through the use of concrete materials. The children learn to count to ten by eye, ear, touch, and movement; to answer questions of number, size, and position in space; and to subtract or add one or two to any number up to ten. It is only in the last year of nursery school, when the children are six years old, that they begin to work with written numbers and with the symbols $+$, $-$, and $=$.

Rest and Play

After lunch, we stood at the door of a dormitory crowded with high, white iron bedsteads and watched the children take their usual two-hour rest. They were supposed to be asleep, but they seemed determined not to succumb. Stripped to their underwear and covered with sheets, they tossed, turned, whispered, sucked their thumbs, asked the nanny for glasses of water, and requested permission to go to the potty—or reported that it was too late.

The nanny treated the bed-wetters and thumb-suckers matter-of-factly. If a child wet his bed, she changed his sheets and underwear with little fuss and no reprimands. She privately asked a few older children to take their thumbs out of their mouths, but when the thumbs were put back in a few moments she seemed not to notice.

After their naps, the children went outside to play. The yard was provided with swings, sandboxes, and little pools of water; there were also gazebos and arbors, tables and chairs, and bookcases full of games, toys, books, and arts-and-crafts materials.

One two-year-old boy, ignoring these enticements, began to wander off the nursery-school grounds. The nanny in charge, a motherly, middle-aged woman, ran after him and brought him back. She scolded him affectionately, threatening to punish him by making him sit still.

"He's such a little one," she said. "He really doesn't understand. It's impossible to really punish him."

Mrs. Shvedova told us later that punishment is meted out only if the children hurt someone or are very dis-

obedient. "The first time a child is bad, we don't do anything. We try to understand. But after a while we must punish, because of the other children. We try to suit the punishment to the child and the situation. We know the children well and we know what each one will consider a punishment." Corporal punishment is frowned on in the Soviet Union, and the usual method of discipline is the temporary withdrawal of affection and praise.

Creativity Training

During the play period, one group of girls five or six years old went to an arts-and-crafts area to color. They were eager to please and to show us their work, which was very neat. When one girl offered to draw us a picture to take home to our daughter, we requested a dog. "I can't," she said. "No one has taught me how."

In Soviet nursery schools, drawing is a lesson—something to be learned. There are exercises on how to draw straight lines, circles, and other forms, and simple figures. These exercises are not considered play, and the teacher keeps a little folder of each child's work to encourage a serious attitude toward it.

Looking through these folders, we found that the children's drawings were all the same. The teacher had shown them how to draw a house, a person, or whatever, and they had done it. Unlike most Americans, who believe that a child will be creative "naturally" if he is given the chance, the Soviets believe creativity is more than a matter of opportunity. It requires training. But they are quick to point out that the object of training is not stilted, narrow drawings like those in the folders at Preschool 67. How to teach creativity properly is a problem now being studied at the laboratory of esthetic education of the Institute of Preschool Education.

However, the development of creativity does not seem to be very high on Soviet preschools' list of priorities. When we asked Mrs. Shvedova what goals Preschool 67 had for its children, she replied, "We want them to be smart and honest. If they are honest, they will be fair. We want them to love beauty, to be real people. We don't want them to be all alike, but originality and creativity are not that important."

Sensory Training

One thing that *is* important is sensory training, which the Soviets define rather more broadly than we would. At the preschool one morning we watched a row of three-year-olds, seated on small benches under an arbor, receive a lesson in sensory training that was also a lesson in language. The teacher showed the children five vegetables and named them: an onion, a beet, a carrot, a cabbage, and a potato. Then she put the vegetables in a cloth sack and asked a child to draw one out and name it.

When each child and the teacher had named the vegetables several times and repeated the names in unison, the teacher told the children that the five objects together were called vegetables. The class said the word "vegetable" several times and was dismissed.

The four- and five-year-olds had a harder task. After they chose a vegetable from the sack they were asked, without looking at it, to name it and tell everything they knew about it—its color, its shape, how it grows, and how it is eaten. The rest of the children in the group corrected and helped them.

According to the Russians, perception is more than the physical reception of energy by the sense organs. It also involves the organization of perceptual signals—the way a person selects and systematizes certain characteristics of perceptible reality so that he can use them in such activities as speech, music, art, and work. For the Soviets, then, perception means not only "perception" as we usually think of it; it includes a number of cognitive functions as well. When a child learns to perceive, he learns to orient himself in the world of the senses.

The Russians will allow that this can occur spontaneously, as a by-product of normal activity. But they do not believe that spontaneous development is very efficient or very effective. As A. V. Zaporozhets, director of the Institute of Preschool Education, explained when we talked with him, "Our nursery schools differ from most of those in the West, where there is no special program of education and it is believed that, given the chance, a child will ask questions and learn through his own initiative."

Soviet psychologists, Zaporozhets continued, disagree with both Jean Piaget and Maria Montessori. According to Piaget, the kind of thinking a child is capable of depends on his age. If beans are poured from a short, fat jar into a tall, thin one, a child of four is likely to think the tall jar contains more beans, while a child of six or seven will not be fooled. Piaget attributes this to the fact that the older child understands the principle of conservation.

The Russians, Zaporozhets said, do not agree "that a child cannot do such and such until a certain age. We think that teaching plays a decisive role in learning, and that a child can do quite a bit more than we previously imagined he was capable of."

They do think it is *easier* to develop certain abilities at certain ages, although they are not sure which abilities are easiest to develop at which age. As a working policy, they try to develop intuition and sensory abilities in early childhood, leaving abstract thought for later on. "We believe that thought is a hierarchical structure. For a complete intellect, the entire system, from the most concrete to the most abstract, must exist. You don't have to rush to the third stage when you haven't gotten through the first."

Like Montessori, Zaporozhets said, the Soviets think

sensory abilities should be developed during early childhood. But "Montessori believed that the child is born with all his sensory abilities and that training will simply strengthen them. We think this is incorrect."

As the handbook for nursery-school teachers written by Institute psychologists, *Sensory Training*, explains, the Russians find the Montessorian system of training too formal, too "pure," too far removed from the everyday world in which the child must use his senses. They believe it is not enough to acquaint the child with an endless variety of sensory data. He must be taught a generalized method of orientation and investigation—an approach to the world of the senses—that will efficiently give him the information he needs. This is best done informally, within the context of regular nursery-school activities such as making models, drawing, constructing things with sand or blocks, singing, dancing, and storytelling.

Abstract exercises in which the child discriminates triangles from circles in an unanalyzed way are thought to teach him very little. In the Russian nursery school, a child is taught not only that red is different from blue but that red is the color of apples and, indeed, that red apples are ripe apples and ripe apples are edible apples.

The child is taught to use his senses, and he is also taught what the things he perceives mean and what words he can use to describe his sensory experiences precisely. At the same time, he is encouraged to generalize and categorize on the basis of his immediate sensory experience—he is taught, for instance, that onion-beet-carrot-cabbage-potato equals vegetable.

Here is a typical elementary exercise in sensory training used with two- and three-year-olds. The object of the exercise, which is preliminary to developing the kind of perception the Soviets are talking about, is to teach the child to use his sensory apparatus to the fullest.

The teacher gives the child two cardboard circles (or triangles, or squares) that are the same size but different colors. She asks the child to put one circle on top of the other so that the edges are even, and to run his finger along the edges of the figures so that he can tell whether he has aligned them correctly or not. Then she gives the child a circle and a square of the same color—say, blue—and shows him a *red* square. His task is to find which of his figures has the same *shape* as hers. The child makes his choice and verifies it by placing it on the teacher's model. If it fits, the child is praised; if not, the teacher suggests he try the other figure.

As *Sensory Training* points out, the object of perceptual training is to prepare the child for future activity. In short, the Russian approach is highly pragmatic and task oriented. Perhaps for this reason, the schools make considerable use of construction exercises. Like drawing, building requires the child to perform a detailed visual examination of the form, size, and spatial arrangement of an object, but *Sensory Training* warns that there is an important distinction between construction and pictorial tasks. A picture always reflects the exterior characteristics of an object as it is visually perceived; construction serves a practical purpose. "Garages are built for cars, barns for animals, houses for dolls. Constructions are made by children to be used—acted with."

Thus a teacher might provide the children with bricks, have the children pile them up in different ways and test the stability of the piles, and then suggest the construction of a road. Or she might give the children beams of different lengths and ask them to build a corral. She would point out the various factors the children should consider if the corral is to serve its purpose—that it must be high enough to prevent the animals from jumping out, that the beams must be close enough together to keep the animals from squeezing through, and so forth.

Although the stress in exercises like these is on purpose and practicality, note that it is also on *activity*, and particularly on physical activity as an important way to develop perceptual skills. The child is an active agent in his own development. *He* places the geometric figures together and runs his fingers around the edges; *he* piles the bricks and builds the corral.

This emphasis on the role of active experience in the child's development has its counterpart in contemporary American developmental theory. Richard Held of MIT, for example, has shown that there is a close relation between motor experience and visual perception, especially when one must coordinate what one sees with what one does. In one well-known experiment, Held provided a man and a woman with special glasses that shifted their visual fields to the right. Then he had the woman sit in a wheelchair while the man pushed the chair around the campus. When the two were tested later, the man—who had had motor experience with the visual shift—was much better than the woman at correcting for the distortion that the glasses created.

In a similar experiment, Held placed two kittens in a circular box whose walls were painted with vertical stripes. One kitten sat in a cart; the other wore a yoke and walked around the box rather in the manner of a water buffalo, moving the cart around as he did so. Although the kitten who got the free ride saw the same

things as the walking kitten, the walking kitten seemed to learn more. When the two were tested later, the kitten that had the motor experience showed superior ability to perform a number of tasks that required visual-motor coordination.

The notion of the child as an active agent in his own development also occurs in the work of Jerome Bruner of Harvard. Just telling the child a set of facts, Bruner says, does not produce real learning. The child must operate on his environment in such a way that he discovers solutions to the problems it poses. As the child searches for solutions, his approach becomes more sophisticated and also more effective. For example, young children who have not learned how to gather information efficiently play Twenty Questions by asking about specific items: "Is it the dog?" "Is it Mommy?" Older children try to structure their questions so that each yields a maximum amount of information: "Is it a living American man?" Through a process of active searching, the older children have learned generalized techniques for gathering information.

Much of the research now being done by Zaporozhets and his colleagues at the Institute is based on this general premise that activity leads to learning. There are experiments, for example, on teaching cooperation and consideration of others through role-playing. Several children who are not friendly with each other are asked to perform a joint task—to tell a story together, or to put on a puppet show—in the hope that they will be friendlier after than they were before.

We arrived in the Soviet Union with a mental image of a monolithic preschool system, chiefly Pavlovian in theory, and rigid, regimented, and stifling in practice. Soviet psychology does include some Pavlovian concepts, and Soviet preschool programs do follow a common outline, but these are a much smaller part of the whole picture than we had supposed. In fact, the theoretical and empirical research conducted at the Institute would command the respect of developmental psychologists in Geneva or New York, and the care given the children of Preschool 67 could serve as a model anywhere—anywhere, that is, where children are treated as one of society's most valuable resources.

The Content Is the Medium: The Confidence Is the Message

Harold Bessell

The Human Development Program (HDP), a thirty-six-week guided group experience for young children, is currently being tried out and refined through use in several nursery and elementary schools. It is based on the premise that the child is not primarily a cognitive machine: Rather, he needs to feel that he is successful and has control and responsibility for what happens to him in his environment.

Since the author believes that positive personality traits derive from individual awareness, self-confidence, and social interactions, HDP focuses on these three areas, with a different aspect of each being stressed each week. The goals of the program are the child's greater awareness of his own behavior and feelings, greater awareness of the behavior and feelings of others, and an understanding of the cause-and-effect relationship between what one person does and the feelings produced in the person for whom it is done. The author hopes that children's experience with a program like HDP will produce more confident and effective adults and will reduce the personal dissatisfaction so prevalent in today's youth.

For twenty minutes each day, in nursery school and kindergarten classes where the Human Development Program (HDP) now is in use, there is a special guided group experience—one that any good teacher can lead—which is not a psychological appendage to education but a deceptively easy way to the very heart of learning, to the self-confidence that ensures the motivation to learn. Twenty minutes is not a scientific time-attention span; it is a practical amount of time in the schedule of a school day.

The teacher becomes the facilitator of a modified encounter group after a brief training period, and his course book is the HDP manual, which is more an outline than a plan. Let's look at the HDP week's plan for Awareness of Positive Behavior, one part of a year-long program. On the first day, the teacher brings to the circle a bowl of fifteen peanuts—or candy, grapes, or jellybeans. Children love something that gives them oral gratification. The teacher says: "I'm going to do something that is nice," and she presents a peanut to a child, naming the child and asking him how he feels about the gift. Obviously, very few children feel bad. Children, being egocentric, naturally would rather get themselves food and thus miss the chance to learn they have the power to make someone feel good, or bad. So the teacher says something like: "Who wants to make someone feel good?" until all the children have given away a treat. (The day's fringe lesson—there need be no losers in order to have winners in a group.)

On Tuesday, the group is presented with broken crayon halves and with masking tape, and the teacher shows that something that has been broken can be repaired. On Wednesday, each member of the circle tells about something good he did for someone outside the circle. By Thursday, the children are asking each other: "What can I do for you that would be nice?" They are learning to inquire, consider, and respond. They are learning, too, their own responsibility and power. On Friday, the teacher discusses the significance of the week.

Every child wants to succeed; every child has the same questions when he starts to school: "Am I safe? Can I cope with this? Will I be accepted?" The child is not a cognitive machine. He will feel like a failure unless he perceives success, unless he really feels power and responsibility for what happens to him, and around him. If he feels strong, he *can* achieve far more in school and in life itself.

Rationale for the Program

The Human Development Program grew out of my fifteen years as a psychotherapist whose patients still had the very young child's early school fears: "Am I safe? Can I cope with this? Will I be accepted?" The HDP is an ambitious program, granted, and it is the first time that such a regularly scheduled daily group plan has been used for normal schoolchildren. I see it as the kind of strengthening process during school days that can prevent three problems that patients who come to therapists invariably have in common: insufficient awareness of the motives determining personal behavior; a great need for more real self-confidence; and too dim an understanding of the causes and effects in interpersonal relationships.

The personality-development theory of Karen Horney, who relates personal growth to social relationships, provided the major theoretical basis for this new program, which I developed and tested in partnership with Uvaldo Palomares of San Diego State College. Miss Horney concentrates on the basic drives to achieve mastery and to gain approval; her conviction is that the child with such urges develops a healthy self-concept and the incentive to strive for further self-realization. Thus, and I agree, further successes increase motivation and lead to even further success in an ever-upward spiral.

Our Magic Circle groups aim to dispel what Harry Stack Sullivan described perfectly as "the delusion of uniqueness," the notion people have that they are different from others and therefore somehow inferior. In our circles, children see that others feel unsure and have fears; and each child can perceive that others in the group are much more *like* him than they are different from him. The children also get positive reinforcement through success at every session. Their tasks are challenging, but the chances for success are excellent. (After all, the program is set up to reinforce confidence.)

We also applied the research of William Schutz into the structure of interpersonal relationships. Schutz identified three variables—inclusion, control, and affection—in any dyad, or relationship between two people. Personality difficulties arise when a variable is extremely tilted. The emotional effects of extreme imbalance are obvious: with *inclusion*, too much means violation of a child's privacy, and too little is rejection; with *control*, too much means adult decisions that children could make for themselves, and the reverse is shattering; and with *affection*, the poles are smothering and coldness.

The Program Structure

In sifting a variety of personality theories in efforts to find common attributes and to give our theory universality, we listed those positive, effective personal characteristics that can be measured with some degree of agreement by men of differing theoretical orientations; and we selected characteristics that actually can be rated on a modified Fels Child Behavior Scale. Because major positive traits all derive largely from awareness, self-confidence, and social interaction, we built our Human Development Program, a thirty-six-week daily group plan, around those three critical areas. Each week, a different aspect of each is stressed. Ours is an existential approach, built around what children feel and see. It is *not* moralistic.

In the HDP we use those effective group-therapy and group-encounter techniques that have as their goals the development of greater awareness and a higher level of functioning; and our program is tailored so it is handled within the elementary language and the grasp of children. We have attempted to develop provocative stimuli that are significant but not threatening, and to provide a way to open children to a discussion of life that will leave them confident and not eviscerated, as many adults have found themselves after self-exploration weekends of intensive group encounter.

The experiences in the daily Magic Circle groups always are related specifically to program goals. If teachers did not plan specifically to teach children the letter "P," their students might or might not learn that particular lesson. In the same way, development of responsibility and self-confidence is not left to chance. For instance, it takes only a few sessions for a child to learn that everybody has fears—because that lesson is a planned part of the curriculum.

This same planning anticipates and provides for sharpening of the tools needed for effective adjustment *before* those strengths are needed academically. The child is taught appreciation for what others do for him. And he is taught to be honest about his resentments instead of learning to deny their existence or to repress them. The atmosphere in the Human Development Program is open and free, except that any "acting out" is stopped immediately by the leader. This is a learning program, *not* therapy.

It should be stressed at this point that our program is not geared to produce manners in children that will help them manipulate people. We have no intention of training better psychopaths. The children in the Human Development Program, I am convinced, are learning at an early and impressionable age what adults too often learn painfully through psychotherapy—that both the negative and the positive are natural. In place of socially acquired feelings of guilt, we believe that children can develop in a socially constructive way, with solid feelings of identification, compassion, and empathy.

We decided to begin with children at the earliest age they can be reached by trained personnel. Since verbal expressiveness is considered important and because a degree of mental maturity is desired, the nursery-school age of four was chosen as the logical place to begin. It is highly probable that important work toward establishment of personal effectiveness could be done in earlier years if children can be reached at that time.

It was not a program developed by psychologists and then presented to teachers that we originated, but a combination of education and psychology. The background of Uvaldo Palomares, whose doctoral studies were preceded by experience as a classroom teacher, enabled us to unite practical application with our theory from the beginning.

Our first experimental program was introduced at the Twin Trees Nursery School in La Jolla, California, in 1964. By testing and refinement, we developed a curriculum that explains personality development in simple terms, describes the most common defense maneuvers, suggests constructive interventions for maladaptive behavior, and gives semistructured daily plans for classroom use.

Through experimentation we found that the ideal group consists of ten children. Smaller groups offer the children less opportunity to discover the large range of individual differences in human reactions, while larger groups demand too much patience from the children while they wait to hold the center of attention. The sessions are held daily because repetition is vital to learning, and the same children meet at the same hour with the same adult in order to develop in each child a sense of security. Sessions could run longer than the scheduled twenty minutes but for the demands of the curriculum—one group of four-year-olds broke their circle reluctantly after seventy minutes.

We arrange the children in a circle to avoid the usual teacher-in-front-of-the-room feeling. As we researched the program, it became apparent that when seated in a circle, children make a conscious effort to pull into the group those children who usually hang back and do not contribute to the games.

Our kindergarten curriculum is divided into units of six weeks each. The lessons are designed to strengthen those concepts introduced originally in the earlier nursery school circle (see box). Five-year-olds develop mastery in motor coordination through games of graduated difficulty in which they jump onto boxes, close their eyes and touch their noses, stand on one foot, or pick up two things at the same time with one hand. These same children develop mastery in performance skills with zippers, buttons, and dustcloths and by watering plants to make them grow. Names of objects and people are learned, along with concepts such as many, few, more, and less. Learning takes place within a framework that discusses useful application to the child—as he sees it—of each skill or bit of knowledge.

Mastery is a concept that embodies the acquisition of personally meaningful and useful skills with an accompanying feeling of self-confidence. Self-confidence is inevitably acquired when a child is confronted with a challenge that is difficult enough to be interesting but that he perceives will almost certainly give him success

Awareness of self and others (six weeks)
    Positive feelings
    Positive thoughts
    Positive behavior

Mastery (six weeks)
    Language concepts
    Mathematical concepts
    Performance skills
    Motor coordination
    Health and care of clothing
    Social comprehension

Social interaction (six weeks)
    What did you do that somebody likes?
    What did you do that somebody did not like?
    What somebody did that you liked.
    What somebody did that you did not like.
    Learning to ask for kind behavior.
    Learning to give kind behavior.

Awareness (six weeks)
    Positive feelings
    Negative feelings
    Positive thoughts
    Negative thoughts
    Positive behavior
    Negative behavior

Mastery (six weeks)
    Repetition, on a more sophisticated level, of earlier mastery unit.

Social interaction (six weeks)
    Repetition, on a more sophisticated level, of earlier social interaction unit.

if he tries. Here there is always the personal involvement of "I bet I can whip this problem." When the child then is highly motivated to try, and he succeeds, he is immediately praised by the highly credible and very powerfully perceived teacher, and this deeply reinforces the feeling that "I am a capable person at something, and one who is recognized as such from a socially significant quarter." This is a time-tested and proven formula for the acquisition of self-confidence, and is specifically planned for and allowed to happen. Simple as this may seem, unless the teacher deliberately focuses upon building a genuine sense of "I can-ness," she almost invariably places the emphasis on the acquisition of facts and all too often ignores the more fundamental issue of whether the child is developing an increased belief in himself as a person who can try, who can cope, and who has a sense of optimism about being able to deal with the new and unknown problems that will continually be facing him.

Through games like "You can make him feel bad or good," and "Can you guess what makes him mad?" our five-year-old group members begin truly to understand the cause-and-effect relationship between the behavior of one person and the feelings produced in another person. Children learn that angry feelings are universal and natural and that there always is some reason for them, even though it might not be clear at that moment. Children in the program have the chance to discuss emotionalized experiences in a calm and rational setting; the teacher acts as a nonmoralizing listener and creates what Carl Rogers has called *acceptance*.

A single game may be continued over a period of several days until each child in the group has contributed. Great emphasis is placed upon the need for each child to express himself; children learn best by doing. Whenever a child participates in a game, he is recognized by name and praised for his contribution when he finishes.

Discussions of negative behavior are introduced deliberately into the kindergarten circle. While we have found that sometimes discussion of negative behavior is too threatening for four-year-olds, the negative can be discussed easily by five-year-old children in the second semester of kindergarten. Five-year-old children in our programs then have had eighteen months with HDP in which to talk about positive events, to build self-confidence, and to comprehend and describe emotional reactions.

Pictures of children engaged in negative behavior (fighting, teasing) are shown to the group. The behavior of children in the picture is discussed in an atmosphere devoid of criticism, moralizing, or embarrassment; negativism is seen as a specific behavior that makes different people react in a certain way.

This game has had dramatic results. One boy, after he punched the girl who sat in the chair next to him, announced to his classmates: "It makes me feel good to make her feel bad." Then he said he wanted to be a bad guy when he grew up. Yet within a month, this same boy was sure he wanted to be a good guy, and during the remainder of the school year, his classroom achievement improved. Naturally, so did his acceptance by his teacher and his classmates.

Through continued testing, we have developed a curriculum for the HDP that retains only those tasks and experiences children find exciting. In this sense, the children themselves have written the program.

The Future

Over the past five years, the Human Development Program has been tested and refined in a variety of socioeconomic school settings and now reaches 60,000 school children each year. The curriculum is used in nursery schools, Head Start programs, and public school systems.

Our program for building healthy egos is now used in more than 2,000 nursery schools, kindergartens, and early grades in California, New Mexico, Washington, New York, Canada, and in Australia, where it has been introduced by A. R. Greig, University of Melbourne. Regional workshops in the use of the program are given continuously throughout California and other states, where teachers are taught to use the program through demonstration, lectures, and discussions. It has been introduced into elementary education courses at the University of Southern California, San Diego State College, and New Mexico University.

Teachers now using the program report that disci-

pline problems are reduced markedly and that children show increased personal involvement, greater verbal expressiveness, more self-confidence, higher motivation, far more personal awareness, and an increased degree of comprehension of social interactions.

While these reports are subjective, the development of the Bessell-Palomares Rating Scales has made it possible for us to plan a research program that will yield quantified results. Scales have been designed to rate positive traits numerically and to arrive at an overall developmental index. Administration of IQ tests, of course, is another way to assess HDP results. If our theory is correct, these children will score higher on intelligence tests after participating in the program, not because they will be more intelligent—intelligence is related mostly to heredity—but because they will be more highly motivated. Test scores often reflect the motivation of children.

The Human Development Program now is complete for four- and five-year-olds, and the three basic themes are projected for six more years. Our experimental sessions continue with children in Grades 1 through 6 at the All Hallows School in La Jolla, and in the National City School District. Here data are being gathered for development of a curriculum for the first six grades.

Everyone wonders what results will actually obtain from this approach to specifically build strong and healthy personalities. At Systems Development Corporation the prospect was found to be so exciting that the program has been chosen as one of several educational innovations to study under a seven-year Ford Foundation research grant at Pacoima School in San Fernando.

Historically, mental health has been conceived as that which is left after all the emotional problems have been resolved effectively. In this approach is an assumption that after a person has psychotherapy, he is pretty much the individual he would have been if he had been without serious emotional problems in the first place. This assumption has no supportive evidence, and we believe it has sidetracked us from learning what children would be like if raised from the start under conditions conducive to effective functioning.

The Human Development Program, which may be the forerunner of a more successful approach to the education of effective citizens, is at the Kitty Hawk stage. The hope is that, through testing and refinement, an eight-year program can be developed from our rudimentary beginnings that will produce confident, personally effective people. If we are right, this will mean fewer dropouts, fewer failures, fewer angry young men, and fewer disenfranchised members of the human family.

Can I Come to Summerhill?

A. S. Neill

Mr. Neill, head of Summerhill school and author of the book that made it so well known, makes a clear differentiation between education *and the learning of traditional school subjects. Central to his concept of education is a strong emphasis on freedom—individual, social, and sexual. If the emotions are free, the intellect will take care of itself.*

A basic premise in his educational philosophy is that man is born good but becomes hateful and violent as a result of the harsh and stifling society he has created. Repression of sexual and other life-giving energies and blind conformity of the crowd produce much of the sickness of the world. Summerhill is organized to allow the individual to act in a free way, not tied to the pressures or opinions of the crowd, as long as he does not infringe on the rights of others. An important distinction is made between the freely determined values and attitudes that an individual may hold and the fact that behavior *related to these attitudes may have to be modified to meet the requirements of society.*

Just over twenty years ago I had two books published in New York, *The Problem Teacher* and *The Problem Family*. So far as I could make out, each issue sold a few hundred copies and the rest were sold as remainders at a few dimes each. The press notices I got were either lukewarm or hostile. One called the books old hat. "We have lived through this in the States and there is nothing new for us." Twenty years later the book *Summerhill* became a best seller in the States. Why? I have no idea. I like to think that the United States has come up to date rather than that I have gone out of date. I do not know why I get so large a mail from the United States. It is mostly from young people, and in the seven years since the book was published I can recall only two hostile letters. Many are from schoolchildren. "Can I come to Summerhill? I hate my school. It is all pressurization. The teachers make every lesson dull and dead and originality is frowned upon." Oddly enough, although our British education is all wrong, I never get letters from home children.

The mystery to me is this: Why has America become conscious that its education is not good enough? Why

now and not twenty years ago? Surely the schools have not changed all that much. But is it a case of a change of society? Is society sicker than it was a couple of decades ago? I fancy that that is the deep reason. In all countries youth is rebelling. Alas, too often rebelling against all that does not matter. The hippies, the flower merchants show their protests not against war, not against race discrimination, not against the stupid learning we call education; no, all the challenge is the right to wear long hair and leather jackets and blue jeans. That is the impression I get in this country, but from what I hear and read about America, the young, especially in the universities, are challenging real evils—the insane dollar values, the dead uniformity of the people who have been molded and indoctrinated so much that they are automatic slaves to any ideas thrown out by the press and the TV screens. In Britain I think that the average TV program is geared to a nation of ten-year-olds. Our B.B.C. refused to put on *The War Game* because it told of the horrors of an atomic war and it might upset the nice folks who want to think that God is in his Heaven and all is right with the world. The young feel that they have been cheated by the old, lied to, castrated by their parents and teachers. They no longer accept glib answers—in Vietnam we are saving the world from Communism; in South Africa we are preserving the God-given rights of the superior whites; in America we are battling to preserve the white civilization. It is significant that all these reasons involve hate and war and possibly ultimate death to humanity. Youth sees a world full of savagery. Hitler's six million Jews paved the way for a world that accepted torture and death as almost commonplace factors in our modern life. In short, the world is very, very sick, and youth feels it but, alas, cannot do much about it. Summerhill's good friend Joan Baez, recently in prison, has no power over the hate merchants; all she can do is to march in protest and then be carted to prison. It is the helplessness of youth that so often brings despair.

In this American *Stimmung* the book *Summerhill* was launched in 1960. It caught on because it was voicing what so many of the young had felt but had not intellectualized, had not made conscious. For its theme was freedom—real freedom, not the sham thing so often called democracy. Freedom for all to grow at their own pace; freedom from all indoctrination, religious, political, moral; freedom for children to live in their own community, making their own social laws. To many a youth Summerhill became synonymous with Paradise. I hasten to say that it isn't—*Gott sei Dank!* Most of the rebellion stems from home, from what Wilhelm Reich called the compulsive family, the family that strangles youth, fears youth, often hates youth. From my mail I am led to believe that the American family is more dangerous than the British one. I never get the sort of letter I had two days ago from New York. "I am seventeen and I am allowed no freedom at all. I have to be in at certain hours and if I am late my father hits me. I hate my parents." A girl of a middle-class family. I have had scores of similar letters. A boy of fifteen writes, "I hate school and cannot concentrate on my work and my parents bully me all the time because they say that I must go to college and get a good job." I have no idea how much truth is in Vance Packard's *The Status Seekers*, but even if a tenth of it is true it gives a terrible picture of American civilization. A Cadillac-civilization with its sequel, dope and drugs and misery for those who cannot accept the god of cars and furs and wealth.

This looks like an attack on a country by an outsider and it may well be resented by some readers, but I do not mean it as an attack; it is a case of trying to think aloud the answer to the question: Why did the Summerhill book catch on in the United States? At home we have our own miseries and troubles. The growing race hate due to the immigration from Jamaica. The futility of a culture that dwells on bingo and football crowds, on infantile TV programs; a culture that gives the cheap sensational press millions of readers while the more cultured papers—*The New Statesman,* the *Observer,* the *Sunday Times*—too often struggle to keep themselves alive. World sickness is not confined to North America. Russia has its teen-age gangsters also.

One reason why Summerhill appealed to Americans may be that it is, so to say, antieducation. The great American educationists, Dewey, Kilpatrick, and their kind were mostly pre-Freudian in their outlook. They kept linking education to learning, and today in all countries educational journals concentrate on the learning process. I escaped that trap. I was and I am ill-versed on what the educationists did. I never read Rousseau or Pestalozzi or Froebel; what I read in Montessori I did not like, partly because it made play the mate of learning. Learning what? Summerhill is not a seat of learning; it is a seat of living. We are not so proud of David who became a professor of mathematics as we are of Jimmy who was hateful and antisocial and is now a warm-hearted engineer with much charity and love to give out. Summerhill puts learning in its own place. I have more than once written that if the emotions are free, the intellect will look after itself. What a waste it all is! Sixty years ago I could read some Latin and Greek. Today I can't decipher the Latin words on a tombstone. Our schools teach children to read Shakespeare and Hardy and Tennyson, and when they leave school the vast majority never read anything better than a crime story. For my part I'd abolish nearly every school subject, making geography and history matters for the school library, and quadratic equations a luxury for the few boys and girls who loved math. Abolish exams—and my school will have only creative teachers —art, music, drama, handwork, and so on.

Every man has a bee in his bonnet. It was comforting to read in Erich Fromm that Freud had to be in the station an hour before his train was due. My original bee was psychology. In the 1920s my home was Vienna and my associates the psychoanalysts. Like all young fools I thought that Utopia was just 'round the corner. Make the unconscious conscious and you have a world full of love and fellowship with no hate. I grew out of that phase but did retain the belief that education must primarily deal with the emotions. Working for many years with problem children made my belief stronger. I saw that the aim of all education must be to produce happy, balanced, pro-life children, and I knew that all the exams and books in a million classrooms could not do a thing to make children balanced. A B.A. could be a hopeless neurotic—I am an M.A. myself. A professor could remain at the age of ten emotionally. The emotional level of the British Cabinet or the American Pentagon is anyone's guess; my own guess is a low one. Today in any school anywhere it is the head that is educated; every exam paper proves the point.

Now, one cannot flee from reality. I cannot say to prospective parents, "Exams and school subjects are not education and I refuse to teach the ordinary school subjects." That is what the Americans would call flunking out, and, by the way, I get too many letters from students in the United States saying, "I can't go on with my college career. The teaching is too dull; I am flunking out. I want to be a child psychologist." I answer that they won't let one be a child psychologist unless one accepts their qualification demands. I wrote to the last man who had flunked out, "If you haven't the guts to walk through the muck heaps, how can you ever expect to smell the roses you value so much?"

I do not find this flunking-out element in old Summerhill pupils. One of my first pupils spent two years standing at a mechanical belt in a car factory. He is now a successful engineer with his own business. His brother, who wanted to be a doctor, had to pass an exam in Latin. In just over a year he passed the matriculation exam in Latin. "I hated the stuff but it was in my way and I had to master it." That was over forty years ago, when students did not as a rule flunk out. I do not think that youth has become defeatist; rather, it is that society has reached a point of futility and cheapness and danger where youth, frustrated by the mundane standard of success, simply gives up in despair. "Make Love not War" is a most appropriate motto for youth even if youth feels it is a hopeless cry, and it is a hopeless cry; the hate men who make wars force youth to die for country, but when the young demand freedom to have a sex life, holy hypocritical hands are held up in horror. Youth is free to die but not to live and love.

I fear I am rambling, not sticking to the point. My consolation—too many who stick to the point make it a blunt one. I ramble because I am trying to evaluate Summerhill as a factor in the sick world, really asking what value freedom has for youth. One is naturally apt to think that one's geese are swans; one tends to forget or ignore the outside world, so that when a lecturer in education in an American college wrote and told me that over 70 percent of his students thought that Summerhill was all wrong, it came as a shock. I had repressed the idea that when the young are conditioned and indoctrinated from cradle days, it is almost impossible for them to break away, to challenge. Few can stand alone without a supporting crowd behind them. "The strongest man is he who stands most alone." Ibsen.

I like to think that freedom helps one to stand outside the madding crowd. Symbolically one sees differences. The conventional suburban office-goer with his striped trousers and his neat tie and his neater mind on one side. On the other, the creator, the artist to whom exterior things mean but little. Compare the tailoring of L. B. J. with that of a film director or a Picasso. Symbols, but characteristic. Put it this way: Summerhill gets hundreds of visitors, but I do not think that any visitor ever notices that my staff never wear ties. Summerhill hasn't got to the Old-School-Tie stage. But one cannot carry such phantasying too far; my old friend Bertrand

Russell wears a tie, and no one would claim that he is a crowd man.

I think that one aspect of Summerhill is that, rightly or wrongly, it gives pupils an anticrowd psychology. I could not imagine any old pupil following a Hitler or for that matter a Kennedy or a Reagan. This sounds incongruous because the chief feature of Summerhill is the self-government, the making of laws by one and all from the age of five to eighty-four. Pupils become ego-conscious and at the same time community-conscious. Bill can do what he likes all day long as long as he does not interfere with the freedom of anyone else; he can sleep all day if he wants to, but he is not allowed to play a trumpet when others want to talk or sleep. It is as near democracy as one can get; every child is a member of parliament able to speak "in the house." No doubt because this democracy is real and honest, our old pupils cannot tolerate the sham we name politics. Because politicians have to rely on votes, nearly every urgent reform is delayed for two generations. In England a Member of Parliament has—say—a predominantly Catholic constituency or a Baptist one. How can he act honestly when faced with some reform—a bill to abolish punishment for homosexuality, a much-needed reform of the divorce and abortion laws? Was any great man a politician? Any Darwin, any Freud, any Einstein, any Beethoven? Was any big man ever a crowd-compeller, a demagogue?

When children are free they become wonderfully sincere. They cannot act a part; they cannot stand up in the presence of a school inspector because they will not countenance insincerity and make-believe. Tact forces them to make minor adaptations, as it does with you and me. I dutifully doff my hat to a lady although I realize that it is a meaningless, even dishonest, gesture, hiding the fact that in a patriarchal society a woman is inferior in status, in pay, in power. To tell a social white lie is often a necessity but to live a lie is something that free people cannot do. And my pupils feel that to be a member of a crowd must involve living a lie.

This crowd psychology angle is important. It is at the root of the sickness of the world. A neighboring country insults your flag, and many thousands of young men die for the honor and glory of their fatherland. National hatreds everywhere, Greek versus Turkey; Israel versus Arabs; Rhodesian white versus black. And it is not only the nationalism crowd. Our football grounds are full of irrational, partisan hate and violence. Gang warfare is not confined to Chicago. Yet in a way violence is minor. It is the violence that a crowd inflicts on its members that frightens, the violence of intimidating, of molding. A school uniform means: We are members of a crowd, a crowd that will not tolerate opposition. We must all dress alike, think alike, act alike. For the great law of any crowd is: Thou shalt conform. The world is sick because its crowds are sick.

Education therefore should aim at abolishing crowd

psychology. It can do this only by allowing the individual to face life and its choices freely. Such an education cannot lead to egocentricity and utter selfishness, not if the individual is free within the confines of the social order, an order made by himself. The slogan "All the way with L. B. J." shows the iniquity of the crowd, a system that makes crowd members sheep who can feel the most elementary emotions without having the intellectual capacity to connect such emotions with reason. Today our schools educate the head and leave the emotions to the crowd-compellers—the press, the radio, the TV, the churches, the commercial exploiters with their lying advertisements. Our pop heroes and film stars have become our leading schoolmasters, dealing with real emotions. What teacher in what school could have a few hundred hysterical females screaming their heads off when he appeared?

The danger today is undeveloped emotion, perverted emotion, infantile emotion. Millions scream in Britain every Saturday afternoon when their favorite football teams take the field. If the evening paper had a front page in big lettering "Atom War Very Near," most of the spectators would turn to the back page to see the latest scores. Crowd emotions are not touched by news of starvation in India or China. It is this same unattached, unrealized emotion that makes the crowd numb to any realization of a likely atomic war. Crowd emotion is not shocked by our inhuman and un-Christlike treatment of criminals in prison; it does not even realize that the inhumanity is there. And none of us is guiltless. I do not cut down my tobacco and give the savings to the starving nations. We are all in the trap, and only the more aware of us try to find a way out. My own way is Summerhill, or rather the idea behind Summerhill: the belief that man is originally good, that, for reasons no one so far knows, man kills his own life and the lives of his children by harsh and antilife laws and morals and taboos. It is so easy to cry, "Man is a sinner and he must be redeemed by religion" or whatnot. God and the Devil were comfortable explanations of good and evil.

One thing I think Summerhill has proved is that man does not need to become a "sinner," that man does not naturally hate and kill. The crowd in Summerhill is a humane one. In forty-seven years I have never seen a jury punish a child for stealing; all it demanded was that the value of the theft be paid back. When children are free they are not cruel. Freedom and aggression do not go together. I have known a few children who were reared with self-regulation, that is, without fear and outside discipline and imposed morality. They seem to have much less aggression than most children have, suggesting to me that the Freudians with their emphasis on aggression must have studied the wrong children.

Even in Summerhill, where very few pupils were self-regulated, there is a peacefulness, a minimum of criticism, a tolerance that is quite uncommon. When a

Negro pupil came from the States, not even the youngest child seemed to notice her color. Our TV showed white faces full of hatred when black pupils were being stoned in the deep South. This is alarming. We can condition children to hate and kill by giving them a hate environment. But we can also give them another sort of environment—were I a Christian I'd call it a love-your-neighbor environment. But then, what is a Christian? Catholics and Protestants beat children in home and school—didn't Jesus say suffer the little children? The Christians see that they suffer, all right. But to narrow the life negation to religion is wrong. A humanist can hate life and children; he can be as anti-sex as any Calvinist.

Summerhill has not answered many questions, the biggest one being: Why does humanity kill the life of children, why does it take more easily to hate than to love? Why did jackboot Fascism conquer a nation of 60 million?

One answer to the question of world sickness is sex repression. Make sex a sin and you get perversions, crime, hates, wars. Approve of children's sex as the Trobriand Islanders did under a matriarchal system and a Malinowski will fail to find any trace of sex crime or homosexuality before the missionaries came and segregated the sexes. Wilhelm Reich, to me the greatest psychologist since Freud, dwelt on the necessity for a full, natural orgastic life as a cure for the sickness of an antilife society. Then came the new American Interpersonal Relationship school of Sullivan and Horney, with long case histories of patients who seemed to have no sex at all. I have a book on problem children written by an Adlerian; I failed to find the word sex in it. And in all this divergence of views on sex, what can one believe? One can make the guess that the torturers of German Jews were sex perverts, but can one safely conclude that the men in the Pentagon are Hawks because of their sex repressions?

I have gone through many phases in the last fifty years, the most exciting my long friendship with Homer Lane and then with Reich. Now, at eighty-four, I simply do not know the truth about sex. Is a teacher who canes a boy's bottom a repressed homosexual or a sadist or simply a man who has never been conscious of what he is doing? I ask because my father in his village school tawsed children with a leather strap, and when I became a teacher I automatically did likewise without ever once wondering if it were good or bad. Looking back now, I see that one motive was fear, fear of losing one's dignity, one's power; fear that any slackness would lead to anarchy. I cannot see anything sexual in my tawsing.

Summerhill society is a sex-approving society. Every child soon learns that there is no moral feeling about masturbation or nudism or sex play. But every adolescent is conscious of the fact that if approval meant the sharing of bedrooms by adolescents, the school would be closed by the Establishment. One old boy once said to me: "The fear of closing the school if pregnancies occurred gave us a new form of sex repression." The difficulty was and is this: How far can a school go in being prosex in an antisex society? Not very far, I fear. Yet one factor is of moment; the pupils are conscious of our attitude of approval. They have had no indoctrination about sin or shame, no moralizing from Mrs. Grundy. Their free attitude shows itself in minor ways. In our local cinema a film showed a chamber pot. The audience went into fits of obscene laughter but our pupils did not even smile; one or two asked me later why the people laughed. Free children cannot be shocked—by cruelty, yes, but by sex, never.

Summerhill products are often said to be quiet, unaggressive, tolerant citizens, and I wonder how much their rational attitude on sex has to do with their calmness of life. They prove that censorship is the product of a life-hating civilization. I never see our adolescents taking from the school library *Lady Chatterley* or *Fanny Hill*. A girl of sixteen said they were boring.

Most of our old pupils are pacific. They do not march with banners against the H-bomb or against racial discrimination. I cannot imagine any of them ever supporting warmongers or religious revivalists or censors. But how much this has to do with a free attitude to sex I cannot know. Certainly sex is the most repressed of all emotions. Most of us were made antisex when in our cradles our hands were taken from our genitals, and it is an arresting thought that the men who have the power to begin a nuclear war are men who were made sex-negative long ago. Anglo-Saxon four-letter words are still taboo in most circles, maybe partly for class reasons; a navvy says fuck while a gentleman says sexual intercourse.

I confess to being muddled about the whole affair of sex. I do not know whether if we all experienced Reich's perfect orgasm, there would be an end to war and crime and hate. *I hae ma doots.* Yet it is true that people who have a prosex attitude to life are the ones most likely to be charitable, to be tolerant, to be creative. Those who do not consider themselves sinners do not cast the first stone. For charity I would go to Bertrand Russell rather than to Billy Graham.

Billy naturally leads to religion. Summerhill has no religion. I fancy that very few religionists approve of it. A leading Church of England priest once called it the most religious school in the world, but few parsons would agree with him. It is interesting to note that I have had many letters of approval from Unitarians in the United States. I asked one Unitarian minister what his religion was. Did he believe in God? No, he said. In eternal life? "Good heavens, no. Our religion is giving out love in this life," and I guess that is exactly what the Church of England priest meant. It is our being on the side of the child (Homer Lane's phrase) that has

aroused so much antagonism among religionists. The other day a Catholic school inspector told a meeting of Catholics that corporal punishment was practiced much more in their schools than in Protestant ones. "We beat the body to save the soul." In the days of that life-hater John Knox I would have been burned at the stake. The widening interest in the freedom that Summerhill stands for fits in with the lessening belief in religion. Most young people, outside the Roman Catholic faith, have no interest in religion. To them God is dead. God to them was father, molder, punisher, a fearful figure. The gods and fathers were always on the side of the suppressors. In Britain the enemies of youth, those who

call for the return of beating with the cat, those who want to censor plays and films and language, those who demand strict punishment for the teen-age delinquents, they are not the young; they are the old, the old who have forgotten their teen-age period.

I am sure that the growing interest in freedom for children coincides with modern youth's rejection of a joyless, repressive religion. A religion that has become perverted. Christ's "love your neighbor as yourself" has become: Okay, so long as he isn't a Jew or a black. "Let him who is without sin among you cast the first stone" has become: Censor plays and novels and measure bathing costumes. Owing to the threat of universal incineration, youth today is possibly more prolife than it has ever been. Juvenile crime is really at bottom an attempt to find the joy of life killed by morals and discipline and punishment. In the days when Summerhill had many delinquents they went out cured simply because they were free from adult standards of behavior. Religion must be rejected because it tells the young how to live, but it does not need to be religion; I have known humanists who gave their children sex repression; I know agnostics who believe in beating children. Really, what one believes does not matter; it is what one is that matters. After all, religion is geographical; had I been born in Arabia I'd have had three wives and, alas, no whisky.

There is a comic element in religion even if there isn't a joke in the Bible or the Prayer Book. The true believer must know that Bertrand Russell will roast in hell for eternity while Billy Graham sits at the right hand of God. With Russell to look after, the familiar words "poor Devil" will have a real significance.

What is the outlook for freedom? Will the minority ever take over from the majority? And if it does, will it retain its belief in freedom? Doesn't Ibsen say somewhere that a truth remains a truth for twenty years, then the majority takes it up and it becomes a lie? Summerhill has sixty-four children who are free from molding: the world has millions of children who have little or no freedom, millions of adults who frankly are sheep. One tragedy of life is that men have followers. Men who remain disciples are always inferiors. The Pharisee who thanked God that he was not as other men may have been a conceited ass, but on the other hand he may have got hold of something. There is something wrong when millions who praise the Beatles never heard of Milton or Freud or Cézanne, when millions kill the life of their babies, when thousands of young men die in a battle for they know not what. Antilife is all around us, and I wish I knew why. I wish I knew why mankind kills what it loves. I do not know the answer; all I know is that when children are free they do not kill life; they do not condemn their fellow men. They do not want to tell others how to live. It is significant that old pupils do not seek jobs where they will boss others; few have gone into business. I used to

daydream of one's becoming a tycoon and endowing the school, knowing all the time that he would be so hard-boiled that he would not endow anything.

I am not trying to sell Summerhill. I am trying to say that the cure for the sickness of man does not lie in politics or religion or humanism; nay, the cure is freedom for children to be themselves. Like many others I once thought that the Russian Revolution would bring Utopia to youth, for it began with freedom for children, self-government in the schools. Then, according to Reich, the psychologists took charge, and youth became sacrificed to political antilife, so that today communism has no connection with naturally growing individual freedom. Indeed I often wonder why the Americans are so scared of communism. Both systems believe in the terror of the bomb; both discipline and castrate children; both believe that education means subjects and exams and acquired knowledge. The only difference I can see is who takes the profit? The Russian Revolution proved that the sickness of the world cannot be cured by politics.

The only answer that I can think of is freedom for children, individual freedom, social freedom, sexual freedom as in a small way practiced in Summerhill.

I said that I thought Wilhelm Reich the greatest psychologist since Freud. His diagnosis of man's sickness is deep and wise. Man flees from natural sex by armoring himself against joy in life, stiffening his body, fearing any signs of genitality, changing good emotions into "emotional plague," in short, becoming antilife, hence wars and many diseases and child-beating. Even if one accepts Reich's diagnosis, the question arises: What can be done about it? How can we prevent folks from becoming antisex and antilife? Analysis of any school is not the answer. What effect on humanity have all the case histories ever published? Do all the things Melanie Klein found in babies have any bearing on the education of children? So far, psychology has been a matter of diagnosing without any salient suggestions for a cure. Ah, yes, some cases of cures of individual neurotics, but the cure for a sick world, none. A Scientologist has just told me that he could cure any problem child in my school in ten days!

Are we all fakers? Self-deluders? Do the hundreds of books on psychology published every year have any effect at all? I am inclined to say none, but I am biased, for I cannot read a book on psychology now.

The psychologists have narrowed the science—or is it an art? The doctors have limited psychology to the consulting room and the rich and those with time to spare. How many psychoanalysts have opened schools? A few—Anna Freud, Susan Isaacs, for example, but the main body of Freudians has done nothing in the way of prophylaxis. The Summerhill Society of New York issues a list of schools claiming to have self-regulation and self-government. Some may be excellent but, as I have not seen any of them, I cannot give an opinion pro or anti. I do not think that they belong to any special schools of psychology and I sincerely hope that they don't. I am sure that the list does not contain the name of the school that claimed to be Summerhillian and washed out a boy's mouth with soap and water when he swore.

The future of psychology should lie not in the consulting room or the hospital for neurosis but in the infant bedroom and the infant school. Mr. Brown's phobia of spiders may fascinate his analyst, but his phobia is as nothing in a world of millions of half-alive children.

To return to Summerhill, it went through the stages of the century—the faith in analysis, the futile attempt to find the original trauma in a young thief. I read them all—Freud, Jung, Adler, Rank, Stekel, Reich—and got more and more confused by their psychological jargon. I never learned the meaning of words like manic-depression, compulsive neurosis, hysteria. Never knew how specialists could draw the line between one and another. Oh, so many were brilliant in their diagnosis and treatment, but in the end what did one learn? And today I feel as confused about the Interpersonal Relationship folks, for, if men like Stekel seemed to overemphasize sex, they seem to denigrate it altogether. So I left schools of thought and concentrated on Summerhill, forgetting theory and avoiding words like complex. "Everyone is right in some way," Reich used to say, the corollary being that everyone is wrong in some way.

Let us face the truth, that we are all little men, even the greatest among us. We do not know how and why the super Rolls Royce, the human body, ticks. We know nothing about life and how it began, nor can we account for the universe. We do not know why Brown dies of cancer and his brother of diabetes. In the psychological realm we cannot account for a Bach or a Milton or a Hitler. We know little about heredity or the origins of love and hate. A doctor does not know what causes a headache. So that we should be wary of panaceas of all kinds—Zen Buddhism, Scientology, Theosophy, psychoanalysis, Moral Rearmament, and a few score of other isms and ologies. We must go on enquiring, searching for the truth, but if we follow a creed, if we become disciples, if we label ourselves Freudian or Reichian or Hubbardian or any other ian we have stopped growing, stopped enquiring; we become "yes" men. It worries me to hear of schools in the United States that call themselves Summerhills. One should take from others what one feels is good. No one should accept any creed, religious or political or psychological. I got much from Homer Lane; later I got much from Reich. But in both men were views that I could not accept, and thus I escaped discipleship. If a teacher claims that Summerhill inspired him, good, I wish him

luck, but if a school claims to be a new Summerhill I fear it will fail. There is a pioneer in each of us, an explorer, a visionary. As in sport we pay others to play the game for us, so in pioneering; we find it easy to look for a leader and be content to be a humble follower of Billy Graham, Sigmund Freud, Barry Goldwater, Karl Marx. Fans are arrested creators, arrested pioneers. And the big question is: in a world in which the vast majority are fans, how can a few independent people set about "curing" the Establishment?

We must remember that the Establishment has the ultimate power. A bureaucratic Ministry of Education could close my school on material grounds alone: not enough lavatories, not enough cubic feet per child in a bedroom. To be fair, the Ministry has not interfered with me in the forty-four years Summerhill has been in England. But now that the National Union of Teachers and many Labor M.P.s demand the closing of all private schools, pioneering in education is going to have a bad time. Had there been no private schools, there could not have been a Summerhill; the state, the Establishment will allow new methods of teaching history or math but it is unlikely to tolerate new methods of living in a school. Really I should vote Tory, for the Tories will not lightly give up their Etons and Harrows, and as long as we have the public schools like Rugby, the smaller private schools will be protected. Alas, the private school is, I fear, doomed by lack of finance alone. Summerhill would have died seven years ago had not the publication of *Summerhill* in the United States brought a flood of American pupils. Today people in England do not have the money to support private schools. Those who do, select the established schools, the public schools, and the big co-ed schools with their well-equipped libraries, labs, etc. Parents in all countries East and West, like teachers, still look on education as learning. Educational journals seldom mention the child or freedom or creation. When I write a letter about the teaching of English I get quite a few replies, but when I write an article on the psychology of the child no teacher answers.

I want to claim that Summerhill has for forty-seven years demanded that character is of more moment than the ability to learn subjects. I have never denigrated learning; all I have done is to put it in its second or tenth place. But what effect the school has had on education I cannot judge. Some say that the permissiveness of some schools stems from Summerhill. Who can know? I like to think that it isn't Summerhill, that it is the *Zeitgeist*, the longing of youth for freedom. Maybe some history of education in the year 2000 will have a footnote about a school called Summerfield run by a mad Scot called S. A. Neale. Sorry I won't be there to laugh at the footnote.

What Does a Summerhill Old School Tie Look Like?

Emmanuel Bernstein

A visitor to Summerhill arrives with the same kind of question that many readers of A. S. Neill's book have raised: Can children educated in this setting of permissiveness ever accept the responsibilities of life outside the school? After visiting the school itself, the author interviewed fifty former students of Summerhill currently living in the London area to ask their views of their educational experience.

Almost all the former students were employed—in a variety of positions ranging from the arts to manual labor—and almost all were living satisfying lives. When asked if there were a typical Summerhill personality, half the group mentioned tolerance as a main trait, and a quarter mentioned sincerity. In their attitude toward Summerhill, 20 percent felt completely positive, while 14 percent felt it had been harmful. A shorter stay seemed to be of greater benefit than a long one, especially if the stay occurred during adolescence. The major complaint raised by the alumni was that the school was academically weak, both in program and teaching.

One day in 1965 I walked down the tree-arched driveway leading to Summerhill School. A boy shot by me on a bicycle. I passed fields where other children roamed freely, climbing trees or nailing together private shacks. Next to a sunny corner of the main building stood an old sofa, its stuffing sticking through the worn cover. There in the morning sunlight sat a small girl of eight who, with deep concentration, was picking out more of the stuffing.

I had come to England to see Summerhill School and to meet some former students. I hoped, through interviews with former students, to answer some of the recurrent questions I have had ever since I read A. S. Neill's book, *Summerhill*. In this school, children were never required to do anything they did not wish to do. And they were allowed to do almost anything they wished as long as they did not infringe upon the rights of others. No one was required to attend any classes.

And so I wondered. Given such freedom, could children ever accept the responsibilities and limits of society? Could the products of such a permissive atmosphere adjust to the realities of life: a job, marriage, parenthood? Could they learn to cope with the authority of a traditional school?

Filled with such questions, I entered the large, vacant hall of the main building. I was shocked to find a series of bulletin boards filled with page after page of single-spaced, typed rules—with accompanying penalties. One fifteen-year-old boy told me: "There are more rules in a free school than anywhere else, even though we make them all for ourselves."

It was an interesting day. At one point I wandered into a tiny room where teen-agers were playing pianos, guitars, and harmonicas while seven- and eight-year-olds leaned against chairs and stared into space, apparently intoxicated by the music. Several of their contemporaries, who sat in overstuffed chairs, amused themselves by tipping each other over.

One girl of eight was dancing the twist with another girl, her face aglow with laughter. Someone whispered in her ear. She stopped dancing, her eyes filled with tears. Her parents had arrived to take her home—a week early. Several children quickly surrounded her, trying to give comfort. Earlier this girl had told me of her activities at the school: music, dancing, writing, reading, acting, and painting—and of her boyfriend.

But for others the outlook did not seem so optimistic. Summerhill could be lonely. One group of teen-age boys told me they were bored; their lives had become centered around their tape recorders. There was the dark, thin boy with horn-rimmed glasses, who stared blankly out of a window. And the sad little red-haired girl alone on the front steps.

In the evening I attended the weekly meeting, where children air all personal and school problems, make new rules and abolish old ones. The hall was filled with seventy-five children, sitting ten deep on the floor, up the stairway, filling every inch of space. A. S. Neill's tall, stooped figure waded slowly through his children. Occasionally he took a large pipe from his mouth to exchange a word or two. The loud talking stopped as Neill took his place on a chipped, green kitchen chair.

A boy of twelve opened the meeting. Arguments began about bedtime hours. There were complaints from a group of teen-aged boys who said they felt like "zoo animals on display" for visitors. This was discussed in relation to the practice of one enterprising group that charged a shilling apiece to see their rooms. A committee to investigate stealing was abolished; perhaps ten new rules were established; and just as many were liquidated or revised, all by "ayes" and "nays."

Later I asked Neill what happened to the children after they left the school. "They go into the arts," he replied. When asked if there was a "Summerhill personality," he said that his students came out well-balanced and sincere.

Back in London, I began my follow-up study in earnest. Officers of the Summerhill Society gave me a few names, and these persons gave me more. There are no follow-up school records. I bought an old motor scooter and a large map of the London area and began visiting the household of one former student after another. By the end of the summer, I had seen fifty Summerhill products.

Because the interview took the form of an informal discussion, the study is a subjective one. I gave no tests of any kind. But I was able to find out how former students feel about their experience at the school and just what had become of fifty children who attended Summerhill.

Most interviews lasted about four hours and took place in the homes of these former Summerhill students. I talked to twenty-nine men and twenty-one women, from sixteen to forty-nine years of age. The median age was twenty-three. The average number of years spent at Summerhill was four and three-tenths; the median was seven years. (Children may enter Summerhill as early as six and they usually leave before they are seventeen. No one "graduates" from Summerhill.) Most of the group had attended the school within the last twenty years, though their entrance years ranged from 1924 to 1963.

In the following weeks my initial impressions were strengthened. Some students found Summerhill ideal, but it failed to meet the needs of others.

Effect on Personality

If there is a quality that could be said to make up the Summerhill personality, it would have to be *tolerance*. This characteristic was mentioned spontaneously by twenty-four of the former students as most typical of a Summerhillian. Their definition of tolerance was accepting people as they are, without regard to race, religion, or other label. Twelve mentioned *sincerity* as the outstanding characteristic of a Summerhillian.

My analysis showed that ten former students—according to both their own feelings and my observation—had benefited most. They felt strongly that Summerhill had given them confidence, maturity, and had enabled them to find a fulfilling way of life. One felt the school had helped him to break away from an overdomineering mother and to think for himself. Another former student, who recalled having been a bully at Summerhill, said, "It got the hate out of me, somehow." Others said typically: "It helped me to grow out of the need to play continuously," and "It led me to explore and be curious about things." Three stressed that the school had given them a healthy attitude toward sex.

These ten who had nothing but praise for Summerhill talked of the free environment that helped them develop into more complete personalities through following their natural bent. They were highly communicative people who usually had definite ideas and direction before they came to Summerhill. The average age of this group was twenty-seven.

On the opposite side, seven felt that Summerhill had been harmful. They charged that the school had not helped them to grow, but instead had led them to find more difficulty in life than they might otherwise have experienced. Most of these complained of the de-emphasis on academic subjects and the lack of good teachers. Most complained of the lack of protection against bullies. One said, "It made me lose the little self-confidence I had." Another, "I think it gave me the habit of not following through, giving up too easily." These were the more dependent, shy people—both before and after their Summerhill experience. The average age of this group was twenty-six.

Thus, the gregarious, aggressive people seemed to benefit the most, while the school seemed to have a negative effect on the more withdrawn, quiet ones. There were a few exceptions: occasionally Summerhill triumphed by suggesting to some shy pupil the pleasant rewards of becoming gregarious.

Effect of Length of Stay

Perhaps the most striking finding of this study came out of interviews with the six who left before they were twelve and returned to traditional schools. A shorter stay seemed more beneficial than the completion of schooling at Summerhill. These children had spent at least three years at Summerhill. All but one were enthusiastic about how the school had helped them. Five felt that there were no adjustment problems to the ordinary local schools and were enthusiastic about having learning presented in an organized way. Although usually "behind," they were easily able to catch up to the other children, learning the required academic skills within the first year.

Typical of this group was Connie, now a twenty-seven-year-old housewife, who left Summerhill because of the financial difficulties of her parents. When asked about her adjustment to the regular state school, she replied:

I loved the way learning was presented! It was something new and fresh! And, you know, it was strange; I couldn't understand why all the other children stopped working when the teacher left the room.

To Connie, the teacher was an instrument for learning. When I talked to Connie's mother, she told me how surprised the teachers and headmaster were, for Connie "soaked up knowledge like a sponge."

The single exception to the record of successful adjustment by this group was, interestingly, Connie's brother, Henry, who attended Summerhill from the time he was seven until he was twelve. He was the only person I encountered who ever ran away from Summerhill. Nor did he adjust to the local school.

Henry, a thin, shy twenty-four-year-old, said he was immobilized by the sudden rigid discipline when he left Summerhill and tended to stay in the background, afraid to ask questions. He was difficult to talk to; his mother was in the room, and she always answered for him, even interrupting him when he did start to speak. Henry felt he had lost two years when he entered the regular school and that only sheer effort and determination had brought him to his first year of postgraduate physics at London University.

When I compared the statements of the eight who entered Summerhill *after* their twelfth birthday, I discovered that the four who stayed the least number of years claimed to have benefited most. Two who stayed for one year felt that Summerhill enabled them to find themselves, as did the two who remained at the school for two years. All but one of those who entered as teenagers and stayed three or more years had been in continuous personal and vocational difficulty since leaving Summerhill.

A country doctor who entered the school in 1925, when he was thirteen, easily passed his examinations for university entrance when he was sixteen. He summed up his feelings about Summerhill:

The freedom was a wonderful thing. It was a good experience for me. But I must say there was very little direction from adults. I taught myself what I knew I should know.

Jane, a housewife who married another Summerhill student, left a strict girls' boarding school when she was twelve to enter Neill's school.

I feel Summerhill saved my life. I was a nervous child and probably ready for a nervous breakdown . . . Naturally I went wild with the new freedom at first, playing outdoors continually and never opening a book, but I gradually settled down within a few months. For the first time in my life, I was enjoying comfortable, matter-of-fact relationships with boys.

Those who attended Summerhill the longest appeared most likely to have difficulty and tenacious adjustment problems. Of the fourteen who spent over ten years at Summerhill, five felt they had "fairly severe" problems adjusting to society for at least a year after they left. Four still were definitely unsettled and having personal and job problems. They were in their mid-twenties.

Adjustment to the Outside

Yet half of the fourteen had little or no trouble adjusting and considered themselves adjusted at present. My observations confirmed this. Most of these ex-students were in their thirties or forties.

When the replies of the other ex-students were added to this group, I found four additional students who complained of fairly severe adjustment problems lasting more than a year; six who had minor problems that were resolved in less than a year; eight who said either their adjustment to the world was easier because they attended Summerhill, or denied any problem at all. In addition, twenty were not sure how their life at Summerhill had affected their later adjustment to society.

A lawyer who spent the years between six and sixteen as a Summerhillian said he had no adjustment problem at all. When he thought about his years at the school, he recalled the happy times at Summerhill and went on to say that "some never wanted to leave that little paradise."

The son of Corky Corkhill, one of the few teachers unanimously acclaimed by his former students, grew up at Summerhill. He said that he had rarely attended classes, but instead spent his time taking Neill's car apart and working with his hands. After he left Summerhill in 1939 when he was seventeen, he served a three-year apprenticeship in skilled metal work. He worked for the same company until three years ago, when he opened his own highly profitable repair business.

A young man of twenty who spent ten years at Summerhill told me that procrastination was an attitude easily picked up at Summerhill.

You know, I think one can stay at Summerhill too long. It was easy to be led astray by new students who did little or no studying.

He did point out that his entire group passed the 11+ exam with above average grades. This crucial examination decides an English child's future; he cannot enter a university unless he passes.

When the positive remarks among the fifty former students were tabulated, five items were mentioned more than any others. Leading the list of benefits were a healthy attitude toward sex and relationships with the opposite sex; a natural confidence and ease with authority figures; and a natural development in line with personal interests and abilities. Close behind was the feeling that Summerhill helps in growing out of the need to play continuously and makes it possible to settle comfortably into more serious pursuits. The tabulation showed the belief of former students that their Summerhill experience had helped them to understand their own children better and to raise them in a wholesome way.

Most of the former students I interviewed seemed able to cope with authority effectively. This ability to handle authority continued into adulthood. At the age of twenty-four, one Summerhillian was promoted to a junior-executive position despite his lack of college education. The president of the company told him: "You're the only one on this staff who is not afraid to tell me what you're thinking and how you really feel about things."

Academic Insufficiencies

The majority of Summerhillians had only one major complaint against the school: the lack of academic opportunity and inspiration, coupled with a dearth of inspired teachers. This was stressed by twenty-six of the students interviewed. I discovered that the school attracted a variety of teachers. Some padded about in sandals, growing long beards, content when the children cut class. Others ran about the school grounds, plucking children from trees and trying to lure them to their lessons. One former student told me that when he first learned to read and write, it was in German—because he liked the German teacher so well.

In spite of the complaints that Summerhill was academically weak, ten of the fifty former students interviewed had passed university entrance examinations. Four of the ten felt they had lost two or more years cramming to pass. Eight had graduated from universities.

An electrical engineer who had spent eight years at Summerhill told me: "Summerhill is good for children up to about the age of ten. After that it's too weak academically."

Although Neill has stated that his former students left Summerhill to go into the arts, less than 20 percent of those I interviewed could be placed in this category. There was a Sadler-Wells dancer with top billing who learned his first ballet steps and Nijinskilike leaps at Summerhill. There was a young musician who played his piano and composed. And there were two artists, an interior decorator, and a writer. But there were two truck drivers, an apprentice bricklayer, two salesmen, a radio technician, and a construction worker as well. There was a noted zoologist who has pioneered in research on the Nigerian snail-disease problem. Six were housewives. Two teen-agers were unemployed, although one of them found a job driving a taxi the week of his interview.

Alumni as Parents

Although three of the eleven couples interviewed had been divorced, most seemed happily married. Two of the divorced group had remarried, with apparent success.

Without exception, former Summerhillians were raising their own children in a self-directive way. Their interrelationship was warm; the children appeared happy and spontaneous. I found a free and easy kind of relationship in most Summerhill homes.

Of the eleven former students who had become parents, all but one felt that their children were unafraid of them. Most of the parents had conflicting feelings about discipline, and all but two had felt guilty at some time when punishing their children. (This is rather typical of *all* parents.) None of the parents customarily used corporal punishment, although three mentioned an occasional situation when permissiveness had led to physical punishment. One mother said:

I believe in giving as much freedom as possible, but I have had great conflicts. For example, I don't believe in hitting children, but I have lost my temper and "coshed" them a bit or yelled. Then I felt terribly guilty afterwards.

Only three of the parents had sent their own children to Summerhill. Two others said they would seriously consider sending their children at a later time. Most of these parents offered a belief in freedom as their reason for sending their children to the school, as had most of their own parents.

Those three Summerhillians who had entered their own children in Summerhill had removed them before they reached the age of thirteen. The removals were almost wholly due to the conviction that not enough emphasis was placed upon academic learning and that Summerhill lacked fine teachers and good equipment.

One second-generation Summerhillian who had spent three years at the school was now preparing to study law.

I hardly opened a book at Summerhill, especially at first. Guess I learned to hate learning at the strict ordinary school and that's why Dad sent me to Summerhill.

At the end of his third year at Summerhill, he decided himself to go back to the regular school in his neighborhood. His reason was simple: "I was ready to learn."

Of the six parents who did not plan to send their children to Summerhill, five felt that children should be with their parents. Three of these said they enjoyed their own children too much to send them away.

The eleven-year-old daughter of one former student told me:

I go to a Quaker boarding school. I don't think Summerhill would have agreed with *me*. It sounds a little too loose and unorganized.

The ages of the parents among the group of former students ranged from twenty-five to forty-nine. The average age was thirty-three. Their children were as young as two and as old as twenty-one. The average age of these fourteen children was eight.

Upon completing the five weeks of interviews, my

feelings were mainly positive. Almost all the former students were working, raising responsive children, enjoying life.

The Summerhill Approach Adjusted

Yet I felt that something was lacking in Summerhill's completely free approach. Neill has said that the goal of good education should be *happiness*. And he has said that happiness is *interest*. It seemed to me that this is where Summerhill's philosophy could be improved. A child cannot be interested in anything until he succeeds. Then he can find satisfaction in anything—even in arithmetic.

(The Summerhill experiment does not stand alone. Between 1933 and 1941, some 1,500 graduates from thirty experimental schools across the United States were compared in the Aiken study with 1,500 graduates of control schools, carefully matched with the experimental group. Students were matched not only for age, grades, and IQ, but for social and economic status, community size and geographical area.

Three hundred colleges—including the Ivy League's Harvard, Princeton, and Yale—accepted students from these experimental, sometimes gradeless, schools on the basis of the school's recommendation. Students from the experimental schools did better in college by every measure of academic success: grades, academic honors, participation in activities, orientation toward occupational choice. And researchers found that the more *experimental* his secondary school was, the better the graduate performed in college.)

When, the next fall, I faced my ungraded New England class of seven- to twelve-year-olds with reading and emotional problems, I began to apply some of the lessons I learned in England. Don struggled for hours over a single page of arithmetic. When told he did not *have* to do any arithmetic, he left the workbook in his desk for a month without opening it. Suddenly he began doing ten to fifteen pages of problems each day, racing with another student. In less than two months he had mastered a year's work.

But not all children can handle complete freedom. Frank just wanted to draw. With new confidence, I told him how good his picture was and asked him how high the school building was. He guessed wildly, as he did when I asked him the length of our schoolroom.

Others in the class began wondering, and rulers began to appear from desks. The room was measured. At recess, Frank and a friend climbed down the fire escape to measure the height of the building in yards. Now they had to learn division in order to change the yards to feet.

Frank was told he could draw, but only after the division problem was done. If Neill were observing, he would surely say, "This is certainly not a Summerhill classroom." But if he came back an hour later, he would find Frank busily drawing, his division mastered.

And Jimmy, who wanted to spend all his time on scientific experiments! I ordered him to write up all his experiments, giving the date, the procedure, and the results. He struggled, but within a week he began to see the importance of recording what day the mold began to grow in his test tube filled with yeast and sugar, and how it became fuzzy and changed from day to day.

Would Neill say that Jimmy was not self-directed, that he wrote only for *me*? Or would he see a child learning new satisfactions, finding new horizons open? I would hope the latter, for there *is* a middle ground. A compromise with Summerhill, a guided freedom, might bring together the best of both approaches to education.

Political Attitudes
in Children

Robert D. Hess

Some 12,000 elementary-school children, representing different geographical regions and social classes in the United States, were questioned to find the extent of their political knowledge and their attitudes. These children generally have a very positive attitude about the United States government. They believe it to be benevolent and responsive to the individual vote; they know little about political parties or pressure groups. This highly idealized view comes about, the author believes, as the result of attitudes learned in school and through the child's need, because of his position as an inferior and weak member of society, to see the government as helpful and protective of him.

Although some realization of discrepancy between the ideal and the actual begins to develop toward the end of the elementary-school years, children continue to deny the existence of conflict or disagreement between political parties or candidates. Their belief in the effectiveness of the individual vote continues to increase; this is especially true of children from higher social classes and of higher IQ. On the basis of the teachers' beliefs (the teachers answered the same questions as their students), the author suggests that there is insufficient discussion of group versus individual power in government.

Sandra, in what way could our country be harmed?"
"By war, we can be harmed, and if the President of the United States don't do the right job that he should be doing he can lead us into trouble too."

"Which is worse?"

"I think war is worse. No, wait—I don't think war is worse. I think the other one is worse, because in war you can fight back but when the President doesn't do his job right, there can be nothing done about it. You just can't get a new President—you just have to wait."

Sandra is a sixth-grade girl from the working class, the daughter of a police detective in a large Midwestern city. She is somewhat more sophisticated about political matters than many children her age. It is unusual for an elementary school child to suggest the possibility that the President might not "do his job right." More typical is Sandra's implicit assumption that the United States would be on the defensive side in the event of war. Most young children believe that the government and its representatives are wise, benevolent, and infallible, that whatever the government does is for the best, and that the United States is a highly effective force for peace in the world.

The average child would agree with Sandra that, if something *is* wrong, "you just have to wait." They know that a citizen can write letters to the President

and to Congress, but they see virtually no other way to influence political affairs in the period between elections. They know almost nothing about pressure groups, for instance. In fact, group political activity of any sort, including that of political parties, seems unimportant to them. They believe that the way the citizen affects the government is through the vote, the individual vote; that is almost the only thing that counts, and it counts very heavily indeed.

Political socialization, the process by which attitudes like these are learned, is a special, socially oriented form of political learning. It is accomplished *by* the society and *for* the society, mostly through the institution of the schools. Its purpose is to transmit to each new generation the political attitudes and behavior patterns that the society deems useful in its adult citizens. That is, political socialization is based on and is intended to preserve stability and consensus in the adult population.

In the United States today, stability and consensus are conspicuously lacking. There is strong, open conflict between ethnic groups and the dominant society, between the affluent and the poor, and between generations. The conflict concerns wealth and other material resources, but the basic issue is the division of political power.

In my opinion, children in this country are being

socialized in ways that contribute to the very fragmentation that political socialization is meant to prevent.

In 1961 and 1962, David Easton and I, together with Judith Torney and Jack Dennis, collected data on the political knowledge, attitudes, and behavior of 12,000 children in grades two to eight. The children were from eight cities, two in each major region of the United States. In each region we used a large city and a small one; and in each city, two schools from working-class areas and two from middle-class areas.

We found, among other things, that elementary-school children have a highly idealized view of the government and a very high estimate of the power of the individual vote, combined with an ignorance of other legitimate channels of influence. These views are unrealistic (a fact that is becoming increasingly obvious today to children themselves), and they do not offer a good foundation for active, effective participation in a democratic process. They seem to point more toward compliance and complacency on one hand, and toward disillusionment, helplessness, anger, and perhaps even rejection of the system on the other.

The child's early conception of the nation and its government is vague but very favorable. In the early grades, almost all children agree that "the American flag is the best flag in the world," and that "America is the best country in the world." As one girl put it, "if it wasn't for the United States, there probably would be a lot of wars and regular Dark Ages."

"President" and "government" are almost synonymous for the young child. Both are regarded as powerful and benevolent, though there is some confusion about the functions they perform:

"Judy, do you know of anyone in the United States government?"

"Well, the President."

"What do you know about the President?"

"Well, that a . . . oh, dear . . . he . . . ah, makes laws and a . . . and . . . ah . . . well, he tries to do good."

"Tommy, what is the government?"

"The government is like the President, but he isn't actually a President. . . . Maybe he makes the laws of the country. Maybe he tells the numbers on the license plates. . . . I heard on the radio that he's in charge of the income tax. He can higher it or lower it."

"What does he spend the money on?"

"How should I know? Like, the government doesn't know what we spend our money on. He spends it for food, clothing, things for his wife, and that sort of thing."

In the second grade, the average child believes that the President would be nearly as helpful to him as a policeman or his father if he were in trouble. Children express strong emotional attachment to the President and expect him to protect them. They think he is personally responsive to children's wishes; if necessary they could even go to the White House and talk to him.

Responses to one question show especially clearly how concerned children think the President is about them. The question was: "If you write to the President, does he care what you think?" The possible answers were that he cares "a lot," "some" or "a little." Three-fourths of the children in second grade and 43 percent of those in eighth answered "a lot." (Interestingly, this answer was also chosen by 47 percent of the teachers.)

Laws, like government, are viewed as powerful and benevolent. They are helpful and protective, just and unchanging. Most young children think laws were made a long time ago, probably by the President, and his stamp of approval carries weight: "The President okays them before they're obeyed, so I guess if it is good enough for him, it is good enough for anybody."

The young child's idealization of the figures and institutions of government is supported by what he learns in school, but it does not seem to originate there. Its source is probably the child's psychological need to compensate for his own inferior and vulnerable place in the system. Attachment to the President, for example, begins with an awareness that there is a very powerful "boss" of the United States. If he is benevolent and concerned with the child's welfare, the child need not be afraid of him. The child apparently sees his own position in the nation as similar to his position in the family, a conclusion borne out by what we learned from children with working-class backgrounds. Working-class children tended to have less positive attitudes toward their fathers than children from the middle and upper classes, and to invest the President with correspondingly more paternalistic qualities. They expressed very strong emotional ties to him.

In the later grades, children begin to transfer their allegiance from officials to offices and institutions. The average seventh-grader thinks that the Supreme Court and the government know more and are less likely to make mistakes than the President. Since support for offices rather than for particular officials is an important ingredient in peaceful political change, the transfer of allegiance from personal figures to roles and institutions is a step toward political stability.

However, older children have not so much abandoned their belief in the benign qualities of governmental authority as redirected their expectations of protection toward institutions. In all grades, 80 to 90 percent of the students agreed that "the United States government knows what is best for the people." Agreement on a related item, "What goes on in government is all for the best," declined with age, from 90 percent in grade three to 76 percent in grade eight, but this is still a very high percentage. (Among teachers, agreement had dropped to 46 percent.)

An idealized acceptance of the authority, omniscience, and benevolence of the political system does not fit well with the need, in a democratic society, for a critical examination of public policy. Without abandoning his positive attachment to government, law, and structures designed to regulate dissent, the citizen must see a need to watch—and to influence—the government's actions.

Older children do show more awareness than younger ones that all is not necessarily perfect. Though agreement with positive statements about how the system *should* be stays high in all grades, perceptions of how things actually are become more realistic with age. Most children in all grades agree that the policeman's job is to make people obey laws, but the belief that punishment inevitably follows crime declines from 57 percent in second grade to 16 percent in eighth (and to 2 percent in teachers). Similarly, children of all ages agree that "laws are to keep us safe," but there is more and more reluctance to agree that "all laws are fair." In general, responses to idealized statements of how things ought to be were more stable than perceptions of the way the system really functions.

How Does the System Work?

The discrepancy between the ideal and the actual could be the basis for disillusionment and cynicism, but it might also be an incentive to act. Let us assume the latter—that at least some older children are motivated to do more than admire the status quo and comply with the law. Let us also assume (for the moment) that these children have two other prerequisites to political action, a view of themselves as effective and a view of the system as responsive. What then?

Children believe that democracy is "rule by the people," but they have a limited understanding of how this rule operates. As one sixth-grade boy tried to explain it, "Oh, in the United States the people are supposed to rule the government . . . but that is kind of complicated because the government rules over the people. . . . It is kind of mixed-up, but it's a good set-up, but yet there's no real rule. Everybody has power; that is, everybody's power is limited."

The idea of a reciprocal relationship between an individual citizen and the government is difficult to grasp, even for adults. Young children do not try: they see government at the top and themselves at the bottom, with influence moving down but not up. In general, children in the early grades say that the duties of the citizen are compliance and "good" behavior. Asked what a citizen can do to help the country, one fourth-grader replied, "Well, follow the laws, don't get in accidents, and do practically everything as hard as he can." Children this age, presented with a list of seven characteristics of the good citizen and asked to choose two, opted for "helps others" (48 percent) and "always obeys laws" (44 percent).

Older children said that the good citizen "is interested in the way the country is run" (65 percent) and "votes and gets others to vote" (45 percent). Almost all

eighth-graders think it is important to vote, and most of them are convinced that the ideal citizen "makes up his own mind" about a candidate, rather than turning to parents, teachers, television, newspapers, and so forth. Just where the ideal citizen *does* turn for political information is unclear, though estimates of usefulness of the mass media began to rise in the later grades.

A similar spirit of independence shows itself when eighth-graders are asked what they think of voting along party lines. The ideal citizen, they say, votes for "the man, not the party," and he splits his ticket.

Parties and Pressure Groups

Attitudes toward political parties are fairly late in developing. Most children first learn the words "Democrat" and "Republican" when they label a Presidential candidate as one thing or the other. Young children identify the party with the candidate rather than vice versa; since they see the candidates as different, they also believe the parties are different.

To older children, the Democratic and Republican parties look almost identical. "Well, basically they both want the same things," said an eighth-grade girl. "Just peace and happiness and want our country to be free."

Children are eager to minimize political conflict of all sorts. They usually take sides in a campaign and hope their man wins, but this does not mean they condone strong disagreement between the candidates. Unity and cohesion should surely reign *after* an election, and perhaps before as well. Here, for instance, is what one seventh-grader remembered about the 1960 election: "[I remember] the morning of the election when Kennedy was elected, and Nixon said that Kennedy would be a nice President. Kennedy said how sorry he was that Mr. Nixon wasn't elected. He would have been just as good a President as he was himself, and that he wished they could both be President together. I would have liked them to go together instead of going through this big thing that they go out in the streets and talk to all the people and giving the impression that they got a better impression than the other one. It would have been easy if they both went together. Then there wouldn't have been much quarreling and fighting."

Conflict between parties is just as undesirable as conflict between candidates. One question we asked the children was, "If the Democrats and Republicans disagreed on important things, would it be good or bad for the country?" On a scale from 1 (very bad) to 5 (very good), the responses ranged from a little under 2 in the fifth grade to a little over 2 in eighth. Teachers were better able to tolerate disagreement, and the difference between them and eighth-graders on this item was one of the largest in our data.

Although most older children believe that adults should belong to parties, they think a decision between the two should be deferred until after high-school graduation. Asked to specify the party they would join if they were adults, 32 percent specified "sometimes Democrat, sometimes Republican." This percentage is somewhat higher than estimates of the number of independent voters in the adult population, though much lower than the 55 percent of teachers who reported themselves "sometimes Democrat, sometimes Republican."

Very little material on partisanship and political conflict finds its way into the elementary-school curriculum. Teachers apparently stress the virtue of independent political action oriented toward an assessment of candidates' worth rather than an alignment with a party. They may do this from a desire to avoid controversial issues or to present political material without bias. But the result for the students is an awareness of the need for consensus and majority rule without a complementary appreciation of the role of debate, disagreement, and conflict.

As for pressure groups, children's understanding of the role they play in government is shown in Figure 1. Until the seventh grade, children rated the policeman's influence in law-making as higher than that of any other individual or group except the President and labor unions. In a clear demonstration of faith in the importance of the individual, older children saw the average citizen's influence on law-making as equal or superior to the influence of big companies, rich people, newspapers, and churches. Teachers differed greatly from eighth-graders on this matter, rating the influence of unions, big companies, rich people, and newspapers nearly equal, and much greater than that of the average citizen.

The sharp divergence between students and teachers suggests that this topic, like partisanship, is not discussed at school. Schools concentrate on the formal aspects of government, teaching that Congress makes the laws but not recognizing the influence of interest groups. It is not easy to teach children that groups who promote their own (as opposed to the public) interest can be influential, even decisive, in legislative matters, but it would make for a more realistic view of how a complex democracy operates.

Effectiveness

Exerting an effect on the course of government requires more than an awareness of the need to do so and a knowledge of how to go about it. As I mentioned earlier, it also requires a belief in one's own effectiveness and in the government's responsiveness. A child who thinks the government is benevolent and protective may fail to see why he *should* interfere, but he also believes that if he *does* speak, the government will listen. And a child who thinks the government pays more attention to the average person than to, say, U.S. Steel or *The New York Times* may confine his political activities to the voting booth, but he unquestionably has a high opinion of his own effectiveness.

There is a house-of-cards air to this structure of beliefs; misguidedly or not, however, most children do believe that the government is responsive and that they, as individuals, can be effective in the political arena. Most, but not all. For example: "Richard, if the President did something that people didn't like, what could they do?" "The people can't do anything. They can't go to the White House and tell him what to do because he makes all the decisions. If the people don't like it, too bad for them."

Richard is from a working-class home. A difference in feelings of effectiveness was one of the most striking

Figure 1. Teachers' attitudes and changes in those of children about the relative influence of groups and individuals on law-making.

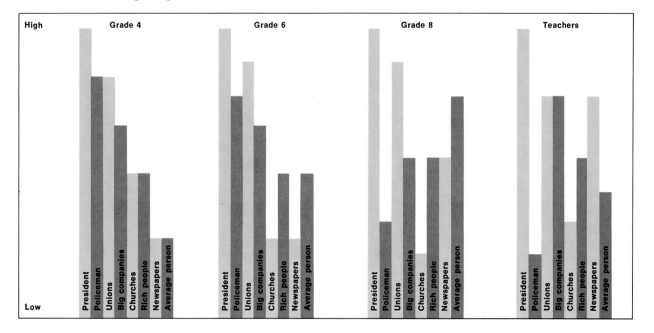

social-class discrepancies in our data, one of the few variables on which there was considerable difference between the middle- and the low-status groups. Even in third and fourth grade, low-status children see themselves and their families as having substantially less ability to influence government than high-status children award themselves; the difference increases with age.

Differences between IQ groups on effectiveness were even more marked than those between social classes, and they also increase with age. Children of low intelligence were three or four years behind children of high intelligence in developing a sense of effectiveness; the eighth-grade child of low intelligence was scarcely above the highly intelligent third- or fourth-grader.

On effectiveness, as on most matters where there were variations by both social class and level of intelligence, the difference between low- and high-status children was less than, but in the same direction as, the difference between children of low and high intelligence (see Figure 2). In addition to feeling less effective, children from the lower class and children with low IQs tend to be more loyal, accepting, and compliant and less interested and involved in politics than children from the middle and upper classes and children with high IQs—in short, to be more trusting and apathetic.

Another way of putting it is to say that children from low-status homes and children of low intelligence are retarded in their socialization to effective participation in the political system. But perhaps they are only a little more retarded than children from other groups.

Children of all classes and all levels of intelligence seem to be learning an incomplete, simplistic, and cognitively fragmented view of the political process, and the situation is likely to persist as long as the schools stress values and ideals, the individual and his vote, and

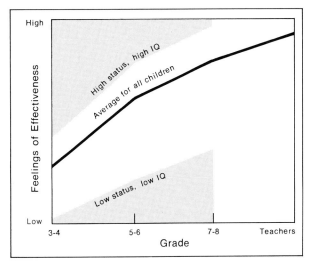

Figure 2. Effect of IQ and social status on feelings of ability to influence government.

the need for compliance and consensus at the expense of social realities, the role of groups, and the uses of controversy and argument.

The strength of current protests against social and political conditions, and the fact that they are focused on institutions, is a sign of vigor: it indicates at least a hope that remedies can be found short of full revolution. However, under the circumstances it makes very little sense to instill in children a superficial faith in the institutions under attack, to gloss over social realities, and to obscure many of the routes effective action can take. More useful would be a candid acknowledgment of political and social facts and, especially, a clear explanation of the ways that institutions can be influenced and changed.

The Computer as a Tutor

Richard C. Atkinson

Computer teaching programs vary in the complexity of the interaction between student and computer system. One type of program has a rigidly fixed series of problems, which never varies from one student to the next. The opposite type of program, still under development though being used in some specific areas (e.g., teaching of geometry), is flexible enough to allow the student to ask his own individual questions of the computer. In the Stanford project reported here, the "tutorial" type of program, somewhere between the two poles in responsiveness, was used. In the tutorial program, although the student must select his answer from a fixed set of responses provided, the order in which problems are presented is modified according to how the student responds to earlier questions. This computer approach is sensitive to individual differences, with some students solving many more problems during a year than others.

The program was used to teach reading to one-half of a first-grade class of children from culturally disadvantaged homes. The other half of the first-graders (the control group) was given the usual classroom training in reading. After one year, the children who were computer trained in reading performed significantly better on standard reading tests.

Another interesting result of the project was that boys and girls did equally well in most tests of verbal skills, whereas it is almost universally true that in classrooms, girls outperform boys. The author suggests that there may be factors unique to this situation that favor the performance of female students.

Last year, for the first time, a sizable number of children received most of their daily reading instruction from a computer. The children were first-grade students at the Brentwood School in East Palo Alto, and most of them came from culturally disadvantaged homes. By the end of the year, they not only had learned to read better than a companion group taught by teachers, but they had shown the project staff a considerable amount about computer-assisted instruction—about how and with what effect computer technology and learning theory can be combined and put into practice.

Concrete research in computer-assisted instruction is badly needed to balance the tremendous number of speculative reports that have appeared over the past few years. The Stanford Project has only begun—it is continuing this year with the new first grade—and much of the initial year must be considered a debugging period for both the computer system and the curriculum material. Nevertheless, the experience has provided us with solid data. My claims will be less grand than many that have been made for computer-assisted instruction, but they will be based on a substantial research effort.

Work on the Stanford Project began in 1964 under a grant from the Office of Education. The purpose of the project was to develop and implement computer-assisted instruction courses in initial reading and mathematics. Because of our individual research interests, my colleague Patrick Suppes has worked on the mathematics curriculum and I have been responsible for the reading course.

Types of Computer-Assisted Instruction

When we began, no lesson material suitable for computerized instruction of either mathematics or reading had yet been developed, and an integrated computer system for instruction had not yet been designed and produced by a single manufacturer. Curricula and system have been developed together over the past three years, and each has had a decided influence on the other.

Three levels of computer-assisted instruction can be defined. The levels are not based on the type of hardware used, but principally on the complexity and sophistication of the interaction between the student and the system. An advanced student-system interaction may be achieved with a simple teletype terminal, and the most rudimentary interaction may require some highly sophisticated computer programming and elaborate student terminal devices.

At the simplest interactional level are the *drill-and-*

practice systems that present a fixed, linear sequence of problems. Student errors may be corrected in a variety of ways, but no real-time decisions are made by the computer for modifying the flow of instructional material according to the student's response history. An example of drill-and-practice systems are the fourth-, fifth-, and sixth-grade programs in arithmetic and language arts that have been developed at Stanford University to supplement classroom instruction. These programs are being used by as many as 2,000 students a day in California, Kentucky, and Mississippi; the entire network is controlled by one central computer located at Stanford University. It takes little imagination to see how such a system could be extended to cover the entire country.

At the other end of our scale of student-computer interactions are *dialogue* programs. The goal of the dialogue approach is to provide the richest possible interaction, one in which the student is free to construct natural-language responses, to ask questions in an unrestricted mode, and in general to exercise almost complete control over the sequence of learning events. Such programs are under development at several universities, but progress has been limited.

The third level of computer-assisted instruction lies between the drill-and-practice and the dialogue programs. Called *tutorial* programs, these have the capacity to modify the sequence of instructional material on the basis of a single response or some subset of the student's response history. Such programs allow students to follow separate and diverse learning paths through the curriculum, based on their individual performance records. The probability is high in a tutorial program that no two students will encounter exactly the same sequence of lesson materials. However, student responses still are quite restricted because they must be chosen from a prescribed set of responses or be written so that a relatively simple text analysis will be sufficient for their evaluation.

Stanford Tutorial System

The computer-assisted reading instruction program at Brentwood School is implemented on the Stanford Tutorial System, which was developed under a contract between Stanford University and the IBM Corporation. Subsequent developments by IBM of the basic system have led to what has been designated the IBM-1500 Instructional System, which soon should be commercially available.

| HARDWARE | The basic system consists of a central process computer with magnetic discs for memory storage, proctor stations for monitoring student performance, and sixteen student stations. The central process computer acts as an intermediary between each student and his particular course material, which is stored in one of the memory discs. A student terminal consists of a film screen, a cathode ray display tube, a light-pen, a modified typewriter keyboard, and earphones (see Figure 1).

The cathode ray tube is essentially a television screen on which letters, numbers, and simple line drawings can be generated under computer control. The film screen is a rear-view projection device that permits the display of still pictures in black and white or in color. Each film strip is stored in a self-threading cartridge and contains over 1,000 images, any of which the computer may select very quickly for display. The audio messages are stored in tape cartridges that contain approximately two hours of messages and, like the film cartridge, may be changed very quickly. To gain the student's attention, an arrow can be generated on the cathode ray screen and moved in synchronization with an audio message to emphasize given words or phrases, much like the "bouncing ball" in sing-along films.

The main responding device used in the reading program is the light-pen, which is simply a light-sensitive probe. When the light-pen is placed on the cathode ray screen, the position touched is sensed and recorded by the computer. Responses also may be made on the typewriter keyboard. However, only limited use has been made of the keyboard in the reading program because we have not yet attempted to tackle the problem of teaching first-grade children to use a typewriter.

The sequence of events in the system is roughly as follows. The computer assembles the necessary commands for a given instructional sequence from a disc storage unit. The commands include directions to display a given sequence of symbols on the cathode ray screen, to present a particular image on the film screen, and to play a specific audio message. After the appropriate visual and auditory materials have been presented, a "ready" signal tells the student that a response is expected. The response is evaluated and, on the basis of this evaluation and the student's past history, the computer makes a decision as to what materials will be presented next.

The time-sharing feature of the system allows us to handle sixteen students simultaneously and to cycle through these evaluative steps so rapidly that from the student's viewpoint it seems that he is getting immediate attention from the computer whenever he makes a response.

| RATIONALE AND MATERIALS | Our approach to computer-assisted reading instruction can be described as applied psycholinguistics. We began by formulating hypotheses about the reading process and the nature of learning to read on the basis of linguistic information, observations of language use, and an analysis of the function of the written code. These hypotheses were tested—and then modified and retested—in a series of studies structured to simulate actual teaching situations. Very little curriculum material ever can be said to be the perfect end product of rigorous empirical evaluation; however, we would claim that the fundamental

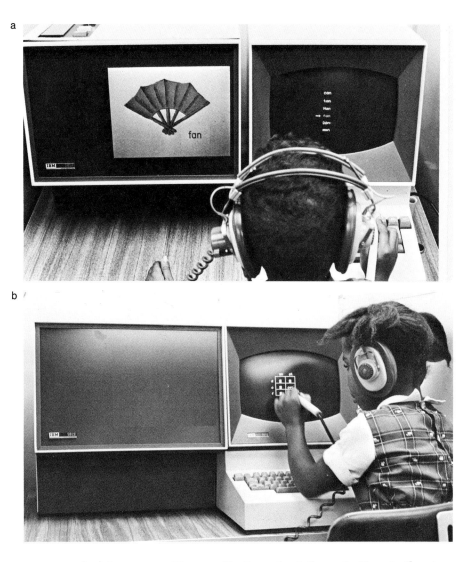

Figure 1. The child's equipment. (a) The child hears a word and simultaneously sees it written and in picture form. (b) The child answers a question by touching a light pen to her response on the cathode ray tube, or by typing it on the modified typewriter keyboard.

tenets of the Stanford reading program are based on considerable empirical evidence, and they will be further modified as more data accumulate.

The instructional materials are divided into eight levels, each composed of about thirty-two lessons. The lessons are designed so that the average student will complete one in approximately thirty minutes, but this can vary greatly. Some students finish much sooner, and others, if they hit most of the remedial material, can take two hours or more. Within a lesson, the various instructional tasks can be divided into three broad areas: decoding, comprehension, and games and other motivational devices.

Decoding involves such tasks as the identification of letters and strings of letters, word-list learning, and phonic drills. *Comprehension* involves such tasks as having the computer read to the child or having the child himself read sentences, paragraphs, or complete stories about which he then is asked a series of questions. The questions deal with the direct recall of facts,

with generalizations about the main ideas in the story, and with inferential questions that require the child to relate to his own experience information presented in the story. Finally, many types of *games* are sequenced into the lessons, primarily to maintain the students' interest. The games are similar to those usually played in the classroom, and they are structured to enable the computer to evaluate the developing reading skills of the child.

Let us consider an example of what a student sees, hears, and does on one of the decoding tasks in a lesson (see Figure 2). This task, called "matrix construction," provides practice in learning to associate orthographically similar sequences with appropriate rhyme and alliteration patterns. Rhyming patterns are presented in the columns of the matrix and alliteration patterns are presented in the rows. The matrix is constructed one cell at a time. The initial consonant of a consonant-vowel-consonant word is called the initial unit, and the vowel and the final consonant are called the final unit.

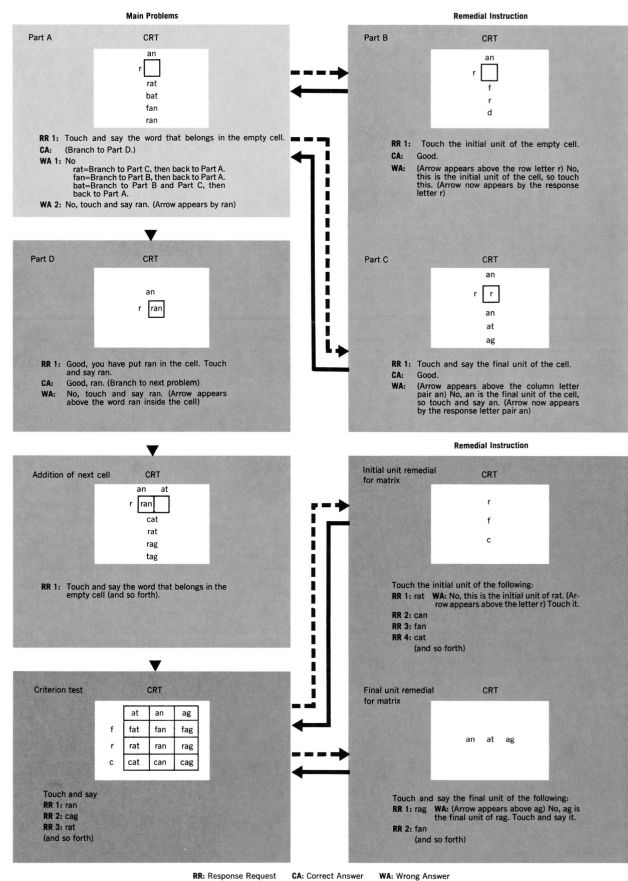

Figure 2. Matrix construction. Note the patterns of remedial instruction differentiating between mistakes on initial units and on final units.

The intersection of an initial unit row and a final unit column determines the entry in any given cell.

The problem format for the construction of each cell is divided into four parts: Parts A and D are standard instructional sections, and Parts B and C are remedial sections. Parts B and C are branches from Part A, and may be presented independently or in combination.

On the cathode ray screen the student first sees an empty cell with its associated initial and final units and an array of response choices. He hears a message to touch and say the word that belongs in the empty cell. If the student makes the correct response, in this case touches *ran* with his light-pen, he proceeds to Part D, where he sees the word written in the cell and is told "Good, you have put *ran* in the cell. Touch and say *ran*."

The array of multiple-choice responses in Part A is designed to identify three types of errors: final unit incorrect; initial unit incorrect; both initial and final units incorrect.

If in Part A the student responds with *fan* instead of *ran*, he is branched to remedial instruction (Part B), where attention is focused on the initial unit of the cell. If a correct response is made in the remedial section, the student is returned to the beginning for a second attempt. If an incorrect response is made in the remedial section, an arrow is displayed on the screen to indicate the correct response, which the student then is asked to touch.

If in Part A the student responds with *rat* instead of *ran*, he is branched to remedial instruction (Part C) on the final unit of the cell. The procedure is similar. However, it should be noted that in the remedial instruction the initial letter is never pronounced by the audio system, whereas the final unit always is pronounced. If the student responds in Part A with *bat* instead of *ran*, then he has made an error on both the initial and the final units, and he is branched through both sets of remedial instruction.

When the student returns to the beginning after completing a remedial section, a correct response will advance him to Part D. If a wrong response is made on the second attempt, an arrow is placed beside the correct response area and held there until a correct response is made. If the next response is still an error, a message is sent to the proctor terminal, and the sequence is repeated from the beginning.

When a student has responded correctly in Parts A and D, he is advanced to the next cell of the matrix, which is a problem identical to that just described. As a student makes correct responses, he constructs a matrix of word cells. When the matrix is complete, the rows and columns are reordered and the full matrix is displayed. The student is asked in a criterion test to identify the words in the cells. He completes the entire test without interruption, even if he makes mistakes. Errors are categorized as initial, final, and other. If the

percentage of total errors on the criterion test exceeds a predetermined value, then appropriate remedial exercises are provided. After working through one or both of the remedial sections, the student is branched back for a second pass through the criterion matrix. The second pass is a teaching run, and the student receives additional correction and optimization routines.

| COMPUTER PROGRAM | Let us consider briefly the problem of translating the curriculum materials into a language that can be understood by the computer. The particular computer language we use is called Coursewriter II, a language developed by IBM in close collaboration with Stanford University. A coded lesson is a series of Coursewriter II commands that cause the computer to display and manipulate text on the cathode ray screen, to display images on the film screen, to position and play audio messages, to accept and evaluate keyboard and light-pen responses, to update the performance record of each student, and, with a set of switches and counters, to implement the branching logic of the lesson.

A typical lesson in the reading program, which takes the average student about thirty minutes to complete, requires more than 9,000 Coursewriter commands for its execution.

An example from a task designed to teach both letter discrimination and the meaning of words will illustrate some of the complexities of the coding problem. A picture illustrating the word being taught is presented on the film screen. Three words, including the word illustrated, are presented on the cathode ray screen. A message is played on the audio system asking the child to touch the word on the cathode ray screen that matches the picture on the film screen.

Using the light-pen, the student then can make his response. If he makes no response within thirty seconds, he is told the correct answer, an arrow points to it, and he is asked to touch it. If he makes a response within the time limit, the point that he touches is compared by the computer with the correct-answer area. If he places the light-pen within the correct area, he is told that he was correct, and goes on to the next problem. If the response was not in the correct area, it is compared with the area defined as a wrong answer. If his response is within this area, he is told that it is wrong, given the correct answer, and asked to touch it. If his initial response was neither in the anticipated wrong-answer area nor in the correct-answer area, then the student has made an undefined answer. He is given the same message that he would have heard had he touched a defined wrong answer; however, the response is recorded on his data record as undefined. The student tries again until he makes the correct response, at which time he goes on to the next problem.

To prepare an instructional sequence of this sort, the programmer must write a detailed list of commands for the computer. He also must make a tape recording of all the messages the student might hear during the lesson in approximately the order in which they will occur. Each audio message has an address on the tape that enables the computer to find and play it when required. Similarly, a film strip is prepared with one frame for each picture required in the lesson. Each frame has an address, and the frames can be presented in any order (see Table 1).

While a student is on the system, he may complete as many as five to ten problems per minute. If all of the instructional material had to be coded in detail, the task would be virtually impossible. Fortunately, there are ways of simplifying the coding procedure if parts of the instructional materials are alike in format and differ only in specified ways.

For example, the "bag" and "card" problems (see Table 2) differ in the actual displays and audio messages, but the logical format is the same. They therefore can be defined once, given a two-letter name, and used later by giving a brief macro command.

The use of macro commands cuts down greatly the effort required to present many different but basically similar problems. Macros have two distinct advantages over codes written command by command. The first is ease and speed of coding: the call of one macro is obviously easier than writing the comparable string of code. The second advantage is increase in accuracy: not only are coding errors drastically reduced, but if the macro is defective or needs to be changed, every occurrence of it in the lesson can be corrected by modifying the original macro. The more standard the various problem formats, the more valuable the use of macros becomes. Approximately 92 percent of our reading curriculum has been programmed using about 110 basic macros.

A bank of switches and counters in the computer keeps a running record on each student. Our program includes enough switches and counters to allow some quite sophisticated schemes for optimizing the teaching routines. For instance, we can present a series of words and require five consecutive correct responses to each of the words. Or we can select for presentation certain phrases that previously have produced the greatest number of errors. As a consequence of decisions like these, each student pursues a fundamentally different path through the reading materials.

Results

Computer-assisted instruction began at the Brentwood School in November of 1966. We selected this school partly because it was large enough to provide a sample of well over 100 first-grade students, partly because the students were primarily from culturally disadvantaged homes, and partly because the past performance of the school's principal and faculty had demonstrated a willingness to undertake educational innovations. Half the first-grade students received computer-assisted instruc-

tion in reading, and the other half, which functioned as a control group, was taught reading by a teacher in the classroom. However, the children in the control group were not left out of the computer project; they received their mathematics instruction from the computer.

Within the lesson material there are a core of problems that we have called main-line problems, meaning problems over which each student must exhibit some form of mastery. Main-line problems may be branched around by passing certain screening tests; they may be met and solved; or they may be met with incorrect responses, in which case the student is branched to remedial material.

At the end of the first year of the project, the fastest student had completed over 4,000 more main-line problems than the slowest student. We also found that the rate of progress, as measured by the number of main-line problems solved per hour, was essentially constant for the median and slow students but showed a steady increase for the fast students (see Figure 3). Whether this last result is unique to our particular curriculum or is characteristic of computer-assisted instruction needs further investigation.

Differences in rate of progress through the curriculum must not be confused with the rate of response to individual questions. The difference in response rate among students was very small. The average response rate was approximately four per minute and was not correlated with a student's rate of progress through the curriculum. The differences in total number of main-line problems completed can be accounted for by the amount of remedial material, the optimization routines, and the number of accelerations for the different students. From the standpoint of both the rate of progress and the total number of problems completed during the year, the computer curriculum appears to be quite responsive to individual differences.

It has been a common finding that girls generally acquire reading skills more rapidly than boys. The sex differences in reading performance have been attributed, at least in part, to the social organization of the classroom, and to the value and reward systems of female primary-grade teachers. It also has been argued on developmental grounds that first-grade girls are more facile in visual memorization than boys of the same age, and that this facility aids the girls in the sight-word method commonly used in primary readers.

If these two arguments are correct, then one would expect that placing students in a computer-assisted environment and using a curriculum that emphasizes analytic skills instead of memorization by rote would minimize sex differences in reading. To test this hypothesis, the rate-of-progress scores in our program were evaluated for differences according to sex. The result, which was rather surprising, is that there was no difference between male and female students in rate of progress through the computer curriculum.

TABLE 1   Detailed Commands for Portion of Instructional Sequence

Computer Commands	Explanation
PR	**Problem** Prepares machine for beginning of new problem.
LD O/S1	**Load** Loads zero into the error switch (S1).
FP FO1	**Film Position** Displays frame FO1 (picture of a bag).
DT 5,18/bat/ DT 7,18/bag/ DT 9, 18/rat/	**Display Text** Displays "bat" on line 5 starting in column 18 on the CRT. Displays "bag" on line 7 starting in column 18 on the CRT. Displays "rat" on line 9 starting in column 18 on the CRT.
AUP AO1	**Audio Play** Plays audio message AO1. "Touch and say the word that goes with the picture."
L1 EP 30/ABCD1	**Enter and Process** Activates the light-pen; specifies the time limit (30 sec.) and the problem identifier (ABCD1) that will be placed in the data record along with all responses to this problem. If a response is made within the time limit the computer skips from this command down to the CA (correct answer comparison) command. If no response is made within the time limit, the commands immediately following the EP command are executed.
AD 1/C4	**Add** Adds one to the overtime counter (C4).
LD 1/S1	Loads one into the error switch (S1).
AUP AO4	**Plays message AO4** "The word that goes with the picture is bag. Touch and say bag."
DT 7,16/→/	**Displays arrow** on line 7, column 16 (arrow pointing at "bag").
BR L1	**Branch** Branches to command labeled L1. The computer will now do that command and continue from that point.
CA 1,7,3,18/C1	**Correct Answer** Compares student's response with an area one line high starting on line 7 and three columns wide starting in column 18 of the CRT. If his response falls within this area, it will be recorded in the data with the answer identifier C1. When a correct answer has been made, the commands from here down to WA (wrong answer comparison) are executed. Then the program jumps ahead to the next PR. If the response does not fall in the correct area, the machine skips from this command down to the WA command.
BR L2/S1/1 AD 1/C1	Branches to command labeled L2 if the error switch (S1) is equal to one. Adds one to the initial correct answer counter (C1).
L2 AUP AO2	**Plays audio message AO2** "Good. Bag. Do the next one."
WA 1,5,3,18/W1 WA 1,9,3,18/W2	**Wrong Answer** These two commands compare the student response with the areas of the two wrong answers, that is, the area one line high starting on line 5 and three columns wide starting in column 18, and the area one line high starting on line 9 and three columns wide starting in column 18. If the response falls within one of these two areas, it will be recorded with the appropriate identifier (W1 or W2). When a defined wrong answer has been made, the commands from here down to UN (undefined answer) are executed. Then the computer goes back to the EP for this problem. If the response does not fall in one of the defined wrong answer areas, the machine skips from this command down to the UN command.
AD 1/C2	Adds one to the defined wrong answer counter (C2).
L3 LD 1/S1	Loads one into the error switch (S1).
AUP AO3	**Plays message AO3** "No."
AUP AO4	**Plays message AO4** "The word that goes with the picture is bag. Touch and say bag."
DT 7,16/→/	**Display arrow** on line 7, column 16.
UN	**Undefined Wrong Answer** If machine reaches this point in the program, the student has made neither a correct nor a defined wrong answer.
AD 1/C3 BR L3	Adds one to the undefined answer counter (C3). Branches to command labeled L3. (The same thing should be done for both UN and WA answers. This branch saves repeating the commands from L3 down to UN.)
PR LD O/S1 FP FO2 DT 5,18/card/ DT 7, 18/cart/ DT 9,18/hard/	**Prepares the machine for next problem** These commands prepare the display for the second problem. Notice the new film position and new words displayed. The student was told to "do the next one" when he finished the last problem so he needs no audio message to begin this.
L4 EP 30/ABCD2 AD 1/C4 LD 1/S1 AUP AO7 DT 5,16/→/ BR L4	**Light-pen is activated** These commands are done only if no response is made in the time limit of 30 seconds. Otherwise the machine skips to the CA command.
CA 1,5,4,18/C2 BR L5/S1/1 AD 1/C1 L5 AUP AO5	**Compares response with correct answer area** Adds one to the initial correct answer counter unless the error switch (S1) shows that an error has been made for this problem. The student is told he is correct and goes on to the next problem. These commands are executed only if a correct answer has been made.
WA 1,7,4,18/W3 WA 1,9,4,18/W4 AD 1/C2 L6 LD 1/S1 AUP AO6 AUP AO7 DT 5,16/→/	**Compares response with defined wrong answer** Adds one to the defined wrong answer area and the error switch (S1) is loaded with one to show that an error has been made on this problem. The student is told he is wrong and shown the correct answer and asked to touch it. These commands are executed only if a defined wrong answer has been made.
UN AD 1/C3 BR L6	**An undefined response has been made if the machine reaches this command** Adds one to the undefined answer counter and we branch up to give the same audio, etc., as is given for the defined wrong answer.

TABLE 2   Macro Commands for Instructional Sequence in Table 1

| Command | Audio Information | | Film Strip | |
	Address	Message	Address	Picture
Problem 1 CM PW]FO1]bat]bag]rat]AO1] ABCD1]AO4]AO2]AO3]7]1,7,3,18]C1]	AO1	Touch and say the word that goes with the picture.	FO1	Picture of a bag.
	AO2	Good. Bag. Do the next one.		
	AO3	No.		
	AO4	The word that goes with the picture is bag. Touch and say bag.		
Problem 2 CM PW]FO2]card]cart]hard]] ABCD2]AO7]AO5]AO6]5]1,5,4,18]C2]	AO5	Good. Card. Do the next one.	FO2	Picture of a card.
	AO6	No.		
	AO7	The word that goes with the picture is card. Touch and say card.		

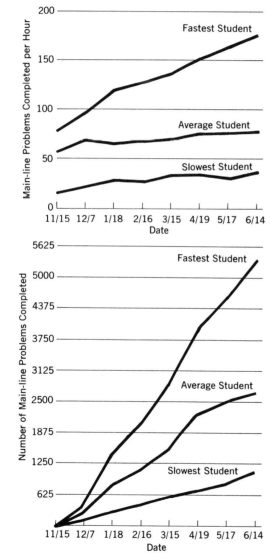

Figure 3. Rate of learning throughout the course. Note the wide range of speeds and total problems completed, showing the great potential for the individual child to learn to capacity.

We also wanted to see whether sex differences affected accuracy. On four standard types of problems—letter identification, word-list learning, matrix construction, and sentence comprehension—the only difference between boys and girls that was statistically significant was for word-list learning. These results, while not conclusive, do lend support to the notion that when students are removed from the normal classroom environment and given computer instruction, boys perform as well as girls in overall rate of progress. The results also suggest that with computer-assisted instruction the sex difference is minimized as the emphasis moves toward analysis and away from rote memorization. The one kind of problem on which the girls achieved significantly higher scores than the boys, word-list learning, is essentially a memorization task.

How did the computer-instructed first-graders compare with the control group? Both groups were tested extensively before the project began and again near the end of the school year. The two groups were not significantly different at the start of the year, but at the end of the year the group that received computer-assisted reading instruction performed significantly better on almost all of the reading achievement tests, including the California Reading Test, the Gates-MacGinitie Test, and the Hartley.

The average Stanford-Binet IQ score for the students (both experimental and control) was 89. There was considerable variation, but by and large these were not exceptional or gifted children. Students, teachers, and parents reacted quite favorably to the introduction of computer-assisted instruction into the classroom.

Initially, students were given only a few minutes per day on the teaching machines. The time was increased to twenty minutes after the first six weeks; in the last month we allowed students thirty to thirty-five minutes. We wanted to determine how well first-grade students would adapt to machine instruction for relatively long periods of time. We found that they adapt quite well, and this year we have been using thirty-minute periods for all students. This may seem like a long session for a first-grader, but our observations suggest that their span of attention is well over a half-hour if the programming is dynamic and responsive to their inputs.

Various optimization routines were evaluated during the year. These evaluations, in turn, have suggested a number of experiments and analyses that might be profitable. Such analyses, combined with the potential for additional research under the highly controlled conditions offered by computerized instruction, could lay the groundwork for a theory of instruction truly useful to the educator. The theory will have to be based on a highly structured model of the learning process, and it must generate optimization strategies that are compatible with the goals of education. The development of a viable theory of instruction is a major scientific undertaking, and substantial progress in this direction could well be one of psychology's most important contributions to society.

III

The Development of the Individual

The Young Monkeys

Harry and Margaret Harlow

The program of research with nonhuman primates carried on by the Harlows is designed to illuminate social and emotional development in human children. They focus on three basic social responses of primates—innate patterns of behavior, which may, as they have shown, be modified by experience. The first of these, affection, develops in the infant monkey by the end of the second month, by which time he will form attachments with his age mates, if the living situation provides the possibility. As a result of such social attachments and play, differences in sex roles emerge, for while sex differences basically depend on anatomical and physical differences, much of sex role behavior is learned through play and socialization with peers. The second basic social response, aggression, appears after sexual differentiation is learned. This aggressive behavior is generally playful, with violent behavior occurring only as a response to threat. Affection, aggression, and fear, the third basic response, have been studied by the authors in a series of investigations of the effects of social and physical isolation. The presence of monkey mothers and/or age mates during the first months of life is shown to have important consequences for later development.

When we watch a newborn rhesus monkey with its mother, the infant seems to display signs of affection almost at once, clinging to the mother's body and climbing into her arms. The slightly older infant cries piteously when separated from its mother. Still later, as the maternal bond weakens, the young monkey reaches out to others its own age for companionship and, finally, for sexual satisfaction.

These examples illustrate the three basic social responses of primates—affection, fear, and social aggression. In fact, the responses usually emerge in that order as the infant monkey matures.

Affection, the reaction to cuddling, warmth, and food, comes first in these broadly based and sometimes even overlapping categories. Then comes fear, as the infant begins to explore a sometimes dangerous world. And finally, there is social aggression when the monkey is older, more exploratory, and better able to handle itself.

These responses obviously are not the simple component behavior patterns that B. F. Skinner has described, nor are they like Pavlovian reflex reactions. Rather, they are highly complicated and built-in patterns of behavior that can be modified by learning. Under certain circumstances, normal development can be blocked, and the patterns disrupted. When this is done under experimental conditions, we can learn more about the sensitive, vital process of socialization.

Certainly monkeys are not people, but they are the next highest form of animal life, and we can perform complex experiments with them, manipulating their environment with a freedom not possible when using people as subjects. For example, we can put monkeys into isolation as they develop, we can add to or take away from their basic emotional needs. And as we learn more about the basic emotions of monkeys, we can profit from this knowledge in our ever-active search to find out more about ourselves in the world.

The Beginnings of Affection

The first sign of affection by the newborn rhesus monkey is a reflex action that facilitates nursing. The infant grasps its mother's fur and moves upward on her body until restrained by her arms. This brings the baby monkey's face close to the mother's breast, and the infant begins to nurse. Throughout the first two or three weeks of life, the response of infant to mother continues to be based on reflexes, although the baby gradually gains voluntary control of its motor behavior. But even after the young monkey is skilled enough to walk, run, and climb by itself, it continues to cling to its mother. The bond of affection between infant and mother continues to grow stronger instead of weaker during the next few months.

The mother monkey warmly returns her infant's affection, and this reciprocal affection operates in a way that helps prepare the young monkey for participation in a more complex social environment. The mother shows her fondness by cradling, grooming, caressing, and protecting her baby. At first, this affection is primarily reflex behavior and is stimulated by the touch, sound, and sight of the baby. Interestingly, the baby need not be the female monkey's own, for preadolescent, adolescent, and adult females are attracted to all the infants in their group. Given the opportunity, even females who have not recently borne young will adopt infants, and this indicates that hormonal changes associated with parturition are not essential to the establishment of maternal affection.

Fear

Fear responses show themselves after the young rhesus has matured intellectually and has had enough experience to recognize objects that are strange and dangerous. In its first two months a young rhesus shows little or no fear. But by the third or fourth month of life, unfamiliar places, persons, and objects as well as loud or unusual noises make the infant screech and cling to its mother. Young monkeys separated from their mothers will cry frequently and clasp themselves. An infant that has previously known only its mother can be frightened by other monkeys, but if the young rhesus has previously been part of a group, it will be afraid of other monkeys only when threatened by them, or actually hurt.

Making Friends

By the time they are two months old, young monkeys that have been allowed to live in groups show an interest in other monkeys, especially infants. First contacts are usually brief, beginning with physical exploration, which can be one-sided or mutual. From these early experiences come more complex play behavior and the development of affection for other young monkeys. Emotional attachment to monkeys of the same age usually appears before the emergence of fear. However, if such attachments are not permitted to develop—if, for instance, the young monkey is kept apart from his peers—there is some possibility that this friendly emotion will not emerge at all. Nevertheless, the infant that has received a good deal of maternal affection can sometimes make friends even when the normal age for doing so has passed.

Emotional bonds among those of the same age usually grow stronger as the maternal relationship begins to ebb. The infant's first emotional experience, the attachment to its mother, is quite distinct from later emotional ties. For example, the peer relationship originates in and develops through play. Young monkeys that have not been permitted to establish relationships with other infants are wary of their playmates when finally allowed to be with them, and these deprived monkeys often fail to develop strong bonds of affection. Yet monkeys that have been deprived of mother love but provided with early contacts *can* develop ties with their peers that seem comparable to the bonds formed by mother-reared infants.

Affection of age mates for one another is universal within the entire primate kingdom. It starts early in all species of monkeys and apes, and it is evident throughout the life span. The beginnings of human sociability, however, are more variable because children's opportunities to contact their age mates differ from family to family and from culture to culture. Four decades ago, research by Charlotte Buhler and her associates in Vienna showed that human infants in their first year of life generally are responsive to one another. This can be confirmed informally by anyone who looks in on a pediatrician's waiting room where healthy young children contact one another quickly. If held, they strain toward one another, and if close together, they reach out to one another. They smile at each other, and they laugh together.

Sex Roles

In early infancy, the child's sex is relatively unimportant in social interactions: Human boys and girls, like male and female monkeys, play together indiscriminately at first. Though this continues for several years in humans, behavioral differences begin to appear in monkeys by the third or fourth month and increase steadily until the animal is mature.

Male monkeys become increasingly forceful, while the females become progressively more passive. A male will threaten other males and females alike, whereas females rarely are aggressive toward males. During periods of play, males are the pursuers, and the females retreat. As they grow older, increasing separation of the sexes becomes evident in friendship and in play.

During their juvenile period, one to two years of age, and even after, rhesus monkeys as a rule form pairs and clusters of friends of the same sex. Only in maturity when the female is in heat does the pattern change, and then only temporarily. Male-female pairs dominate until the mating period ends. And then the partners return to their own sex groups. With humans, too, friendships with those of the same sex predominate in childhood, adolescence, and maturity. Even when men and women attend the same social event, men often cluster together with other men, while women form groups by themselves. Clubs for men only, or for women only, further demonstrate this sexual split.

At both the human and subhuman levels, this separation is undoubtedly based on common interests, which in turn are based on anatomical and physical differences between the sexes. For example, male primates of most species are larger and stronger than the females and better equipped physiologically for feats of strength and physical endurance. This probably leads the male to more large-muscle activities. Culture influences do not create differences in behavior between the sexes, but they do mold, maintain, and exaggerate the natural differences. Thus boys, not girls, are encouraged to become athletes, and women boxers and shot-putters are generally regarded as oddities.

The importance of peer relationships in monkeys cannot be overemphasized. All primates that live in groups achieve much of their communal cohesiveness and adult sexual social behavior through affectionate relationships with others of the same age. Monkeys learn their sex roles through play. By the third or fourth month of life, male and female sexual behavior are beginning to be different. By the time they are a year old, most monkeys who have been reared in groups display mature and specialized sexual behavior, except that male intromission and ejaculation do not occur until puberty, at about four years of age.

Social Aggression

Sexual differentiation usually is learned by monkeys before social aggression appears. After numerous and varied studies at the University of Wisconsin, we have concluded that unless peer affection precedes social aggression, monkeys do not adjust; either they become unreasonably aggressive or they develop into passive scapegoats for their group.

Rhesus monkeys begin to make playful attacks on one another almost as soon as they are old enough for actual contact, and their aggression increases steadily throughout the first year of life. The young monkeys wrestle and roll, pretend to bite one another, and make threatening gestures. But they do not hurt each other, even though their teeth are sharp enough to pierce a playmate's skin.

If the young rhesus has had normal group contact during infancy, it will show restraint toward both friends and strangers. Only if threatened, or to protect weaker members of its group, will it fight.

While in the group the young try to find a place in the hierarchy, and as dominance is established, a relative peace ensues. In contrast, monkeys who have been socially deprived may seriously injure one another when placed together at this stage.

Isolation Breeds Fear

One experimental rearing condition that throws much light on the problems of aggression and peer affection is total social isolation. At birth, the monkey is enclosed in a stainless steel chamber where light is diffused, temper-ature controlled, air flow regulated, and environmental sounds filtered. Food and water are provided, and the cage is cleaned by remote control. During its isolation, the animal sees no living creature, not even a human hand. After three, six, or twelve months, the monkey is removed from the chamber and placed in an individual cage in the laboratory. Several days later it is exposed for the first time to peers—another monkey who has been reared in isolation and two who have been raised in an open cage with others. The four are put in a playroom equipped with toys and other apparatus designed to stimulate activity and play (see Figure 1); they spend usually half an hour a day in the room five days a week, and these sessions go on for six months.

Fear is the overwhelming response in all monkeys raised in isolation. Although the animals are physically healthy, they crouch and appear terror-stricken by their new environment. Young that have been isolated for only three months soon recover and become active in playroom life; by the end of a month they are almost indistinguishable from their control age mates. But the young monkeys that had been isolated for six months adapt poorly to each other and to the control animals. They cringe when approached and fail at first to join in any of the play. During six months of play sessions, they never progress beyond minimal play behavior, such as playing by themselves with toys. What little social activity they do have is exclusively with the other *isolate* in the group. When the other animals become aggressive, the isolates accept their abuse without making any effort to defend themselves. For these animals, social opportunities have come too late. Fear prevents them from engaging in social interaction and consequently from developing ties of affection.

Monkeys that have been isolated for twelve months are very seriously affected. Although they have reached the age at which true aggression is normally present, and they can observe it in their playmates, they show no signs of aggression themselves. Even primitive and simple play activity is almost nonexistent. With these isolated animals, no social play is observed and aggressive behavior is never demonstrated. Their behavior is a pitiful combination of apathy and terror as they crouch at the sides of the room, meekly accepting the attacks of the more healthy control monkeys. We have been unable to test them in the playroom beyond a ten-week period because they are in danger of being seriously injured or even killed by the others.

Our tests have indicated that this social failure is not a consequence of intellectual arrest. In the course of thirty-five years of experimentation with and observation of monkeys, we have developed tests of learning that successfully discriminate between species, between ages within species, and between monkeys with surgically-produced brain damage and their normal peers. The tests have demonstrated that the isolated animals are as intellectually able as are monkeys of the same age raised in open cages. The only difference is that the isolates require more time to adjust to the learning apparatus. All monkeys must be adapted to testing, but those coming from total isolation are more fearful, and so it takes longer for them to adjust to the situation.

From Apathy to Aggression

We continued the testing of the same six- and twelve-month isolates for a period of several years. The results were startling. The monkeys raised in isolation now began to attack the other monkeys viciously, whereas before they had cowered in fright. We tested the isolates with three types of strangers: large and powerful adults, normal monkeys of their age, and normal one-year-olds. The monkeys that had been raised in the steel isolation cages for their first six months now were three years old. They were still terrified by all strangers, even the physically helpless juveniles. But in spite of their terror, they engaged in uncontrolled aggression, often launching suicidal attacks upon the large adult males and even attacking the juveniles—an act almost never seen in normal monkeys of their age. The passage of time had only exaggerated their asocial and antisocial behavior.

In those monkeys, positive social action was not

initiated, play was nonexistent, grooming did not occur, and sexual behavior either was not present at all or was totally inadequate. In human terms, these monkeys, who had lived unloved and in isolation, were totally unloving, distressed, disturbed, and delinquent.

Sexual Inadequacy

We have found that social deprivation has another long-term effect that is particularly destructive—inadequate sexual behavior. This is found in all males and most females reared in total or semi-isolation. Whereas some of the females that had been in semi-isolation still show a certain amount of sexual responsiveness, this is probably due to their easier role in copulation. The separate actions required for copulation begin to appear in young infants, but these actions are not organized into effective patterns unless early social play—particularly of a heterosexual nature—is allowed. Monkeys that fail to develop adult sexual patterns by the time they are twelve to eighteen months old are poor risks for breeding when they are mature.

For example, we found in one study that semi-isolated females that are placed with breeding males avoid social proximity and do not groom themselves. They often engage in threats, aggression, and autistic be-

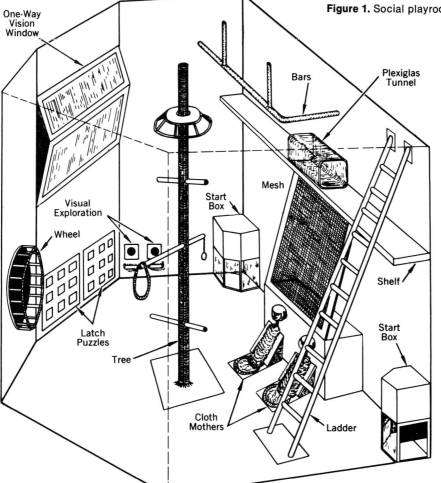

Figure 1. Social playroom for the young monkeys.

One-Way Vision Window

Bars

Plexiglas Tunnel

Visual Exploration

Wheel

Start Box

Mesh

Latch Puzzles

Tree

Shelf

Start Box

Cloth Mothers

Ladder

havior such as clutching and biting themselves, and they frequently fail to support the male when mounting occurs. In contrast, normal females seldom threaten males, are not aggressive, and do not engage in autistic behavior; they maintain social proximity, groom themselves, and provide adequate support for the mounting male.

Parallel tests with males show that socially deprived males are even more inadequate than their female counterparts. Compared to the normal males, they groomed less, threatened more, were more aggressive, rarely initiated any sexual contact, engaged in unusual and abnormal sexual responses, and—with one exception—never achieved intromission.

The sexual inadequacies of the socially deprived monkeys did not come from a loss of biological sex drive. High arousal was often seen, but it led to inappropriate responses—autistic behavior, masturbation, and violent aggression—all in a frenetic sequence lasting only a few seconds.

Monkeys Without Mothers

In another series of experiments on the emotional bases of social development in monkeys, we raised some infants with continuous peer experience and no mothers. Two, four, and six monkeys were reared together in groups. The groups of two tended to cling together in the first few weeks, chest to chest, and this behavior persisted long after normally raised infants would have stopped clinging to their mothers. The two young monkeys moved about like Siamese twins joined at the chest. When some external force turned up to break the two apart, or one rhesus attempted to explore an object, the other quickly tried to resume the clinging posture. This immature behavior continued until the animals were put in separate cages, although we found that it could be drastically reduced if the pairs were reared together for a fixed period of time, separated for another specified time, and then subjected to alternate togetherness and separation.

We also found that four or six infant monkeys living together in one cage tend very soon to form a line in which one rhesus leans forward and the others get behind him in a single file, each clinging to the back of the animal in front of him. If the first monkey moves without breaking loose, the whole group usually moves in unison with it, but if the lead rhesus frees itself, the pattern breaks up, to be re-formed shortly.

While monkeys reared in pairs play very infrequently —the tight clasp they have on one another restricts movement—the infants raised in larger groups play extensively. In one respect, the monkeys that have been raised in the larger groups are quite precocious: Their sexual behavior is perfected at an early age and as adults they breed readily. This is in sharp contrast with

the absence or insufficiency of sexual activity in male and female isolates.

Throughout our studies, we have been increasingly impressed by the alternative routes monkeys may take to reach adequate social behavior, which by our criteria includes affection toward peers, controlled fear and aggression, and normal sexual behavior. In protected laboratory conditions, social interaction between peers and between mother and child appear to be in large part interchangeable in their effect on the infant's development. A rhesus can surmount the absence of its mother if it can associate with its peers, and it can surmount a lack of socialization with peers if its mother provides affection. Being raised with several age mates appears to compensate adequately for a lack of mothering, although it is likely that animals reared in this way would be at a disadvantage if confronted by monkeys that had had a mother and early experience with others their age as well.

From an evolutionary point of view, there is an advantage to the animal in having two independent sources of affection—mother and peers. Each in part compensates for the deficiencies of the other. Mothers vary considerably in the depth and type of their attachment to their children. A rhesus mother denied normal affection in her early life may be so detached from her infant and, in many cases, may be so brutal that the effects could be devastating for her infant unless there were companions available for play. Human mothers may also exhibit detachment and physical abuse, which pediatricians refer to as the "battered baby" syndrome —a much more prevalent phenomenon than police and court records indicate.

Isolation studies that begin at birth and continue until some specified age provide a powerful technique for the analysis of maturational processes without interference from an overlay of learning. Indeed, the isolation experiment is one of the few methods by which it is possible to measure the development of complex behavior patterns in any pure or relatively pure form. While it is commonly thought that learning shapes preestablished, unlearned response patterns, this is barely half the picture, at least as far as social learning is concerned.

One of the most important functions of social learning in primates—and perhaps in all mammals and many other classes of animals as well—is the development of social patterns that will restrain and check potentially asocial behavior. These positive, learned social patterns must be established before negative, unlearned patterns emerge. In this sense, social learning is an anticipation of later learning: The inappropriate exercise of negative behavior can be checked within the social group while the same behavior is permitted toward intruders threatening from without.

Sex-Role Identity

Jerome Kagan

In establishing one's sexual identity, not only are the physical signs of sexuality considered, but psychological characteristics are also taken into account. The combination of these objectives and subjective signs is then matched against an idealized image of what masculinity or femininity should be, as determined by the particular values of the culture in which the individual lives. One part of the present article discusses the factors that contribute to differences in the firmness of an individual's sex-role identity.

How does the child learn these culturally derived sex-role standards? The author suggests that such learning occurs in much the same way as does any conceptual learning. Thus, sex roles are defined by the different physical attributes and the different functions or behaviors of men and women—including characteristic opinions, feelings, and motives. Despite the importance of learning in developing idealized sex-role standards, the author points out, many of these sex-related differences are found both across cultures and across species, as discussed, for example, in the preceding article.

Every person wants to know how good, how talented, and how masculine or feminine he or she is. Of the many attributes that go into the concept of self, sex-role identity is one of the most important.

It may seem odd that anyone should be unsure of his sex-role identity. A human who is five feet and eleven inches tall, eighteen years old, and who has X and Y chromosomes, testes, penis, and body hair is, by definition, a male. It would seem that all such men should regard themselves as equally masculine. But the human mind, in its perversity, does not completely trust anatomical characteristics and insists upon including psychological factors in the final judgment. Man is as foolish as the cowardly lion, who had to be reassured of his courageous qualities by the Wizard of Oz.

A sex-role identity is a person's belief about how well his biological and psychological characteristics correspond to his or her concept of the ideal male or female. The definition of the ideal—the sex-role standard—is influenced by the values of his particular culture. A Kyoto girl is taught that gentleness is the most important feminine quality; a Los Angeles girl learns that physical beauty is an essential quality.

A person is said to have a strong or firm sex-role identity when his subjective judgment of himself comes up to the standards of the ideal. If there are major discrepancies between the ideal and a person's view of himself, he has a weak or fragile sex-role identity.

To get at the dynamic significance of a person's sex-role identity, we must confront four questions: (1) How does a person initially learn sex-role standards? (2) Just what is the content of the standards? (3) Are some sex-role standards generalized across cultures? (4) What are the implications of a firm sex-role identity and a fragile one?

Learning Sex Roles

A child learns sex-role standards the way he learns many other concepts. He learns that an object that is round, made of rubber, and bounces is called a ball. He learns more about the definition of a ball by watching how it is used, by listening to people talk about it, and by playing with one himself. By the age of two he has learned that certain humans are called boys and men; others, girls and women. He learns the definition by noting what they do, how they look, and what they wear, and by listening and watching as others discuss the sexes. The categorization of human beings into the two sexes, usually in place by two and a half years, is one of the earliest conceptual classifications a child makes.

Sex roles are defined not only by physical attributes and behavior but also by opinions, feelings, and motives. Most American girls regard an attractive face, a hairless body, a small frame, and moderate-sized breasts as ideal physical characteristics. American boys regard being tall and having large muscles and facial and body hair as ideal.

Some psychological traits that differentiate males from females are changing in American life. Aggression is one of the primary sex-typed behaviors. The traditional sex-role standard inhibits aggression in females but licenses and encourages it in boys and men. It is difficult to find a psychological study of Americans that fails to note more aggressive behavior among males than among females.

These differences over aggressive and dependent behavior are reflected in a person's action, and in a reluctance to perceive these qualities in others. As part of an extensive personality assessment, seventy-one typical middle-class American adults watched while some pictures depicting aggression and some depicting dependency were flashed onto a screen at great speed. Each person was asked to describe each picture after it was flashed seven times. The women had greater difficulty than the men in recognizing the aggressive scenes; the men had greater difficulty in recognizing the dependency scenes.

Sex-role standards dictate that the female must feel needed and desired by a man. She must believe that she can arouse a male sexually, experience deep emotion, and heal the psychological wounds of those she loves. The standards for males also stress the ability to arouse and to gratify a love object, but they also include a desire to be independent in action and to dominate others and to be able to control the expression of strong emotions, especially fear and helplessness.

The American male traditionally has been driven to prove that he was strong and powerful; the female to prove that she was capable of forming a deeply emotional relationship that brought satisfaction and growth to the partner—sweetheart or child.

These values are reflected in the behavior of young children from diverse cultures. John and Beatrice Whiting of Harvard University observed children from six cultures and found that the boys were more aggressive and dominant than the girls. The girls were more likely than boys to offer help and support to other children.

Young children agree that males are more dangerous and punishing than females. This view also persists at a symbolic level: Six-year-olds believe that a tiger is a masculine animal and that a rabbit is feminine. In one experiment, pairs of pictures were shown to young children. On the first run, the child selected from each pair the picture that was more like his father. The second time, the child selected the picture that was more like his mother. In the third run, he picked the one more like himself. Boys and girls alike classified the father as darker, larger, more dangerous, and more angular than the mother. The boys classified themselves as darker, larger, more dangerous, and more angular than the girls.

Cross-cultural Comparisons

These perceptions are not limited to our culture. Charles Osgood of the University of Illinois showed similar pairs of abstract designs or pictures to adults from four different language groups: American, Japanese, Navajo, and Mexican-Spanish. He asked each adult to indicate which picture of the pair best fitted the concept of man and which fitted the concept of woman. As the children had done, the adults from all four cultures classified men as large, angular, and dark and women as small, round, and light.

Dependency, passivity, and conformity are also part of the traditional sex-role standard. Females in America and in most European countries are permitted these qualities; boys and men are pressured to *inhibit* them. Thus men experience greater conflict over being passive; females experience greater conflict over being aggressive.

In one study, my colleagues and I observed two-year-old boys and girls in a large living room. The girls were more likely than boys to stay in close physical contact with their mothers during the first five minutes. Then a set of toys was brought into the room and the children were allowed to play for a half hour. Most children left their mothers immediately and began to play. However, after fifteen or twenty minutes many became bored and restless. The girls tended to drift back to their mothers, while the boys preferred to wander around the room. Michael Lewis of Educational Testing Services has reported similar differences in children only one year old. Linda Shapiro of Harvard studied pairs of two-year-olds (two boys or two girls) in a natural setting and found the girls more trusting, more cooperative, more nurturing, and less fearful of each other than the boys.

It is interesting to note that the rhesus monkey and the baboon, who are not taught sex-role standards, display behavioral differences that resemble those observed in young children. Harry Harlow and his colleagues at the University of Wisconsin have found that threatening gestures and rough-and-tumble contact play are more frequent among young male than among young female monkeys, whereas passivity in stress is more frequent among the females. (See the Harlow article, "The Young Monkeys," in this section.)

Some of the differences between males and females seem to stretch across cultures and species, suggesting that sex-role standards are neither arbitrary nor completely determined by the social groups. Each culture, in its wisdom, seems to promote those behaviors and values that are biologically easiest to establish in each of the two sexes.

Implications of Firm and Fragile Identities

The individual's sex-role identity, as noted, is his opinion of his maleness or femaleness, not a summary of his physical attributes. In one study, Edward Bennett and Larry Cohen of Tufts University asked American adults to select from a list of adjectives those that best described their personalities. The women described themselves as weak, fearful, capable of warmth, and desirous of friendly and harmonious relationships with others. The men described themselves as competent, intelligent, and motivated by power and personal accomplishment.

Sex-role identity differences among children arise from three sources:

First, a family-reared child is predisposed to assume

that he or she is more like his or her parent of the same sex than like any other adult, and is inclined to imitate that parent. If a father is bold and athletic, his son is more likely to believe he possesses these masculine attributes than is a boy whose father is not athletic.

Second, the child is vulnerable to the special definition of sex roles shared by his peer group. A boy who is clumsy on the playing field is more likely to question his sex-role identity if he lives in a neighborhood devoted to athletics than he is if he lives in a community that values intellectual prowess.

Third, sex-role identity depends heavily on the quality of sexual interaction in adolescence. The sex-role identity has two important six-year periods of growth: one prior to puberty when acquisition of peer-valued sex-role characteristics is primary, and one during adolescence, when success in heterosexual encounters is crucial. If the adolescent is unable to establish successful heterosexual relationships, he will begin to question his sex-role identity. To the adult, the potential for attracting the affection of another and entering into a satisfactory sexual union is the essence of the sex-role standard.

Let us consider the implications of a firm sex-role identity and a fragile one. Each of us tries all the time to match his traits to his notion of the ideal sex role. This is but one facet of the human desire to gain as much information about the self as possible. When one feels close to his ideal standard, his spirits are buoyed. He is confident he can come even closer, and he makes the attempt. If he feels he is far from his standard, he may turn away from it and accept the role of a feminine man (or a masculine woman). Acceptance of a culturally inappropriate role reduces the terrible anxiety that comes from recognizing in one's self a serious deviation from an ideal that cannot be obtained. The only possible defense is to redefine the ideal in attainable terms.

The continuing attempt to match one's attributes to the sex-role ideal allows men to display a more intense involvement than women in difficult intellectual problems. Males are supposed to be more competent in science and mathematics; as academic excellence is necessary for vocational success, it is therefore an essential component of a man's sex-role identity.

Adolescent girls view intellectual striving as a form of aggressive behavior because it involves competition with a peer. Since many females believe they should not be overly competitive, they inhibit intense intellectual striving. A visit to college dining halls often reveals males arguing so intensely that the air crackles with hostility. Intense debate in the female dining hall is less frequent because it threatens the girl's sex-role identity. Men seem to be better able to argue about an issue because they do not always take an attack on an opinion as an attack on the person.

Although intense intellectual striving is more characteristic of adult men than it is of women, this is not the case among young children. In the primary grades, girls outperform boys in all areas. The ratio of boys to girls with reading problems ranges as high as six to one. One reason for this difference is that the average American six- or seven-year-old boy sees school as a feminine place. On entering school, he meets female teachers who monitor painting, coloring, and singing and put a premium on obedience and suppression of aggression and restlessness. These values are clearly more appropriate for girls than for boys. Studies of children affirm that they see school as feminine, and seven-year-old boys naturally resist the complete submission it demands. If this is true, a community with a large proportion of male teachers should have a smaller proportion of boys with serious reading retardation. Some American communities (Akron, Ohio, is one) are testing the hypothesis.

Depression and anxiety affect the sexes differently. Women are likely to suffer psychological stress when it is suggested that they are not attractive, loving, or emotional. Some women experience serious depression after giving birth because they do not feel strong love for the infant and they question their femininity. Men become anxious at suggestions that they are impotent or not competent, successful, or dominant. Depression is likely to follow a man's career failure.

Changes in Societal Sex Roles

The sex-role standards of a society are not static, and changes in the standards that surround sexuality and dependence are just becoming evident. The American woman has begun to assume a more active role in sexual behavior; her mother and grandmother assumed passive postures. This reach for independence has extensive social implications. Some college-educated women feel that dependence, especially on men, is an undesirable feminine trait. They want to prove that they can function as competently and autonomously as men, and this pushes them to develop academic and career skills.

Why? The intense effort spent on getting into and staying in college has persuaded the young woman that she should use her hard-won intellectual skills in a job. Technology has made it less necessary for a woman to do routine housework and has forced her to look outside the home for proof of her usefulness.

Most human beings seek the joy of accomplishment. A man tries to gratify this need in his job, and he has something concrete with which to prove his effectiveness—an invention, a manuscript, a salary check. Woman once met her need to be useful by believing that her sweetheart, husband, or children required her wisdom, skill, and personal affection. Instant dinners, permissive sexual mores, and freedom for children have undermined this role. It is too early to predict the effect of this female unrest. It should lead to a more egalitarian relation between the sexes. It could make each partner so reluctant to submerge his individual autonomy and admit his need for the other that each walks a lonely and emotionally insulated path. Let us hope it does not.

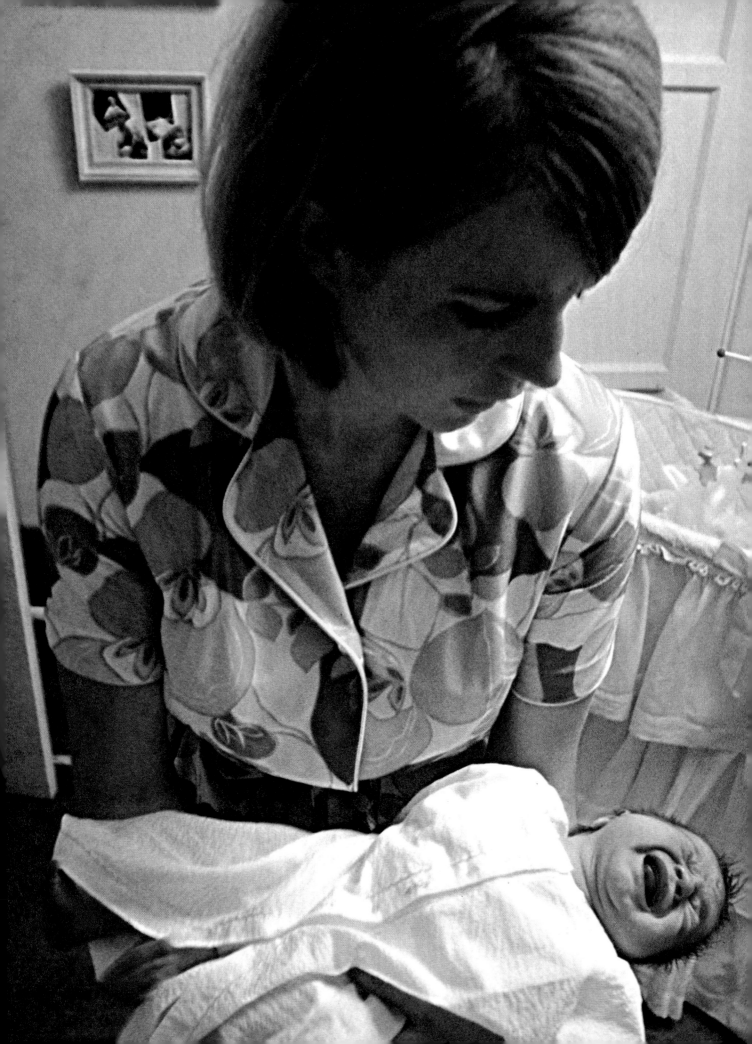

Mrs. Oedipus

Matthew Besdine

Freud, reflecting the ethos of the Victorian era, focused on Oedipus and his father in his construct of the Oedipus complex, largely ignoring the role of Jocasta, the mother. It is doubtful that women of Jocasta's ilk were ever as passive and nondynamic as Freud suggests; certainly today women play an increasingly active role in our society.

The author reviews the Oedipus myth and sees in it a potential new universal construct: a particular kind of mothering pattern, similar to that of Jocasta as depicted in myth and drama (but not by Freud), may be critical for the development of creativity in the child. This pattern of Jocasta-mothering stimulates and encourages the child to higher and higher levels of creative productivity because the relationship fulfills the intelligent, sensitive mother's needs for emotional intimacy and intellectual sustenance. The author traces the developmental consequences of such an intense mother-child attachment through childhood, adolescence, and later life and indicates how the early, almost symbiotic, relationship can result in both great artistic feats—and intense personal misery. He points out many Jocasta sons in the arts and uses Michelangelo and Jesus Christ as representative.

Let us call him Patient XY and consider him a composite of countless patients in analysis, or of a legion of troubled men. XY's father was dim, distant, or remote—either absent from the home physically, or absent as a paternal masculine force because of weakness, irresponsibility, or deep involvement in a successful career. XY's mother was a bright, warm, intelligent, forceful woman, but for one reason or another, these gifts of intellect and love were not laid at the feet of friends, society, or husband; they were poured out almost exclusively for her son, who was an only child, or the first child to survive, or a child born late, after earlier children had grown up and had left the home.

XY himself is intelligent and sensitive, but his relations with himself and with others are stormy, unhappy, or at least highly ambivalent. He craves a deep, binding, exclusive intimacy with others and yet continually jeopardizes such intimacy—when he doesn't repel it entirely—on the slightest of pretexts. Then he frantically seeks it once again, often succeeding once more in frightening away or exasperating the loved one.

He finds the possibility or fact of marriage almost nightmarish, and establishes close bonds only with women who are "safe"—with married women, known lesbians, or with women much older than he is. He is capable of lust only with women who can lay no claim to him as a permanent partner: whores, women of defective intelligence or much lower social position, or one-night stands of one kind or another.

He has a very strong homosexual streak, either overt or ferociously suppressed. All or most of his deep emotional and intellectual friendships occur with men. He tends to be paranoid, masochistic, and laden with a veritable crush of guilts. He often has some quasi-ruinous addiction—to gambling, to drink, to drugs, to crackpot schemes, or to wild extravagances of some kind. When this guilty activity has been indulged, he punishes or redeems himself by fantastic bouts of work, often equally ruinous in terms of health or temper.

XY is also capable of rich, childlike humor and fantasy; he often plays with words or ideas or the observed world as though with bright and very special toys. If you are walking down the street with him, he will often seem to perceive the environment quicker than you do. He may notice and call attention to a strange face, to a weird old tree, to a marvelously shaped rock or cloud. His attention seems to flit quickly, almost as though he were speed-reading the world. Yet he will retain a staggering amount of detail. Little bits and pieces of past experience continually pop up to be recombined in curious or witty ways. It is almost as though the whole of his experience must be kept in touch with, run through associatively like prayer beads.

XY tends to have a sharp tongue and is intolerant of people or things he dislikes. He tends to be—or appears to be—forceful, aloof, moody, cold, or snobbish among strangers, and sometimes even among friends. When he speaks of himself, he may often mention events or aspects of his childhood. And he will frequently mention his mother.

XY could be any number of analysands. He could be one of countless thirty-year-old decorators, architects, hairdressers, or musicians experiencing some typical homosexual panic or climacteric.

But XY could also be Christopher Marlowe, Goethe, Heinrich Heine, Leonardo Da Vinci, Michelangelo, André Gide, Balzac, Marcel Proust, Dostoevsky, Lytton Strachey, Oscar Wilde, Jean Paul Sartre, or Sigmund Freud.

Freud's Oedipus

Shortly after his father's death, Freud created and gave to the world his retelling or reinterpretation of the Oedipus myth. The result was a new emphasis on childhood sexuality, on the boychild's lust for his mother, on patricidal feelings, and on the role of the father as a second love object, threatening ogre, and crucial wedge separating the child from its all-enveloping maternal surround. Freud thus created a whole new focus not only for the "story" of man but for literary biography. In the light of his theories, many of the recorded lives of great men appeared lopsided, if not wholly inadequate; multivolume biographies were, in a sense, thick at the wrong end.

But it is not belaboring the obvious to point out that Freud was a late Victorian, that late-Victorian middle- and upper-class society had a strong patriarchal character, as well as deeply rooted myths and taboos about women, and that Sigmund Freud's Oedipus was just as much his own as Sophocles' was, or Michelangelo's "David" was. Like all great created "characters," Freud's Oedipus is both universalized and unique.

Partly as a result of his culture and partly as a result of his own character gestalt, Freud more or less edited out Jocasta, the mother of Oedipus. He allowed Jocasta to remain in plush obscurity, and this obscurity has become quite apparent in the altered lights of our own time and culture. Mid-twentieth century American society has quite consciously called attention to the altering, commingling roles of father and mother, husband and wife; it has watched with glee the spectacular death of the so-called paterfamilias.

In the orthodox Freudian view, Jocasta is merely the passive recipient of the oedipal lusts; her sexual, emotional, and intellectual life is almost wholly lacking in detail and dynamic. She merely subserves the larger, masculine plot. But the facts are there, both in the myth and in Sophocles' play. Jocasta's husband, warned by the Oracle that a manchild born to him would kill him, abstained from all sexual intercourse with his wife. However, a drunken orgy led to the birth of a child, Oedipus. Jocasta was then forced to abandon her child on the cruel mountain. In the play, she actually turned Oedipus over to a retainer for this purpose. She remained thereafter childless, then husbandless, until the grown Oedipus turned up, whereupon she bore him four children.

The bare bones of a character structure are there: a presumed craving for children, the absence of a normal sex life, grief for a child presumably dead and "half-murdered," as it were, and finally the complete removal of the husband.

Freud did not really apply his imagination to this set of facts; he did not consider sympathetically enough the fact that the Jocasta of Sophocles' play is a woman of considerable personal force and insight, and above all, that it is *she* who speaks the ripe words that all men dream of lying with their mothers.

What would happen if one placed the spotlight upon Jocasta as well as Oedipus and viewed them as an integral unity, as mother and child? This question came to mind as I studied the life of Michelangelo. The first ten years of Michelangelo's life had been almost unexplored, and a great deal of suppression and distortion continues to cloud the events of those years. It was known, however, that the infant Michelangelo was mysteriously expelled from the Buonarotti family and turned over to a stonecutter's wife, much as Oedipus of legend was found and raised by the childless queen of Corinth. Further investigations revealed similarities in the childhood and subsequent lives and works of many strikingly creative people. I have begun strongly to suspect that the mothering pattern typical of "Jocastas" may be in some ways essential to creative productivity, particularly in the field of the arts.

Jocasta-Mothering

We must clearly distinguish the complex configuration I call Jocasta-mothering from other kinds of mothering that have similar features. At one extreme, there is total rejection of the infant. Rejecting mothers may cling pathologically to a child, but they are aware only of their own needs; they are insensitive to cues and signals from the child. There is far more hate than love in such a relationship, and the child's intellectual development is retarded and distorted, often to the point of schizophrenia. That is certainly *not* Jocasta-mothering.

Somewhere in the middle of the mothering continuum is the mother who loves her infant tenderly but whose life is fulfilled in other loving relationships. She willingly allows her child to grow and to separate himself from her, and she consciously or unconsciously exposes him to appropriate masculine models. This is not Jocasta-mothering either.

Jocasta-mothering has had a number of not entirely satisfactory tags applied to it: overevaluating, overprotective, binding, overindulgent, doting, seductive, narcissistic, momistic. These terms, while accurate enough, do not seem to suggest strongly enough a peculiar but identifiable configuration having its own limitations, its own dynamics, and its own strange richness.

Jocasta-mothering presupposes a sensitive woman who is emotionally, sexually, and intellectually starved. It also presupposes or requires a bright, sensitive child, who can respond successfully to the subtly escalating demands of such a mother.

What happens, simply enough, is that the all-enveloping, intensely warm, intimate and tender mother-son interaction of symbiosis, so typical and necessary in the first year, is extended far beyond the normal cut-off point. It can continue through adolescence, even into manhood. The Jocasta mother becomes her child's companion, tutor, and principal emotional source. This exclusive mothering process nurtures and cultivates the fullest creative potential. Just as a gardener snips all but the central bud to secure prize flowers, the Jocasta mother devotes herself almost exclusively to her chosen child.

Quite often she introduces the child very early in life to her own delight in art, music, painting, or literature. The child become precocious, or intellectually mature and sensitive for his age, thus further reducing his chances at successful relations with his peers or with weak, dull, ineffectual, or harsh masculine models. As the child grows, both he and the mother become increasingly dependent upon one another for a satisfying life of the mind and emotions—and increasingly aware of this dependency.

The mother becomes frightened by this intimate dependency and periodically repulses the child; the child finds that vital intimacy cruelly shattered, then born again. He comes more and more to regard this marvelous blessing as two-faced, as half-suffocating or half-crippling. Yet it is the only close, tender, enriching relationship in his experience; he must constantly exceed himself to renew or recapture it. The prodigies of effort needed to do this seem to enlarge or train lifelong drives or capabilities; greater and greater effort is needed, more and more grandiose success is envisioned, and quite often accomplished.

Studies of the mothers of geniuses indicate that not only the intensity but also the *quality* of Jocasta-mothering is very high. These Jocasta mothers are often women whose originality, aliveness, and deep, wide-ranging interests make them outstanding people in their own right—as were the mothers of Goethe, Heine, Freud,

Proust, and Lytton Strachey, to name but a few.

Indeed, the character, gifts, and quickness of the mother, and her ability to interact with her gifted child in increasingly stimulating, complex, and imaginative ways during the first years of life, and her need and ability to continue that relationship well into adolescence and beyond, seem to furnish the soil in which the seeds of intelligence and creativity flourish most spectacularly.

The pattern of mothering I call Jocasta-mothering has frequently been cited as causing or contributing heavily to homosexuality. And we do indeed find among men of real creative originality that overt homosexuality, strong bisexuality, extreme marital difficulties, or an unusual incapacity to relate to women as peers occurs far too frequently to be coincidental or irrelevant.

My experience with analysands and with those who walk in from the pages of biography has led me to a number of tentative, more or less grudging, conclusions on this subject.

As the intense, tender, highly stimulating mother-son symbiosis extends into the oedipal period (five to seven years) and beyond, the son of a Jocasta finds himself increasingly looking at the world through the window of a room that is essentially and irreversibly *feminine*, in the good sense of that word. A love of fabric, color, form, scent, subtlety of design, indirection, suggestion —all the tangibles and intangibles of vibrant female life—form a cluster of sensations and stimuli that becomes home base for the child. (The domain of sheer intelligence, of powerful, acute, rational thought—to which the mother has usually introduced the child quite early—is, I believe, essentially sexless or neuter, though usually considered to have a male gender.) The vigorous masculine world becomes for the son of Jocasta increasingly a world seen from afar, in tantalizing or agonized glimpses. And as the absence of an undoubtedly masculine world becomes more and more acutely felt, male models or companions increasingly become the property of imagination, rather than of personal experience.

A search for idealized friends or companions begins usually in the world of imagination itself—in literature or art. This search becomes a lifelong impulse, often assuming the proportions not only of hero worship but of hero creation.

Since the one manifest impossibility of the Jocasta mother-son relationship is the satisfaction of physical lust, the sexual object must be found elsewhere, or else eschewed entirely.

In the *actual* experience of the Jocasta son, this object is often a woman who is quite unlike the mother in terms of sensibility, talent, or warmth. The sex object is often slovenly, or beneath notice as a human being. And it is often a man. The fact that lust may be more quickly and noncommittally satisfied by a homosexual partner can, however, only partially account for the choice of male love objects by so many sons of Jocasta.

It is the *imaginative* experience of Jocasta sons that seems to be crucial in explaining their actual love lives. Imagination is the realm of ideals, and for Jocasta sons the ideal tends to be a synthesis of what was lacking, and what was known. Such sons scramble through an often grubby sexual underworld looking for a companion or relationship that is or has all things: Apollonian maleness; physical beauty of a lithe, sensuous, graceful, or heroic sort; force of character and accomplishment; the kind of youthfulness or boyishness always lacking in children mature beyond their years; complete understanding, and, of course, an ego-dissolving love like the richly sensual intimacy characteristic of the first fused or symbiotic state.

Since life but imperfectly mimics art or imagination, such an impulse toward an ideal comrade or lover remains more or less unrealized in real life. In an environment that can be mastered and controlled—the artist's medium, in other words—such an ideal crops up again and again, sometimes disguised, sometimes not. This ideal hides in the absorbing metaphor, the ambiguous line, the Gioconda smile in all its ageless, infinite variety.

Michelangelo as a Jocasta Son

Michelangelo, for example, was much more at home with the heroes of his imagination, Jesus, David, Brutus, Hercules, and Moses, than with the father figures or the lovers of his "real" life. As a boy of twelve, or younger, he sought out the older artist, Granacci; as a teen-ager, the luminaries of the Plato Academy; and later, Pope Julius II, who employed him to do his Tomb (containing the "Moses") and the ceiling of the Sistine Chapel.

As Michelangelo grew older, he was attracted to a series of young men, usually in their teens. Not till his sixty-third year could he establish even a platonic friendship with a woman. Though he died just short of ninety, he never married.

The pendulumlike "agony and ecstasy" of all his relationships is best documented in the letters, sonnets, painting, drawings, and marbles inspired by Thomasso Cavalieri, a teen-ager whom Michelangelo fell in love with at the age of fifty-seven. Snapping out of a suicidal depression, the artist wrote: "You are . . . matchless and unequaled, light of our century—paragon of the world . . ." He revealed in a poem, beginning "The horseman always riding in the night," that Cavalieri was his dream lover. In a letter to Cavalieri, he shows his symbiotic attachment and dependence, and confesses: ". . . the boundless love I bear you . . . Your name nourishes body and soul filling both with such delight that I am insensible to sorrow or fear of death. . . ." To a friend, he wrote ". . . if he were to fade from my memory, I think I should instantly fall dead."

The patterns of love are presented even more pointedly in the Cavalieri sonnets and drawings. The "Phaeton," the "Tityos," and the "Rape of Ganymede" are quite open. In the last of the drawings, Michelangelo portrays young Cavalieri as the godlike, all-powerful lover who sweeps down, overwhelms and seizes him, taking him off to heaven to be his lover. It is quite similar to rape fantasies found in certain female patients. The awesome, all-powerful, godlike Cavalieri was an idealized, imaginative creation of the artist with which, in the flesh, he was bound to be frustrated, disappointed, and furious.

The way in which Michelangelo saw and felt mother figures is characteristically grim, aloof, and distant. They never look lovingly at the infant in their arms. The glowing ecstatic mother in adoration, a theme so common to his contemporaries, is never attempted. Most of his life women were for him distant Madonnas untouched with eroticism. On the other hand, his male nudes on the Sistine ceiling, in the "Doni Madonna," the "Bacchus," the "David," and the "Battle of Centaurs," have that nuance and erotic quality men usually find in women. One has only to compare the hairless adolescent Adam and the newly created Eve of the Sistine vault, for they tell their own story of the psychosexual reality of Michelangelo. At no point in his life did he create a female adolescent the equivalent of the "David" or the "Ignudi."

Michelangelo's sense of guilt showed constantly in his life and work. In a self-portrait, he sits upon a horse, a Roman soldier crucifying St. Peter. In the statue of the "Victory," he is a vanquished old man, crushed by his love of Cavalieri and other adolescents. Obsessed with his sinfulness, he cries out in agony, "So near to death and yet so far from God." He shudders in terror at his expectancy of doom, fearing "the double death" of his body and immortal soul.

In expiation he seeks a saintly life, portraying himself as the martyred Saint Bartholomew in the "Last Judgment." In another self-portrait, he is St. Nicodemus in the service of the martyred Jesus. In real life, he devoted himself for his last seventeen years in saintly service as chief architect of St. Peter's, accepting no earthly reward; a labor of love to please the Popes and the Father in heaven for the "good of his soul." His deepest agonies compelled him to create his most beautiful masterpieces, hopefully expecting to be accepted and loved rather than repulsed and punished.

Art from Torment

For the Jocasta son, be he a Michelangelo or not, the real world is unstable, ambivalent, and extreme in a primitive, emotionally regressed way. He is constantly seeking to bind it up, to make it one. Hence you tend to get from him the kind of comprehensive, synthesizing, metaphoric thought represented not only by Plato (or Freud for that matter) but also by the major religions of the world.

Indeed, it could be argued that the life of the historical Nazarene, as we know it from the Gospels, bears the clear imprint of Jocasta-mothered genius. There is, for instance, the ineffectual, older father; the astonishing intellectual precocity; the rebellious parting from the mother; the absence of any sexual relations with women yet the intense sympathy for the prostitute; the vanity, the egocentricity, and fig-blasting temper; the exclusively male band of disciples and companions; the beautiful, profound, lovingly simple stories; the emphasis on childlikeness; the search for an all-loving, all-wise, and powerful father; the guilt, the atonement, the courting of and achievement of personal destruction. And finally, the staggering accomplishment: the creation of a complex picture or image in which men for two thousand years have read the death of the body on the cross or pinwheel of the world, and the entrance into a proper spiritual home through that necessary death.

It is all very curious. It would seem that Jocasta-mothering represents a deviation or pathology in terms of the mothering process. Nevertheless, it seems to create drives or force fields of personality that, though producing mostly misery and torment in real life, express themselves in the realms of art and thought as extraordinarily potent, comprehensive, or beautiful things.

Jocasta sons cannot wholly trust and yield to intimacy because they get caught in it in the same consuming, ego-dissolving way in which they first experienced love. They are inordinately demanding; when the loved one cannot meet these demands, they withdraw, deeply hurt and angry. The defenses go mile-high—from paranoid fury to complete dissociation of all emotional states— and soon enough come crashing down again. Their actual world is constantly receding from them, or shattering into bits. Therefore they must, *somehow*, create an unambiguous, comprehensive world or resting place that will hold and heal their experience, and they *must* work for and win that lover, who is somewhere. Such a world is built of canvas and paint, or Carrara marble, or wood, or words; more often than not, so is the lover.

As a practicing analyst, I would be the last to deny that most people who have the character structure so typical of homosexuality are lonely, miserable, unrealized people, sadly and trivially withered on the vine of human potentiality. Yet far too many truly creative people have to some degree the same personal dynamic or gestalt, a dynamic whose genesis I prefer to locate in the kind of mothering I attribute to Jocasta.

The Child as a Moral Philosopher

Lawrence Kohlberg

Investigators of moral development have been faced with the impossibility of identifying distinct moral traits: a person who is "honest" in one situation may or may not be honest in another. Professor Kohlberg approaches the development of moral thinking by focusing on the forms and structures of thought and attempts to avoid aspects of moral judgment that are primarily culture determined. The approach is similar to that of Piaget and others concerned with cognitive development, in that an invariant sequence of levels and stages is hypothesized. Professor Kohlberg identifies three levels of moral development, each of which is divided into two stages. Levels are defined in terms of the degree to which the rules of the culture have been internalized and the extent to which moral judgment is separated from the dictates of authority. Each progressive stage is more differentiated, more integrated in itself, and more general or universal than any preceding stage.

Applying this scheme to research investigations, the author found that the majority of an individual's moral thinking will be at one stage at a given time, regardless of the specific content of the moral issue. He also investigated the six stages of development in cultures as divergent as Taiwan and Mexico, and in different social classes. The findings indicate that although the rate or speed of development varies from one group to the next, the order of development through the stages is consistent across groups, suggesting that these are universal principles underlying the development of moral judgment.

How can one study morality? Current trends in the fields of ethics, linguistics, anthropology, and cognitive psychology have suggested a new approach that seems to avoid the morass of semantical confusions, value bias and cultural relativity in which the psychoanalytic and semantic approaches to morality have foundered. New scholarship in all these fields is now focusing upon structures, forms, and relationships that seem to be common to all societies and all languages rather than upon the features that make particular languages or cultures different.

For twelve years, my colleagues and I studied the same group of seventy-five boys, following their development at three-year intervals from early adolescence through young manhood. At the start of the study, the boys were aged ten to sixteen. We have now followed them through to ages twenty-two to twenty-eight. In addition, I have explored moral development in other cultures—Great Britain, Canada, Taiwan, Mexico, and Turkey.

Inspired by Jean Piaget's pioneering effort to apply a structural approach to moral development, I have gradually elaborated over the years of my study a typological scheme describing general structures and forms of moral thought that can be defined indepen-

dently of the specific content of particular moral decisions or actions.

The typology contains three distinct levels of moral thinking, and within each of these levels distinguishes two related stages. These levels and stages may be considered separate moral philosophies, distinct views of the sociomoral world.

We can speak of the child as having his own morality or series of moralities. Adults seldom listen to children's moralizing. If a child throws back a few adult clichés and behaves himself, most parents—and many anthropologists and psychologists as well—think that the child has adopted or internalized the appropriate parental standards.

Actually, as soon as we talk with children about morality, we find that they have many ways of making judgments that are not "internalized" from the outside, and that do not come in any direct and obvious way from parents, teachers, or even peers.

Moral Levels

The *preconventional* level is the first of three levels of moral thinking; the second level is *conventional*, and the third *postconventional*, or autonomous. While the preconventional child is often "well behaved" and is responsive to cultural labels of good and bad, he interprets these labels in terms of their physical consequences (punishment, reward, exchange of favors) or in terms of the physical power of those who enunciate the rules and labels of good and bad.

This level is usually occupied by children aged four to ten, a fact long known to sensitive observers of children. The capacity of "properly behaved" children of this age to engage in cruel behavior when there are holes in the power structure is sometimes noted as tragic (*Lord of the Flies, High Wind in Jamaica*), sometimes as comic (Lucy in *Peanuts*).

The second, or conventional, level also can be described as conformist, but that is perhaps too smug a term. Maintaining the expectations and rules of the individual's family, group, or nation is perceived as valuable in its own right. There is a concern not only with *conforming* to the individual's social order but in *maintaining*, supporting, and justifying this order.

The postconventional level is characterized by a major thrust toward autonomous moral principles that have validity and application apart from authority of the groups or persons who hold them and apart from the individual's identification with those persons or groups.

Moral Stages

Within each of these three levels there are two discernible stages. At the preconventional level we have:

Stage 1: Orientation toward punishment and unquestioning deference to superior power. The physical consequences of action, regardless of their human meaning or value, determine its goodness or badness.

Stage 2: Right action consists of that which instrumentally satisfies one's own needs and occasionally the needs of others. Human relations are viewed in terms like those of the marketplace. Elements of fairness, of reciprocity, and equal sharing are present, but they are always interpreted in a physical, pragmatic way. Reciprocity is a matter of "you scratch my back and I'll scratch yours" not of loyalty, gratitude, or justice.

And at the conventional level we have:

Stage 3: Good-boy—good-girl orientation. Good behavior is that which pleases or helps others and is approved by them. There is much conformity to stereotypical images of what is majority or "natural" behavior. Behavior is often judged by intention; "he means well" becomes important for the first time, and is overused, as by Charlie Brown in *Peanuts*. One seeks approval by being "nice."

Stage 4: Orientation toward authority, fixed rules, and the maintenance of the social order. Right behavior consists of doing one's duty, showing respect for authority, and maintaining the given social order for

its own sake. One earns respect by performing dutifully.

At the postconventional level, we have:

Stage 5: A social-contract orientation, generally with legalistic and utilitarian overtones. Right action tends to be defined in terms of general rights and in terms of standards that have been critically examined and agreed upon by the whole society. There is a clear awareness of the relativism of personal values and opinions and a corresponding emphasis upon procedural rules for reaching consensus. Aside from what is constitutionally and democratically agreed upon, right or wrong is a matter of personal "values" and "opinion." The result is an emphasis upon the "legal point of view," but with an emphasis upon the possibility of *changing* law in terms of rational considerations of social utility, rather than freezing it in the terms of Stage 4 "law and order." Outside the legal realm, free agreement and contract are the binding elements of obligation. This is the "official" morality of American government and finds its ground in the thought of the writers of the Constitution.

Stage 6: Orientation toward the decisions of conscience and toward self-chosen *ethical principles* appealing to logical comprehensiveness, universality, and consistency. These principles are abstract and ethical (the Golden Rule, the categorical imperative); they are not concrete moral rules like the Ten Commandments. Instead, they are universal principles of justice, of the reciprocity and equality of human rights, and of respect for the dignity of human beings as individual persons.

Up to Now

In the past, when psychologists tried to answer the question asked of Socrates by Meno, "Is virtue something that can be taught (by rational discussion), or does it come by practice, or is it a natural inborn attitude?" their answers usually have been dictated not by research findings on children's moral character but by their general theoretical convictions.

Behavior theorists have said that virtue is behavior acquired according to their favorite general principles of learning. Freudians have claimed that virtue is superego identification with parents, generated by a proper balance of love and authority in family relations.

The American psychologists who have actually studied children's morality have tried to start with a set of labels—the "virtues" and "vices," the "traits" of good and bad character found in ordinary language. The earliest major psychological study of moral character, that of Hugh Hartshorne and Mark May in 1928–1930, focused on a bag of virtues including honesty, service (altruism or generosity), and self-control. To their dismay, they found that there were *no* character traits, psychological dispositions, or entities that corresponded to words like honesty, service, or self-control.

Regarding honesty, for instance, they found that almost everyone cheats some of the time, and that if a person cheats in one situation, it does not mean that he *will* or *won't* in another. In other words, it is not an identifiable character trait, *dis*honesty, that makes a child cheat in a given situation. These early researchers also found that people who cheat express as much or even more moral disapproval of cheating as those who do not cheat.

What Hartshorne and May found out about their bag of virtues is equally upsetting to the somewhat more psychological-sounding names introduced by psychoanalytic psychology: "superego strength," "resistance to temptation," "strength of conscience," and the like. When contemporary researchers have attempted to measure such traits in individuals, they have been forced to use Hartshorne and May's old tests of honesty and self-control, and they get exactly the same results—"supergo strength" in one situation predicts little about "superego strength" in another. That is, virtue words like honesty (or superego strength) point to certain behaviors with approval but give us no guide to understanding them.

So far as one can extract some generalized personality factor from children's performance on tests of honesty or resistance to temptation, it is a factor of ego strength or ego control, which always involves nonmoral capacities like the capacity to maintain attention, intelligent-task performance, and the ability to delay response. "Ego strength" (called "will" in earlier days) has something to do with moral action, but it does not take us to the core of morality or to the definition of virtue. Obviously enough, many of the greatest evil-doers in history have been men of strong wills, men strongly pursuing immoral goals.

Moral Reasons

In our research, we have found definite and universal levels of development in moral thought. In our study of seventy-five American boys from early adolescence on, these youths were presented with hypothetical moral dilemmas, all deliberately philosophical, some of them found in medieval works of casuistry.

On the basis of their reasoning about these dilemmas at a given age, each boy's stage of thought could be determined for each of twenty-five basic moral concepts or aspects. One such aspect, for instance, is "motive given for rule obedience or moral action." In this instance, the six stages look like this:

1. Obey rules to avoid punishment.
2. Conform to obtain rewards, have favors returned, and so on.
3. Conform to avoid disapproval, dislike by others.
4. Conform to avoid censure by legitimate authorities and resultant guilt.

5. Conform to maintain the respect of the impartial spectator judging in terms of community welfare.
6. Conform to avoid self-condemnation.

In another of these twenty-five moral aspects, "the value of human life," the six stages can be defined thus:

1. The value of a human life is confused with the value of physical objects and is based on the social status or physical attributes of its possessor.
2. The value of a human life is seen as instrumental to the satisfaction of the needs of its possessor or of other persons.
3. The value of a human life is based on the empathy and affection of family members and others toward its possessor.
4. Life is conceived as sacred in terms of its place in a categorical moral or religious order of rights and duties.
5. Life is valued both in terms of its relation to community welfare and in terms of life being a universal human right.
6. Belief in the sacredness of human life as representing a universal human value of respect for the individual.

I have called this scheme a typology. This is because about 50 percent of most people's thinking will be at a single stage, regardless of the moral dilemma involved. We call our types stages because they seem to represent an *invariant developmental sequence.* "True" stages come one at a time and always in the same order.

All movement is forward in sequence, and does not skip steps. Children may move through these stages at varying speeds, of course, and may be found half in and half out of a particular stage. An individual may stop at any given stage and at any age, but if he continues to move, he must move in accord with these steps. Moral reasoning of the conventional, or Stage 3–4, kind never occurs before the preconventional Stage 1 and Stage 2 thought has taken place. No adult in Stage 4 has gone through Stage 6, but all Stage 6 adults have gone at least through 4.

While the evidence is not complete, my study strongly suggests that moral change fits the stage pattern just described. (The major uncertainty is whether all people at Stage 6 go through Stage 5 or whether these are two alternate mature orientations.)

How Values Change

As a single example of our findings of stage sequence, take the progress of two boys on the aspect "the value of human life." The first boy, Tommy, is asked "Is it better to save the life of one important person or a lot of unimportant people?" At age ten, he answers "all the people that aren't important because one man just has one house, maybe a lot of furniture, but a whole bunch of people have an awful lot of furniture and some of these poor people might have a lot of money and it doesn't look it."

Clearly Tommy is Stage 1: he confuses the value of a human being with the value of the property he possesses. Three years later (age thirteen) Tommy's conceptions of life's value are most clearly elicited by the question, "Should the doctor 'mercy kill' a fatally ill woman requesting death because of her pain?" He answers, "Maybe it would be good to put her out of her pain, she'd be better off that way. But the husband wouldn't want it, it's not like an animal. If a pet dies you can get along without it—it isn't something you really need. Well, you can get a new wife, but it's not really the same."

Here his answer is Stage 2: the value of the woman's life is partly contingent on its hedonistic value to the wife herself but even more contingent on its instrumental value to her husband, who can't replace her as easily as he can a pet.

Three years later (age sixteen) Tommy's conception of life's value is elicited by the same question, to which he replies: "It might be best for her, but her husband—it's a human life—not like an animal; it just doesn't have the same relationship that a human being does to a family. You can become attached to a dog, but nothing like a human you know."

Now Tommy has moved from a Stage 2 instrumental view of the woman's value to a Stage 3 view based on the husband's distinctively human empathy and love for someone in his family. Equally clearly, it lacks any basis for a universal human value of the woman's life, which would hold if she had no husband or if her husband didn't love her. Tommy, then, has moved step by step through three stages during the ages ten through sixteen. Tommy, though bright (IQ 120), is a slow developer in moral judgment. Let us take another boy, Richard, to show us sequential movement through the remaining three steps.

At age thirteen, Richard said about the mercy killing, "If she requests it, it's really up to her. She is in such terrible pain, just the same as people are always putting animals out of their pain," and in general showed a mixture of Stage 2 and Stage 3 responses concerning the value of life. At sixteen, he said:

I don't know. In one way, it's murder, it's not a right or privilege of man to decide who shall live and who should die. God put life into everybody on earth and you're taking away something from that person that came directly from God, and you're destroying something that is very sacred, it's in a way part of God and it's almost destroying a part of God when you kill a person. There's something of God in everyone.

Here Richard clearly displays a Stage 4 concept of life as sacred in terms of its place in a categorical moral or religious order. The value of human life is universal, it is true for all humans. It is still, however, dependent on something else, upon respect for God and God's authority; it is not an autonomous human value. Presumably if God told Richard to murder, as God commanded Abraham to murder Isaac, he would do so.

At age twenty, Richard said to the same question:

There are more and more people in the medical profession who think it is a hardship on everyone, the person, the family, when you know they are going to die. When a person is kept alive by an artificial lung or kidney it's more like being a vegetable than being a human. If it's her own choice, I think there are certain rights and privileges that go along with being a human being. I am a human being and have certain desires for life and I think everybody else does too. You have a world of which you are the center, and everybody else does too and in that sense we're all equal.

Richard's response is clearly Stage 5, in that the value of life is defined in terms of equal and universal human rights in a context of relativity ("You have a world of which you are the center and in that sense we're all equal"), and of concern for utility or welfare consequences.

The Final Step

At twenty-four, Richard says:

A human life takes precedence over any other moral or legal value, whoever it is. A human life has inherent value whether or not it is valued by a particular individual. The worth of the individual human being is central where the principles of justice and love are normative for all human relationships.

This young man is at Stage 6 in seeing the value of human life as absolute in representing a universal and equal respect for the human as an individual. He has moved step by step through a sequence culminating in a definition of human life as centrally valuable rather than derived from or dependent on social or divine authority.

In a genuine and culturally universal sense, these steps lead toward an increased *morality* of value judgment, where morality is considered as a form of judging, as it has been in a philosophic tradition running from the analyses of Kant to those of the modern analytic or "ordinary language" philosophers. The person at Stage 6 has disentangled his judgments of—or language about—human life from status and property values (Stage 1), from its uses to others (Stage 2), from interpersonal affection (Stage 3), and so on; he has a means of moral judgment that is universal and impersonal. The Stage 6 person's answers use moral words like "duty" or "morally right," and he uses them in a way implying universality, ideals, impersonality: He thinks and speaks in phrases like "regardless of who it was," or "I would do it in spite of punishment."

Across Cultures

When I first decided to explore moral development in other cultures, I was told by anthropologist friends that

I would have to throw away my culture-bound moral concepts and stories and start from scratch learning a whole new set of values for each new culture. My first try consisted of a brace of villages, one Atayal (Malaysian aboriginal) and the other Taiwanese.

My guide was a young Chinese ethnographer who had written an account of the moral and religious patterns of the Atayal and Taiwanese villages. Taiwanese boys in the ten to thirteen age group were asked about a story involving theft of food. A man's wife is starving to death, but the store owner won't give the man any food unless he can pay, which he can't. Should he break in and steal some food? Why? Many of the boys said, "He should steal the food for his wife because if she dies he'll have to pay for her funeral and that costs a lot."

My guide was amused by these responses, but I was relieved: they were, of course, "classic" Stage 2 responses. In the Atayal village, funerals weren't such a big thing, so the Stage 2 boys would say, "He should steal the food because he needs his wife to cook for him."

This means that we need to consult our anthropologists to know what content a Stage 2 child will include in his instrumental exchange calculations, or what a Stage 4 adult will identify as the proper social order. But one certainly does not have to start from scratch. What made my guide laugh was the difference in form between the children's Stage 2 thought and his own, a difference definable independently of particular cultures.

Figure 1 indicates the cultural universality of the sequence of stages that we have found. Figure 1a presents the age trends for middle-class urban boys in the United States, Taiwan, and Mexico. At age ten in each country, the order of use of each stage is the same as the order of its difficulty or maturity.

In the United States, by age sixteen the order is the reverse, from the highest to the lowest, except that Stage 6 is still little-used. At age thirteen, the good-boy, middle stage (Stage 3) is not used.

The results in Mexico and Taiwan are the same, except that development is a little slower. The most conspicuous feature is that at the age of sixteen, Stage 5 thinking is much more salient in the United States than in Mexico or Taiwan. Nevertheless, it *is* present in the other countries, so we know that this is not purely an American democratic construct.

Figure 1b shows strikingly similar results from two isolated villages, one in Yucatan, one in Turkey. While conventional moral thought increases steadily from ages ten to sixteen, it still has not achieved a clear ascendency over preconventional thought.

Trends for lower-class urban groups are intermediate in the rate of development between those for the middle-class and those for the village boys. In the three divergent cultures that I studied, middle-class children were found to be more advanced in moral judgment than matched lower-class children. This was not due to

the fact that the middle-class children heavily favored some one type of thought that could be seen as corresponding to the prevailing middle-class pattern. Instead, middle-class and working-class children move through the same sequences, but the middle-class children move faster and further.

This sequence is not dependent upon a particular religion, or any religion at all in the usual sense. I found no important differences in the development of moral thinking among Catholics, Protestants, Jews, Buddhists, Moslems, or atheists. Religious values seem to go through the same stages as all other values.

Trading Up

In summary, the nature of our sequence is not significantly affected by widely varying social, cultural, or religious conditions. The only thing that is affected is the *rate* at which individuals progress through this sequence.

Why should there be such a universal invariant sequence of development? In answering this question, we need first to analyze these developing social concepts in terms of their internal logical structure. At each stage, the same basic moral concept or aspect is defined, but at each higher stage this definition is more differentiated, more integrated, and more general or universal. When one's concept of human life moves from Stage 1 to Stage 2, the value of life becomes more differentiated from the value of property, more integrated (the value of life enters an organizational hierarchy where it is "higher" than property so that one steals property in order to save life), and more universalized (the life of any sentient being is valuable regardless of status or property). The same advance is true at each stage in the hierarchy. Each step of development, then, is a better cognitive organization than the one before it, one that takes account of everything present in the previous stage but makes new distinctions and organizes them into a more comprehensive or more equilibrated structure. The fact that this is the case has been demonstrated by a series of studies indicating that children and adolescents comprehend all stages up to their own, but not more than one stage beyond their own. And importantly, *they prefer this next stage.*

We have conducted experimental moral discussion classes that show that the child at an earlier stage of development tends to move forward when confronted by the views of a child one stage further along. In an argument between a Stage 3 and a Stage 4 child, the child in the third stage tends to move toward or into Stage 4, while the Stage 4 child understands but does not accept the arguments of the Stage 3 child.

Moral thought, then, seems to behave like all other kinds of thought. Progress through the moral levels and stages is characterized by increasing differentiation and increasing integration, and hence is the same kind of progress that scientific theory represents. Like accept-

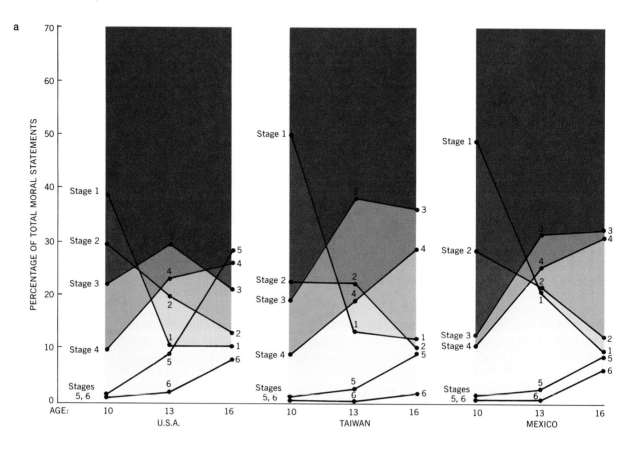

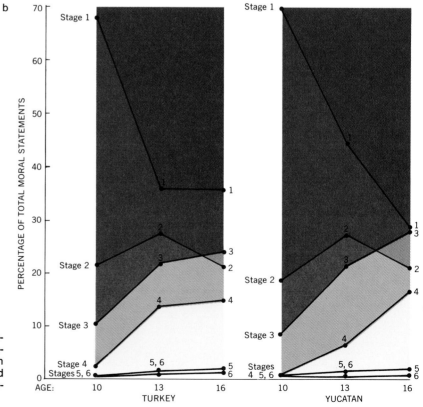

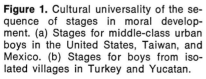

Figure 1. Cultural universality of the sequence of stages in moral development. (a) Stages for middle-class urban boys in the United States, Taiwan, and Mexico. (b) Stages for boys from isolated villages in Turkey and Yucatan.

able scientific theory—or like *any* theory or structure of knowledge—moral thought may be considered to partially generate its own data as it goes along, or at least to expand so as to contain in a balanced, self-consistent way a wider and wider experiential field. The raw data in the case of our ethical philosophies may be considered as conflicts between roles, or values, or as the social order in which men live.

The Role of Society

The social worlds of all men seem to contain the same basic structures. All the societies we have studied have the same basic institutions—family, economy, law, government. In addition, however, all societies are alike because they *are* societies—systems of defined complementary roles. In order to play a social role in the family, school, or society, the child must implicitly take the role of others toward himself and toward others in the group. These role-taking tendencies form the basis of all social institutions. They represent various patternings of shared or complementary expectations.

In the preconventional and conventional levels (Stages 1–4), moral content or value is largely accidental or culture bound. Anything from "honesty" to "courage in battle" can be the central value. But in the higher postconventional levels, Socrates, Lincoln, Thoreau, and Martin Luther King tend to speak without confusion of tongues, as it were. This is because the ideal principles of any social structure are basically alike, if only because there simply are not that many principles that are articulate, comprehensive, and integrated enough to be satisfying to the human intellect. And most of these principles have gone by the name of justice.

Behavioristic psychology and psychoanalysis have always upheld the Philistine view that fine moral words are one thing and moral deeds another. Morally mature reasoning is quite a different matter, and does not really depend on "fine words." The man who understands justice is more likely to practice it.

In our studies, we have found that youths who understand justice act more justly, and the man who understands justice helps create a moral climate that goes far beyond his immediate and personal acts. The universal society is the beneficiary.

Moral Behavior:
A Functional Analysis
Israel Goldiamond

The author distinguishes between those views of moral development that make subjective interpretations regarding the motives or intentions of the individual (see preceding article) and those that attempt to state the functional relationship between the observable antecedent and consequent events. Taking the latter, behavioristic, point of view, he suggests ways in which the procedures and principles of operant conditioning might be used to train moral behavior.

Because moral behavior is related to its consequences in an anomalous way, that is, it does not occur or persist on the basis of overt reward, or reinforcement, the author asks whether a psychology of learning based on reinforcement contingencies can be relevant to moral training. He postulates internalized consequences and describes operant studies of animal learning in which behavior was maintained in the absence of reinforcement, or even in the presence of punishment. He suggests that operant programming of moral behavior is possible and that the use of recently developed errorless programs—instead of the usual trial-and-error methods—may be the most appropriate way to accomplish this learning.

When we speak of someone as following the dictates of his conscience, making a moral decision, we are usually speaking of a puzzling relation between behavior and its consequences. For example, a young man is captured by the enemy, who demand that he betray his fellows. If he gives in, he will be rewarded handsomely. If he does not, he may be tortured or killed. Yet he does not inform. Because he chooses torture over reward, we consider his behavior moral, and we respect him. Even if he is a criminal shielding his accomplices, we may respect him, grudgingly.

In milder form, this kind of nonordinary correspondence between behavior and its consequences is frequent enough to be designated by specific names, such as moral decisions, conscience, altruism, loyalty. We often admire such action, possibly because the cohesiveness of society to a large extent rests upon its occurrence, and possibly because there is something special about it, namely, it violates the customary relation between behavior and its overt consequence.

Violation of this relation is not confined to choice of punishment over reward. The scientist who persists doggedly at his task despite failure after failure exemplifies what would be called, in laboratory terms, the persistence of nonreinforced behavior, or the persistence of behavior in the face of extinction. In common-sense terms, we speak of this relation as indicating determination, will power, or strength of character—traits that are not, of course, limited to scientists. There are yet other cases where it is so difficult to specify the overt consequences that we talk of self-satisfaction and inner direction, as when we solve a puzzle for the sake of solving it.

At times such behavior is called irrational. We can imagine a soldier's captors urging the prisoner to behave sensibly, or reasonably, by revealing what he knows. The captors are not being strictly opportunistic when they use such terms to gain compliance, since a common definition of rational behavior involves weighing the consequences according to some decision rule.

When we talk of conscience, or morality, we usually are speaking of behavior in anomalous relation to its overt consequences. The anomaly is posed by our expectations, which are based on common sense and on such systematized relations of consequences to behavior as classical economics and behaviorist learning theories.

It is becoming increasingly possible to develop operant programs for behaviors that are relevant to human social problems. Since these procedures require systematic use of consequences, to what extent are they relevant to moral outcomes that are anomalously related to consequences?

Laboratory Expectations

Operant behavior may be loosely defined as behavior whose rate or form is governed by its (overt) consequences. The behaviors that concern decision theory are, accordingly, operants. In operant laboratories, one or more behaviors are chosen for measurement, and events that are of consequence to the organism are made *contingent* on these behaviors. With these methods, it has been possible to maintain selected behavior for extended periods of time.

At first glance, it is difficult to conceive of anomalous goals in the experimental animal laboratory. If a rat has a choice between two levers, and pressing the one will bring him food, while pressing the other will bring a brief intense electric shock, we would regard it as unusual if the rat chose shock and spurned the food. If humans sometimes act otherwise, it may be argued that laboratory procedures are irrelevant to human behavior described as dictated by conscience. It might be stated that, yes, we may be able to utilize operant technology to program arithmetic and reading, and possibly even to eliminate such problems as stuttering. But when it comes to conscience, morality, altruism, and regard for others, behaviorism falls short. These behaviors—which make us human—cannot be related to a system of overt and manipulable consequences.

Rather than adopting this sweeping negation, we might state that consequences *do* enter into the outcomes discussed, but that they are *internalized*. On an intuitive level, we avoid guilt feelings and remorse by behaving appropriately, and, indeed, conscience makes cowards of us all by suppressing those behaviors that would lead to internal punishment. The captive who would not betray his colleagues has set up an internal psychological economy in which the loss of his life is outweighed by the lives of his colleagues.

Psychoanalytic theory separates the internal psychological economy governed by the avoidance of anxiety or attainment of gratification from the consequences described as *secondary gain*, which may be external. A neurotic symptom (behavior) may be maintained by the secondary gain (explicit reinforcement) of social control it produces. The symptom may, however, be a defense against certain disastrous internalized consequences. The development of the superego may be partly considered as internalization of external relations.

Such internalized concepts have been extended to explain nonordinary behavior in laboratory animals. The pigeon who pecks continually under extinction, after working on an intermittent schedule, is considered by some theorists to be maintained by hope. Eventually, the reality principle takes over and the hope is replaced by despair. He extinguishes.

Observable conditions that are explained by internalization seem, like human conscience, to be marked by nonordinary relations between behavior and its consequences. However, it is becoming increasingly possible to state the conditions under which they occur and can be programmed. They can be categorized under three major headings; alternate contingencies and consequences; behavioral consequences; and programming variables.

Decision theory has been used to rationalize many of the problems of classical psychophysics through signal detection. In research involving decision theory, the organism makes either of two responses. A person may, for example, buy a stock or a bond. Either purchase may result in gain or loss. For given market conditions, a pattern of purchases may be stipulated that optimizes net income or follows some other decision rule.

In our laboratory we have flashed on a screen rectangles analogous to market conditions of ambiguous sizes. The rectangles we call small (stocks) vary in size around a small mean size, and the rectangles we call large (bonds) vary in size around a larger one. In the training program, a single rectangle is presented each time. The observer is taught to press a button or lever on the left when a small rectangle appears and a button or lever on the right when a large rectangle appears. The distributions then overlap: a rectangle from the large end of the small series will be larger than one from the small end of the large series, but we will treat it as small, regardless of its objective size. The situation is similar to that created by a single radar blip that cannot be distinguished as either a Russian or an American plane. A discriminative response, a decision, must be made, and the decision will have consequences. If the observer calls it large (by responding on the right), the response is considered a false alarm and is penalized. Different consequences are attached to all four possible combinations of responses.

Decision theory specifies a criterion (a pattern of behavior whereby the organism tends to respond with "large" to any rectangle over a given size). A variety of boundaries or criteria between small and large is possible, and in each the net from profits and losses will differ. As we shift the overlap between small and large distributions and change the payoffs, our observers shift their criteria, continuing to optimize net gain.

The subjects in our experiments were humans working for money—and baboons and patis monkeys who worked for food pellets obtained only during hits responding right to large. A false alarm made the apparatus inoperative (time out) for as long as 120 seconds, resulting in varying delays of the opportunity to earn further reinforcement.

Any criteria set when distributions overlap will produce hits, but also errors. Our observers suffered long runs of such losses, *produced by their own behavior,* but these were more than counterbalanced by the long-term gains. Indeed, this same argument of long-term gains often is raised in support of moral behavior. The point is that we were able to program such behavior for laboratory monkeys by manipulating the program of reinforcement.

Avoidance Behavior

Another relevant behavioral pattern is called Sidman Avoidance. A timer may deliver a shock every five seconds. Pressing the bar postpones the shock fifteen seconds. By responding at least once every fourteen seconds, shock is completely avoided. Perfect avoidance is maintained over extended periods.

Complex internalized explanations have been proposed to explain such behavior when there is no environmental change. One explanation is that anxiety builds up as the time for shock approaches. A response at that time, since no shock follows, terminates the inner anxiety and reinforces the behavior, exactly as when a response ends a shock.

A very simple explanation emerges when we examine possible alternatives. If the person or animal in the experiment docs not respond, he will get shocked. If he responds, there is no shock. Hence, he responds.

To assess the extent to which alternatives—rather than anxiety—control behavior, we might substitute for the electric shock consequences not related to anxiety, such as presentation of positive reinforcement. In our laboratory, Donald M. Thompson is doing precisely this. Food is automatically presented every fifteen seconds to a pigeon. When he pecks a disc, he postpones its delivery for five seconds, that is, obtains food five seconds later. If he waits fourteen seconds and then responds, the food will have been delivered nineteen seconds after the last delivery. Accordingly, he waits for delivery, then responds, gets food five seconds later, responds again, and so on. The animal learns in accord with this schedule, exactly as does the shocked animal. In this case, the pigeon maximizes reinforcement frequency, and in the avoidance case, he minimizes shock frequency. No special explanation is required to the effect that internalized escape from anxiety is being built up. Alternatives may also explain some choice of punishment, as Nathan H. Azrin and his colleagues at Anna State Hospital have demonstrated. When they shocked a pigeon every time it pecked, pecking increased. But when punishment was absent, pecking stopped. Such behavior appears masochistic. The explanation is that when shock followed each response, food was also sometimes delivered. When shock was absent, there was no food.

A second key was then made available that provided food without shock. The pigeon switched pecking to this key. If undergoing punishment is the only way to obtain reinforcement, then the animal or a human being may set up the conditions for punishment. If there is an alternative reinforcement, a better way, without punishment, he will choose that instead.

It has been argued, in the human case, that the patient in therapy desires to maintain the disturbing behavior but wants to shed the punishing consequences attached. Our observations suggest that reformulation is required. The disturbing behavior is punished, hence the request for treatment. The suggestion for treatment is to identify, from the disturbing behavior, the maintaining consequence, and make the consequence depend on desirable behavior.

In other words, disturbing or "emotional" behavior may not be irrational. One four-year-old, who could complete a fluent sentence in five seconds, took as long as twenty seconds when he stuttered. His parents, by scrupulously behaving in exactly the same attentive manner whether he stuttered or not, actually reinforced his stuttering. Operant analysis suggested that the stuttering was a means for getting attention. If his parents attempted to extinguish the response by not reinforcing it, another symptom might be substituted. Instead, the parents were urged to continue reinforcing stuttering with attention, but to supply massive reinforcement whenever the child spoke fluently. Within three weeks he was totally fluent.

Results from research on alternate contingencies and consequences pose problems for an analysis in terms of overt consequences if one defines reinforcement only in terms of presentations (or withdrawals) immediately following the response. Implicit acceptance of this narrow equation may have driven reinforcement underground, or, rather, underskin. A broader definition of consequences accounts for the data and preserves their observable, and therefore, manipulable, nature. As we shall see, yet another restriction supports internalization.

When a rat runs an exercise wheel, where is the reinforcing stimulus? When the child works on a puzzle for the fun of it, the same question may be raised. And being virtuous for its own sake, rather than for external blandishments, is a test of moral upbringing, as is resistance to temptation. In such cases, there has been discussion of *intrinsic* reinforcement, or *autonomous* behavior or *autotelic* behavior. There have been numerous attempts to reformulate these terms into stimulus-response links and chains. These attempted reformulations, as well as frankly internalized terms, may rest upon the equation of consequential events with consequential stimuli.

Behavior as a Consequence

Research by David Premack of the University of California, Santa Barbara, has led to formulation of the principle bearing his name. One form of the principle states that given two behaviors with differing probabilities of occurrence, the high probability behavior may be used to reinforce the low probability behavior if it is made contingent upon it. In one experiment, for example, a rat only occasionally pressed a lever (no food was attached), but he often operated a running wheel. The running wheel was now made operative for only a short period of time; pressing the lever released the brake. Lever pressing increased, exactly as it does when it is rewarded with food.

The Premack principle is not a trivial restatement. It rests on a procedural and functional definition of scientific terms. If identical behavior results when we (a) manipulate the presentation of a stimulus (which defines it as a reinforcing event), and when we (b) similarly manipulate the opportunity to behave, then the opportunity may also be defined as a reinforcing event. If I withdraw from a child the opportunity to work on a puzzle and require specified behaviors to produce this opportunity, and the behaviors then increase as they do with similar manipulations of food for pigeons, then the scientific status of the two consequential procedures is identical, and both are reinforcers.

The Premack principle has tremendous practical implications. It suggests that by observing anyone's behavior carefully we may discover what his reinforcers are. These may be the behaviors that he persistently engages in, and are to be distinguished from high-frequency behavior that produces punishment as well as reinforcement, such as stuttering and other disturbing behaviors. The engineering problem is to make the behavioral reinforcers depend upon the behaviors we want the organism to emit.

There is a further implication. All the procedures developed in the laboratory to transfer reinforcing properties from one stimulus to another, to maintain their effects over extended periods of time, and to schedule them may now be used for behavioral reinforcers. Behaviors that seem to be goals in and of themselves can be used as reinforcers to increase and maintain other behaviors.

The Program as a Variable

If we establish a behavioral pattern by reinforcing each occurrence, as we typically do, and then arrange it so that long periods of behavior are not reinforced, the behavior may extinguish. If, however, we gradually program toward this goal, we can maintain control; Jack Findley of the Institute for Behavioral Research was able to maintain behavior when 20,000 responses were required for reinforcement. When the periods between presentations of reinforcement vary, and we decide to extinguish, behavior will persist for extraordinarily long periods of time. This persistence creates a theoretical puzzle by the narrow definition of reinforcement as a separate event attached to behavior (where is the reinforcement?), and solves the puzzle by internalizing the reinforcement. We would say the pigeon is hopeful, or expects reinforcement. When he finally extinguishes, despair has overcome him.

We can, however, explain the behavior on the basis of the schedule and the program used to control it. This explanation is not limited to the hopeful pigeons. On the contrary, it is a statement of tremendous generality. It holds for a variety of species, for a variety of behaviors, and for a variety of different reinforcers. Such resistance to extinction will characterize the behavior of almost any organism programmed toward such an intermittent schedule. Since a scientific explanation describes a functional relation and the conditions under which it holds, we have provided a very explicit explanation that encompasses a variety of findings by stating that the

behavior is a function of the program used.

We might state that the pigeon who persists in a task despite the absence of payoff is stubborn or stupid (the snarl words) or has character (the purr word for the same data). Indeed, when a person persists despite frustration (which is one of the nontechnical terms for extinction) and despite defeats, we state either that he doesn't know when he's licked or that he has character, depending on our relation to him. The programming of intermittent reinforcement suggests to us how we can establish character.

Practically every behavior of the Cub Scout is reinforced. Requirements for merit badges are gradually increased, to the prodigious feats required of Eagle Scouts. The scouting movement builds character.

From the learner's viewpoint, we are speaking of his past history. From the investigator's viewpoint, we are speaking of a *program* used to alter the learner's repertoire, and the program itself is a critical variable.

A dimension along which we may consider the programming variable is the probability of built-in error. This may range all the way from a high probability to almost zero.

Typically, in the laboratory, we establish a new behavior or a new discrimination by reinforcing the correct response and by not reinforcing the incorrect response. Errors are so characteristic of this trial-and-error procedure that the number of errors or number of trials needed to establish the response (which often is saying the same) is used as a measure of learning.

It has been argued that error is indispensable for learning, for it supplies the necessary information and knowledge of results. However, errorless programming procedures systematically investigated by Herbert S. Terrace of Columbia University have questioned this statement. It is possible to produce complex discriminations in such a manner that the trainee never makes a mistake. The program capitalizes upon current strengths by requiring behavior under very similar conditions. The requirements are changed gradually so that we finally wind up with a totally different repertoire, produced in small steps, each within the organism's grasp.

While it is possible to establish identical end discriminations by either trial-and-error or errorless programming, other factors may indicate the superiority of one method of programming over another in some instances.

A child who has been trained to swim by throwing him into a deep lake, pulling him out as he goes under and dunking him again may learn to swim as well as a child gradually introduced to water in current swimming instruction programs. But children taught by the two methods are likely to have very different responses and other behaviors associated with swimming.

Errorless procedures have been used to program a variety of behaviors with humans in both individual and social settings. The learning in these situations occurs without the frustrations and emotional concomitants of extinction.

In the laboratory, an identical discrimination, say choosing yellow instead of green, produced by trial-and-error learning or by errorless programming will be accompanied by differences in the generalization gradients when other colors are presented, as well as by other differences. Ensuing behaviors, as well as the possibility of learning in some cases, become functions not only of the task but of the program, that is, how the task was taught. Theoretically, the question that errorless programming raises is the generality of learning formulations derived from investigations characterized by error during acquisition. The formulations may be quite valid for the value of the programming dimension represented by error. The extent to which the formulations extend to the value represented by errorless programming remains to be seen.

A Better Way to Morality

The substitution of errorless programming for trial-and-error learning may be considered part of a social trend that has gradually seen the substitution of reinforcement procedures for aversive control. It is only recently that slavery has been abolished. As Harvard's B. F. Skinner has pointed out, a wage society has substituted the maintenance of work through positive reinforcement for the slave society's maintenance of work through the negative reinforcement of avoiding the lash, and there is no question as to which is the more productive. It requires far more ingenuity to maintain and alter behavior through continual reinforcement than through extinction and aversive control.

Our discussion has centered around procedures that can be used to establish and maintain the behavioral relations with subtle consequences that define our use of such terms as conscience, morality, altruism, and character. If we can explicitly define these relations, we may be able to start developing programs in which such behavioral relations are our objectives. We would start with the current repertoire of the organism, and step by step reinforce approximations, explicitly specified, in the desired direction. By changing the program where it does not work, we might learn what is involved in the establishment of conscience and how to develop programs toward this end, like other programmed courses now available. Training takes place at present, of course, but the programs may be implicit, may contain irrelevant and unsuccessful items, and often employ aversive control. Rather than exhort or punish, we might try to train effectively.

The possibility of errorless programming of such terminal repertoires, and the probability that much of our programming to date, whether explicit or haphazard (called development of morality), has involved errors, extinction, and aversive control raise some interesting questions.

Certainly, much of the training involved in teaching a child to respond to the dictates of conscience and to internalize outer effects, known as the development of the superego, rests to a large extent upon the use of punishment or its threat, and it is this that may have been picked up by psychoanalysts and systematized around castration anxieties. A task that therapists often face in the case of a person unable to live existentially (that is, respond to immediately available as well as to postponed consequences) and to respond fully to his environment is to release him from such crippling bonds of the superego. The crippling bonds have been regarded as a necessary accompaniment of training processes. It may very well be that these bonds are connected not with the training process itself but with the use of extinction and aversive control in the establishment of the behavior-consequence relations we call conscience.

Laboratory research in behavior analysis suggests that we might turn our attention to the possibility of establishing moral and other discriminations without extinction and aversive control by using errorless procedures that provide continual reinforcement. It may thereby be possible to program behavioral relations with the environment that are dictated by conscience, that are moral, and that are altruistic but at the same time are spontaneous, existential, and free, since they have been programmed without fear or threat.

IV
Contemporary Problems for Youth

The Grim Generation

Robert E. Kavanaugh

The author, a college counselor for many years, observes that carefree and humorous attitudes of earlier student generations are not found among today's students. Rather, the main concern on the campus is a search for meaning and values in life. Six types of campus personalities are distinguished: the disruptive, violent activist; the constructive, nonviolent activist; the materialistic, self-promoting con man; the spiritualistic, self-abnegating flower child; the uninvolved; and the failures. The students move back and forth among these subgroups, sometimes being involved in more than one at the same time. The confusion about roles and identity is traced to the ineffectiveness of our current culture in transmitting clear and firm values, which the student may either accept or reject. The author makes the important point that the difficulty of the normal adolescent rebellion against established values is intensified if these values are unclear and diffuse. Today's students are looking for some way to extricate themselves from the confusion they feel. Their reasonable expectations that the university will provide strong alternative positions or solutions must be met by academicians if the university is to survive.

What are the changes in today's college student? The public is conditioned to see the student in terms of revolt, dope, sex, or the image transmitted by the mass media. But I am a college counselor. I see unsmiling faces, peer into dreamless eyes, hear indictments of parents and country, am frightened by threats of anarchy, listen to pleas for instant friendship, react to demands for student power, and cringe at the nakedness of youth without hope.

There are drastic changes in the students, and they are more than passing whims of a few.

I dare write about the changing student only in light of the adage: "In the land of the blind, the one-eyed man is king." But I write after seventeen years as university lecturer, administrator, campus pastor, and counselor.

There is an absence of mirth on today's campus, a lack of humor. Long before the new student uprisings, even before the recent assassinations, life on campus had become intensely grim. Gone are the sick jokes, gone is the practical joke and the belly filled with goldfish. Humor magazines, planned buffoonery, and silly laughter—long typical of college youth—are as rare as popularity for administrators. A Rowan and Martin "Laugh-In" can trigger giggly smiles, but the self-generated humor of the inner man, which normally helps the self gain perspective, is decidedly rare.

Perhaps the cause lies in the grimness of contemporary life or in the uncertainty of tomorrow. Perhaps it lies in the pressure for grades or in the frustration experienced as values crumble. No matter what the cause, life without laughter is pained and out of focus. Despite an alleged increase in sexual license and party atmosphere on campus, the cared-for student of today is not the carefree student of other years.

Our era of instant communication means instant feedback to the campus of mass media reports about student action. The scene is one of comic tragedy. Selective reporting provides easily memorized stage directions, and students—in search of an identity—seem to become what the commentators on our culture "direct" them to be.

The *malevolent dreamers* are the only students who drive me to say the prayer I read in the eyes of many administrators: "Oh, God, restore to us the apathy of the 1950s." No matter what their label—activists, leftists, radicals, or anarchists—their cause is the overthrow of all authority and every institution, with little regard for means and almost no regard for consequences. Their motivation ranges from philosophical theories of revolution to inner pain and frustrated hurt. A few choose gradualism and nonviolent change, but I see them in astonishing numbers almost psychopathically wed to violence—now. Campus administrators still hopefully advocate dialogue, liberal professors still believe rational debate can direct this admirable energy along nonviolent channels; this stand is being tested hard and many academicians are retreating to the safe ground of the more precise *rule of law*.

Radical students debate mostly with each other or with faculty members of similar philosophy, and administrators get little hearing. Radicals have deep respect for rational debate, but few activists venture to "fly without a flight plan" gained by prior group agreement. And the popular view that unkempt appearance is characteristic of an angry mob pushes the radical groups further away from all outsiders. And even further.

Other students protect the activists, for they share the activist concern for social and political betterment while lacking the activist daring to be heard. They also lack the ability to come up with alternate solutions. The continued stability of campus activism lies in this body of quiet sympathizers.

Black activists seem ambivalent. Sometimes they want to go it alone, sometimes they want the support of white brothers. They walk, speak, and give orders with new confidence; they know that administrators are scurrying to put both more time and more money into minority-student recruitment and support. They know too that faculty planners are desperately arranging curricula in Afro-American studies, that professional schools will admit minority students who are "almost" qualified, and that all academe blushes with shame.

The largest and least often identified type on campus can be called the *kept generation*. The dominant characteristics here are good reputation and moderation. Preoccupation with grades, noninvolvement in extracurricular affairs of a serious nature, and an overriding tone of cynicism are other characteristics. They make mock of the hippy, debunk the activist, berate administrators, con the faculty, and associate only with one another.

Their morality stems from habit and fear, not from internalized conviction. They are adept at the dual standard, attending church only at home, writing letters as family peace and finances dictate, and cribbing on exams. They *ran* the family home and still *command* by phone or letter. In a sense they are what their parents designed.

If members of the kept generation accept an office, it is for personal benefit; if they take dope, it is out of curiosity or conformity; if they make love, contraceptives are more important than passion. They hate war because they must go. They abhor violence because it blights their plans. Though they loudly mock the student left, they fail to articulate the political right. Cynicism marks their typical humor: "Every time I eat a Hershey bar, I project a death wish." Their identity crisis is deferred, their umbilical cord strained but not severed.

The mark of the kept generation is on enough brows to determine the fate of this generation of students. Anarchists warn that if they sleepwalk back to suburbia, they will find it in ruins. And should they awaken to involvement in social problems, it is these kept kids who will tilt the balance of campus upheaval.

There are other students who are monastically hidden in the cells of their own personal concerns and who join the community only for the common prayer of the classroom. They are a taxpayer's delight because they use no campus services other than the academic. Their number is legion; they go uncounted because they are seldom noticed. The *monastic generation* includes the married student who works nights, the shy commuter, the virginal fat girl, and the 4.0 student who studies incessantly. The monks have little to say on campus radicals, answer no polls, and seldom see a psychiatrist. Their views rarely are tinged with cynicism and only infrequently with self-pity. They are the potential dropouts who refuse to drop out.

Benevolent dreamers are the young men and women who have passed through their identity crisis. They have "lost" their parents or "found" them in a new adult relationship. You see them tutoring in the inner city, raising funds to educate minority youth, leading campus governments, editing newspapers, and forming ad hoc committees. They are prominent in every legal and vital facet of campus or community life. They are willing to be measured. With high ideals and dreams for a better world, accompanied by the drive and ambition to make them effective, these students work mightily to avoid the basely utilitarian overtones they despise in their society. Especially is this true of the benevolent dreamers in the ranks of the nonviolent New Left.

They feel threatened and wounded by draft demands, prospects of urban violence, and the "immoral" approval of war, by racism, poverty, and overpopulation. They feel strapped, stifled, and betrayed by their elders. Such students are not unduly fearful of revolution but they opt for peaceful reform of American institutions. They are abrupt with tradition, suspicious of advice, impatient with authority, and disdainful of duplicity.

Because their cause is seldom sensational and their tactics rarely flamboyant, they are not newsworthy. Some of them try drugs in their desperation for answers, but if so they do not continue, for—even if drugs help—they prefer the fight for legality to illegal involvement. They oversimplify life's complexities, switch heroes easily, and, beneath their confident exterior, they are depressed, anxious, and confused.

Small in number but important to the total picture are the *hippies*. Imitated by other students and often confused with nonacademic hippies, the authentic campus hippy is more than a court jester or a whipping boy. He frightens or disgusts those who measure men by garb, and he confounds those who listen patiently to the rationale for his life style. He is trying, albeit naively, to downgrade material concerns.

The hippy hopes to find himself, to discover meaning and sanity in life. His experience with American life has been brief but distasteful. Usually from a home that is broken or breaking, the campus hippy resembles a soft-spoken Isaiah, decrying middle-class foibles. He preaches human love and worth in the face of campus scoffing and community snickers. Though he probably loves others no more than most of us, love is his shibboleth.

The campus hippy provides few answers. He prefers to raise questions. Unable to visualize life in any but simplistic terms of love and community, the hippy regularly locks in to the dream world of his inner self, where felonies, personal inadequacies, selective service, economics, and social shallowness cannot touch him. Most hippies are somewhat paranoid about police and community harassment. They are a joy to counsel if handled respectfully in the framework of their own world.

Interestingly, though the hippy student professes little concern for grades, his marks tend to be above average.

And yet few campus hippies survive a full four years of college pressure. They drop out. But those who successfully negotiate the narrow path to graduation are potentially great people. They are willing to live in poverty, ready to share puff and pad, and they are able to follow their own convictions in the face of ridicule and scorn.

Campus hippies offer interesting predictions about their own future. Precious few forecast their own return to the Establishment when "their thing" is finished. The majority foresee the possibility of a permanent subculture, though they lack the concept of marriage or family that would allow such a continuance.

The saddest group on campus is one I see as the *graveyard generation*: the hippy who is on his way out and no longer can meet academic demands; the overextended student who holds on despite lack of talent or motivation until rescued by a face-saving transfer, by mononucleosis, or by wise counseling; the disillusioned youth, crushed by home problems, ineffective love affairs, or financial duress; the late bloomer in his budding days of failure; the student who punishes overanxious parents by his academic reluctance; and the one who is psychologically ill.

For this group, the gravestone always can be rolled away from the tomb by a meaningful love affair, by

counseling, therapy, or even by survival through development.

I see today's students move with sudden fluidity from group to group, or even reflect several strains at once. I see them belonging to one group while masking affiliation to another.

Many of the changes I see in today's students can be traced to our changed family structure. Crashed or crashing marriages at home intensify the student identity crisis. The failure of the home, the school, and the church to transmit a sound and solid value system further heightens the expected crisis. Today's student lacks a strong parental figure or a deeply indoctrinated sense of values to polarize his identity crisis. Yesterday's authoritarian father and overworked mother, community-backed teacher and "heaven-hell" church generated clearer paths for rebellion or acceptance. Polarization is hardly possible when family authority is vested in "daddy-son" or "mommy-daughter," when teachers are overly accepting, when churches impart vague platitudes. The student is torn between acceptance and rejection and confused by a diffusion of goals and values.

Because of its altered structure and increased mobility, the family creates personal isolation and insulation. At best, today's family offers only limited opportunities for intimate relationships. When these are bungled by conflict or parental incapacity, the laboratory for friendship becomes the large high school, the shifting neighborhood, the dwindling extended family, or a church.

The results show in the demise or changing structure of the fraternity-sorority system, faculty-student aloofness, the grasping and groping for instant friendship, and the solidification of monogamous dating practices. Rare is the student who can cope simultaneously with several close relationships.

A new vision of the family is in the making. Rarely does the campus male animal fight for his woman. Children play an ever decreasing part in the college view of marriage. By admission—and even the reluctant permission—of the male, the wife dominates the married campus couple. And parental benefactors control the campus marriage with financial aid more often than the mendicant lovers realize.

Traditionally, youth uses the future for dreaming, the past for bragging, and the now for living. Yesterday there was little reluctance to permit the present to flow into the future. There was always the promise of a pleasant tomorrow. Some of today's students still enjoy the American dream: the ranch in suburbia, the niche in megapolis, the bench in St. Petersburg, the eternity box at the end. But a growing number believe they have tasted the "capitalistic dream" only to find it embittered by the prospect of war, jail, or emigration. Activists lash out to increase their alternatives. Most students lock in to the present and struggle to manufacture articulate dreams. They have no experience with the world they desire in their tomorrow.

Adoration of the present pervades the campus. The drug user readily admits his need to zero in on the present. Drugs add an intensity and reality to his dreams and fantasies that reality denies. The maximum decibel roar of the stereo provides the hard rock fan with a lesser lock-in. So do the total preoccupation with theoretical math, the endless hours in a lonesome lab, isolated hetero- and homosexual love affairs, attempts at oriental meditation, devotion to alcohol, addiction to cars, and insulated aloofness. Even concern for distant injustices, like the war in Vietnam and poverty in the inner city, makes the present tolerable.

This mania to make the present bearable results in an increased preoccupation with death, both in contemplated suicide and in folk music or other art forms. Violence that does not disturb the present (such as that depicted on movies or TV) is groovy, but fist fights (part of the entertainment on yesterday's campus) are strangely absent.

The search for meaning and values *is* a major factor in student unrest. And the central campus value is this search for values. The framework for the search is one of mutual acceptance: each man has his own bag; don't interfere. (The unpracticed observer can read this non-intervention as a modern version of Cain and Abel, but it is more likely a stand against indoctrination and for individual freedom.) And the search intensifies as the excellence of the campus ascends from junior-college caliber to university level.

Organized religion plays a decreasing role on campus and possibly is saved from extinction only by the superior clergy assigned to most campuses. Scientific humanism attracts numerous students and continues as the "bag" for most faculty members. Political activism and expanding social concern provide new life for the departments of philosophy, political science, sociology, and religion. Oriental cults attract fewer than the press, radio, and TV imply.

Verbalized values are more negative than positive. Students speak out in terms of rights and rarely in terms of duties. There is almost no evidence of a right-wing viewpoint in social, political, or moral matters, even though the confused students seem ripe for simplistic, solid answers.

The much-publicized growing sexual promiscuity is not general practice on the campus. Shyness, introversion, vestigial guilt, self-doubt, and the fear of rejection keep students from the practice of their preaching, even

with pills and intrauterine devices to reduce their fear of pregnancy. Actually, premarital pregnancies are on the wane, "sleeping around" is not admired, and premarital sex is practiced most often in a semiresponsible and monogamous relationship.

Besides the vertical gap between this generation and the last there is a horizontal gap between students of the far left and their middle-of-the-road peers, between the science major and the artist, the engineer and the social scientist. As campus departments insulate themselves in their own concerns and jargon, upper division students share the isolation. A music student put it this way: "Dante could re-create the *Inferno* by putting me in eternity with two engineers."

Students are strangely willing—for the present—to grant the faculty immunity from the rebellious anti-authoritarianism they focus on the administration. This in spite of countless unintelligible or ill-prepared lectures, archaic and haphazard teaching methods, unjust and unscientific grading systems, and sharply limited faculty office hours. *There are signals that this divine right is ending.*

The student of today studies much harder than any college student before him, even that post World War II generation of veterans. The standard of achievement is higher today and today's student worries more.

The 1968 college student already has conquered the American home, exchanging roles with his parents. He has been victorious over his high school, where he found boredom instead of challenge. Now he is poised to lay siege to the American university.

The survival of the university seems to depend on whether faculty and administrators can provide a dream, a hope for tomorrow. Students want—they demand—that their dream include an end to injustice and to the suppression of truth and reality. They no longer want duplicity in morals. They demand a relevant curriculum and a concerned faculty. They want leaders who will take a stand on issues, who can provide meaning, a flame for their apathy, a respect for their right. They want leaders whose lives embody their dreams, leaders who listen. They want leaders who will work with them in the face of the nihilistic anguish of their hopeless present.

Academic arrogance will get us nowhere. These student demands are going to be hard to meet. I am just a counselor who listens. But I know the threat to every tree in the groves of academe if there is no change.

Student Activists: Result, Not Revolt

Richard Flacks

Who are the student activists, what are they protesting against, and what kind of families do they come from? The author does not see the current movement as a typical adolescent rebellion because the dissenting activists are not economically disadvantaged, nor do they wish to deny the values of their parents, who themselves usually have attitudes at variance with the dominant middle-class culture. Investigations by the author and others show the values of activist parents to be humanistic, in contrast to the values of the mainstream middle class, which focus on achievement and materialism. The two groups come into conflict over the issue of self-expression versus self-control. Activist parents encourage free expression of feelings and ideas as a necessity for individual growth, while typical middle-class values stress conformity to rules and authority, with an inhibition of impulsive behavior. Since the values of activist parents differ from those of the dominant middle class, it is not surprising that the values of their children also differ. Activists are seen as the result of their upbringing, not as being in revolt against it.

The scene might have been written by Genet; it was worthy of filming by Fellini. A young man, well clothed and well groomed but with his shirt collar open now, and his tie pulled down, shouted to the audience like an old-fashioned revivalist.

"Come up," he cried, "come up and confess. Put some money in the pot and be saved!"

And they came. The first youth, clutching the green pieces of paper in his hand, recited for all to hear: "My father is a newspaper editor. I give twenty-five dollars." His penitence brought cheers from the assembly. The sin of the next young man was a father who was assistant director of a government bureau. He gave forty dollars. "My dad is dean of a law school," confessed another, as he proffered fifty dollars for indulgence.

The occasion was not a rehearsal for the theater of the absurd but a convention of Students for a Democratic Society. The "sins" that the students confessed were the occupations or the social classes of their fathers. Their origins placed these students in the elite, the high-status group of any community, and yet here

they were, exuberantly adopting a political stance and a style of life that they believed to be the very antithesis of those origins.

Why this should be so, frankly puzzled me and led to research that has confirmed and refined my earliest impression of the social make-up of today's youth in dissent. They are of the middle- and upper-middle class. They are the core of the student movement. They are the dissenters.

That the activist student movement is a small minority of the student population cannot be denied. But it is of great significance—partly because of the movement's social composition, partly because this movement is a phenomenon that was unforeseen by professional social scientists, and *mostly* because many of the themes and ideals of the movement are concurred in by a wide cross section of students.

Are students really in revolt? The simple fact may be that, on the contrary, today's students are tuned in to a developing cultural tradition in the United States, a tradition that has grown all but undetected because certain of our lingering assumptions about American society no longer prevail.

The phenomenon that has come to be called the student movement began in the late 1950s, when Northern white students responded to efforts by Southern Negro students to break down the barriers of segregation. However, as the protest has grown, it has broadened beyond the fight for civil liberties. Now, of course, it includes such issues as nuclear testing, the arms race, campus democracy, the educational quality of the university, and above all the undeclared war in Vietnam.

This evolution to active protest, and to action itself, began even as sociologists and social psychologists were despairing of political commitment among the young. University students of the 1950s were termed "the quiet generation," and experts predicted a button-down-minded generation. Polls showed that students were unconcerned with deep values; they were also complacent, status-oriented, and uncommitted. Conformity was much discussed, as were grey flannel suits, organization men, suburbia, status symbols, and security.

Then, suddenly, young people of the 1960s surprised everyone—they questioned everything and they protested most of the things that they questioned. Theorists were nonplussed, and conventional wisdom about the sources of radical action got a slap in the face.

We are not confronted with youths who are attracted to radicalism because they are economically deprived, or because their opportunities for mobility—or for anything else—are blocked. These highly advantaged youths are indifferent to, or repelled by, the best opportunities for high status and income. Yet these young people cannot be explained and understood as a generation in revolt. This is no effort to break free of the constricting, tradition-oriented, or obsolete values of parents. The parents of student protestors share with their offspring an unusual divergence from conventional religious, political, and social attitudes.

Most activists are recruited from a very special kind of middle- and upper middle-class family. In most of these families both mother and father are highly educated, the father is a professional, and the mother very often has a career as well. Many of these families are Jewish, but regardless of their denominational allegiance, both parents and children tend to be political liberals—there are very few Republicans among them. Activists say that their parents have been permissive and democratic, and the parents' description of themselves agrees.

Our studies indicate that activism, as well as other expressions of youth disaffection, are symptoms of the declining power of those values and goals that traditionally have given direction and meaning to the lives of the American middle class and direction to the American dream. Both students who are attracted to new radical politics and youths who experiment with new styles of Bohemianism—no matter how they may differ in personal history, personality, or perspective—repudiate mainstream middle-class values.

Moving parallel to the line of conventional middle-class values and the families that carry them, there appears to be emerging an alternative value system embodied in certain types of families. These variant families, intentionally or not, create dispositions in their children toward radical social action. This is a *result*, not *revolt*.

Dominant Values

There is a sociological consensus about the substance of middle-class values that derives from Weber's famous analysis of the Protestant ethic. Central in American life remains the value placed on achievement in an occupation.

This emphasis upon career demands a conception of self in terms of occupational status, so that the meaning of one's life centers around activity and achievement in a chosen profession. Thus, experience must be organized in terms of career patterns that demand a strongly future-oriented psychology—present experience is shaped to career requirements. And finally, in this conception, one's full potential for occupational achievement can be realized only to the extent that the emotional life is regulated and rationalized.

To the Weberian emphasis on achievement and self-control may be added the observation of Alexis de Tocqueville: Middle-class Americans are strongly concerned with the opinions of their peers. Increasingly, according to David Riesman and others, efforts to achieve group acceptance depend on one's skills as a consumer. Furthermore, according to Kenneth Keniston, absorption in consumption of material goods within the context of the family provides a much-needed balance to the discipline required in one's occupation.

Humanistic Values

Student activists and their parents are strongly characterized by humanistic values, whereas student nonactivists and their parents are characterized by dominant values. Two clusters of values can be identified within the humanistic subcultures. The first is a basic concern with individual development and self-expression, with a spontaneous response to the world. The free expression of emotions and feelings is viewed as essential to the development and integrity of the individual. Humanistic parents thus raise their children in an environment relatively free of constraints and favorable to experimentation, expressiveness, and spontaneity. They also stress the significance of autonomous and authentic behavior freely initiated by the individual and expressing his feelings and ideas.

Concern with self-development and expression also is reflected in this group's attitude toward aesthetic and intellectual capacities. Creativity in these areas is prized and encouraged in children, who also are given a feeling for their capacity for personal development.

The second group of values within the humanistic subcultures might be called ethical humanism. There is a sincere concern for the social condition of others. This strong humanitarian outlook results in socially and politically aware and active parents, who tend to share their views with their children.

Self-Expression Versus Self-Control

Humanistic values like aestheticism and intellectualism do not appear to be at odds with such dominant middle-class values as career achievement or materialism, but a basic conflict between the humanistic and the dominant attitudes can be seen in the contrast between self-expression and self-control.

In the dominant culture, behavior follows relatively fixed rules of conduct that represent objective authority and that secure the individual against unpredictable and possibly destructive impulses. The humanist, however, rejects such fixed rules. He is more flexible, and he sees the spontaneous flow of feelings and ideas as intrinsically good and necessary for personal growth.

Thus humanistic students are raised in a permissive and egalitarian family environment by parents who encourage them to be expressive and fill them with a sense of their own capacity for self-development. At school and at college these students first discover that the society at large expects them to be centrally motivated around goals and values that they cannot accept. Pursuit of status goals to them means hypocrisy and sacrifice of personal integrity.

In the eyes of humanistic youths, the public world is dominated by large authoritarian organizations, which severely regiment the individual. Subjection to impersonal authority is incompatible with their attitudes toward autonomy and authority. Many of these youths, suspecting that the policy of most organizations does not reflect their own ideals and principles, feel threatened.

Constraints on expression that exist in the world of work threaten youths who have been relatively unconstrained by parents. And they see the university as becoming just another impersonal institution—a big computer. Since so many plan university careers, they want to stop this trend.

Our original study of student activists and their parents, which led to the discovery of the humanistic subcultures, was made in 1965. The activist sample was matched with a control sample by type of college attended, neighborhood of parents' residence, sex, and religion. The interviews with both students and parents averaged about two hours and concerned political attitudes, broader values, and family life.

Parent and student values were not measured identically, although the definitions of values were the same in both cases. The aspirations that parents have for their children frequently were used to ascertain parent values. In most cases, the parents of activist students scored significantly higher on the values we have identified as part of the humanistic subcultures than did the parents of nonactivists. Parents of activists also scored much lower on most of the values we have identified as belonging to the dominant culture.

The values of activist and nonactivist students are very different. Youths active in the student movement have rejected the traditional middle-class values, which still direct the goals of the nonactivist students.

Romanticism, a humanistic value, was identified as a concern with beauty and a sensitivity toward the realm of feelings and emotions. The high romantic was likely to want to become a poet, musician, or artist. He frequently expressed a desire for experience and a love of wandering, an aversion to settling down, and a need to find a liberating social environment in which institutional constraints would be lessened. These themes are traditionally associated with Bohemianism, rather than with radical social action, but our study found them significantly related to student activism.

Parents of activists generally scored higher in romanticism than did parents of nonactivists—none in the latter group could be considered high romantics. Parents who were high romantics were vitally interested in the arts—and hoped their children would be, too. Only a few parents were professional artists; most of them were leisure-time aesthetes.

Intellectualism is high on the list of humanistic values. While romanticism and intellectualism often have been considered mutually incompatible, our data suggest that there is a strong positive relationship between them. Most of the students who scored highest in intellectualism expected to teach and write within a university. They read extensively, particularly in philosophy, the humanities, and the social sciences. The empirical relationship between intellectualism and activism proved to be very strong, as did the link between parent intellectualism and child participation in the student movement.

Parents who were highest scorers talked repeatedly about the importance of books in their own lives and how they had interested their children in books. Their reading interests were the same as their activist youths', and many reported a shared interest with their children in ideas, books, and intellectual discussions.

Authenticity was measured as acute sensitivity to hypocrisy, a wish for self-knowledge and understanding, concern that one's own personal potentialities—as well as those of others—be realized, rejection of imposed standards of behavior, and acceptance of situational ethics.

In appraising the American culture, students who scored highest in authenticity were critical of the political, social, moral, and religious hypocrisies characteristic of middle-class life. Our statistics clearly demonstrate that authenticity is strongly connected with activism and that scores of the children and their parents were closely related.

Parents who scored high on this value viewed their children as autonomous individuals who must have the chance to realize their potentialities. Children of these parents always had been encouraged to make their own decisions, even if they violated parental standards of morality. Like the students, but not to the same degree, these parents were sensitive to hypocrisy.

In student interviews, interpersonal intimacy was explored in terms of both friendship and love. Losing one's self in love and caring deeply were stressed by the highest scorers in this area. The idea of the I-thou relationship as developed by Martin Buber is the most fully elaborated expression of the possibilities felt to be inherent in depth relationships.

The range of interpersonal intimacy correlated less strongly with activism than any of the other humanistic values. But when this area was broken into the separate categories of love and friendship, it was found that concern with deep love was concentrated almost exclusively among the activist students; those concerned with continuous contact with friends were slightly more likely to be nonactivist students. Parents of activist students in turn were slightly more concerned than were nonactivist parents about open and frequent interaction with friends.

Humanitarianism is grounded in a compassion and sympathy for the suffering of others and an outrage at institutions that deprive individuals or groups at any level. In order to separate humanitarianism from activism, we excluded attitudes and actions that related specifically to political ideology or to organized political projects. (This area showed the strongest empirical relationship to activism.) The relationship between parent humanitarianism and activism of children was especially high in the case of fathers.

Occupational Success and Materialism

Occupational success is held up as a major value for boys in the dominant culture, yet difference between the two groups was not nearly as marked as one might expect. And the difference between activist and nonactivist girls is even less pronounced.

Activist and nonactivist males do aspire toward different kinds of careers, however. Nonactivists strive for careers in industry, law, or medicine, while activists lean toward politics, the arts, or the academic life. Only one activist male manifested a strong concern with success in a profession—a Harvard student whose goal is the Nobel prize in physics.

Activist parents consider career just as important as nonactivist parents do. Activist sons, however, tend to be a bit less concerned about a profession than nonactivist young men. Unlike their children, many parents

believe it is necessary to realize the dominant value of career in public life if one hopes to realize humanistic values in private life. The new generation either has not met the necessity for compromise, or *will* not.

Moralism and self-control were measured by studying implicit systems of morality, especially in the area of sexual and other forms of personal expression. Students who scored highest in this category indicated an adherence to a control-dominated moralism and an inflexible personal approach to morality centered around absolute right and wrong. The low-scoring end was for students who rejected conventional morality and who believed in free expression of impulses and emotions. Scores of nonactivist students, obviously, were much higher than those of the activists.

Parents who scored highest were deeply concerned lest the Protestant ethic break down through the weakening of discipline and authority in the institutional world. Low-scoring parents were convinced that traditional morality systems were hypocritical and repressive, and they supported a morality emphasizing expressiveness.

This rating is powerfully related to activism in students and appears to be at the core of value differences between the parents of activists and those of nonactivists. The strong correlation validates our thesis that the central conflict between dominant and humanistic cultures is the opposition between self-control and self-expression (see Figure 1).

In dealing with materialism and status, we explored the concern with making money and the enjoyment of a high level of material consumption, as well as the attainment of social prestige. Those who aspired toward material success included social prestige as an important goal, while those who rejected materialistic considerations were even more emphatic in their rejection of social status. The empirical relationship between materialism-status and student activism was a strongly negative one.

Although parents of student activists score somewhat lower on this scale than do the parents of nonactivist students, the relationship between the parents' material values and the students' activism is not statistically significant. Rather, this is often the major area of disagreement in the families of many students of both sorts. Students view their parents as rooted in an empty and ostentatious suburban life, and parents do not understand their children's rejection of comfort and advantages. Flagrant unorthodoxy in dress and personal appearance particularly disturbs parents. The haircut problem is acute.

Impact of Existentialism

As we tabulated the responses to our interviews, the possibility that existentialism has had a significant impact on the thinking of student activists became more pronounced. The writers who are important to students who scored highest on intellectualism were Dostoevsky,

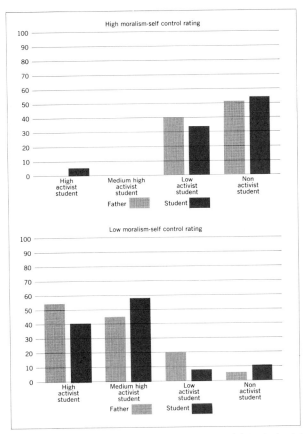

Figure 1. Correlation of activist and nonactivist students' and parents' ratings in terms of conventional morality and self-control versus free expression. The measurements were derived from the study of implicit systems of morality.

Nietzsche, Camus, and Sartre. An existential concern with authentic choice and action showed strongly on the authenticity rating.

In an attempt to discover whether activist students consciously identify with humanism and existentialism, we interviewed a second sample of student activists and again contrasted the sample with a control group. As a part of this interview, we gave students a list of twenty-two "isms" and asked them to list the three items with which they most identified (see Table 1).

The core of the current student movement consists of youths who are searching for an alternative to established middle-class values. And those who are engaged in this search come from families who are skeptical of conventional values. This tradition of skepticism and humanism is growing, and the families that identify with it are likely to increase rapidly in number.

Despite the apparent family roots of humanism and activism in the current student generation, it would be

an error to say that there is a one-to-one correspondence between parental and student values. It would be as great an error to say that parental influence is the sole factor in predisposing youth to radical politics. Children raised in the humanistic subcultures are potential recruits to a wide variety of student deviant, Bohemian, and drug subcultures.

Parental status, values, and practices indicate a predisposition toward humanist values and activist participation by students, but the degree or intensity of their involvement seems to depend on factors that are independent of family background. The college the student attends, the friends and teachers he meets in college, even the dormitory to which he is assigned his freshman year may affect his selection. Other strong influences include the impact of groups and organizations, of books and journeys, of historical events and how the individual experiences them, and of personal experiences such as long illnesses, living and working abroad, or time spent in jail.

The humanist family tradition has contributed a huge share of the initiators of the student movement, and a very large proportion of the most active participants continues to be recruited from middle-class humanistic subcultures.

TABLE 1

Impact of Humanism and Existentialism—Survey Results

Group	First choice (%)		Second choice (%)		Third choice (%)	
	Human.	Existen.	Human.	Existen.	Human.	Existen.
Activists (N = 61)	30	23	22	15	12	15
Nonactivists (N = 55)	16	11	16	5	11	4

Our parent-student research indicates strongly that the movement has a dynamic of its own, which is shaping student attitudes and their commitments. Our data show that the recent protest groups are made up, in part, of a central core of activists who come from humanistic subcultures and have a long history of active protest, and, in part, of a larger group of newly recruited students. Fascinatingly or alarmingly, depending on one's viewpoint, recent recruits more closely resemble the general student population. They come from widely diverse backgrounds, even from conservative and conventional parents. Protest appeals to an increasingly broader spectrum of students. The movement is spreading to the dominant culture.

V
Children with Handicaps

Learning and Lollipops
Todd Risley

Some "enrichment" programs for the culturally deprived preschool child are actually designed for middle-class children and are thus nonproductive for the groups they are supposed to reach. The author describes two programs designed to help the preschool child from a culturally deprived background prepare for entering school. One program was meant to supplement the child's home experiences. The other was a self-help program, which focused on training the mothers as well as the children.

One difficulty commonly faced by children coming from a home milieu drastically different from the educational setting is that the language spoken in the two settings is strikingly different: the children may not understand what is said to them, and they are understood by the teacher only with difficulty. To help these children learn the school language, they were given training in imitation—initially imitating gross motor actions, then more refined motions, and finally speech. In these training programs, food was discovered to be a much more effective reinforcer than social praise. This finding indicates that social approval alone, as generally used in the public schools for motivating students, is unlikely to be successful with children from backgrounds like this. Other techniques involving both mothers and children are described and evaluated.

Play with a play car.

Play with a truck, play with a play car, get on a seesaw and play with a train.

My mama bought them last night when Dan's daddy took her to the Salvation Army.

The Salvation Army is uptown, uptown.

All the way up there in the projects, Dan lives in the projects.

Dan lives across the street from Edward's house.

Me and Dan. Me and Dan went to the store and bought some candy. Here's one that was on the floor.

We found it on the ground.

Some money.

We found it; we found it on the ground. One penny, two penny.

We found it.

A penny.

And we ride the play cars to the store.

Some sugar and a sucker for to eat.

We eat a candy sucker.

These lines are not blank verse, or at least they were not intended as such. They were spoken by a four-year-old boy receiving narration training at a preschool for culturally deprived children. His teacher has asked, "What do you do when you go home from school?

. . . And what else . . . and what else . . . and what else?" This boy is an inarticulate child from an inarticulate family, the kind of child who grows up in our society to be Stanley Kowalski.

As a child grows up, he acquires "culture" chiefly from three sources: from his parents, from his peers, and from the public schools. In view of that fact, it is hardly surprising that those who are culturally deprived as infants usually become culturally deprived adults. Parents and peers cannot easily transmit what they themselves lack, and the public schools apparently offer too little too late—or, to put it another way, too much too soon.

When the culturally deprived child enters kindergarten, he lacks the social and language skills that the schools assume a child of five will possess. Since his parents do not stress the importance of school achievement, he also lacks motivation. In addition, the situation at home may be such that he is not particularly sensitive to the smiles and frowns with which his teacher will attempt to shape his behavior.

One way to attack this problem is to find a way to

modify the behavior of the deprived preschool child so that when he enters school, he will be in a better position to learn what is being taught there. This is the purpose of the Juniper Gardens Children's Project.

The residents of Juniper Gardens, an area located in northeastern Kansas City, Kansas, have the lowest median annual income in the city: 90 percent of them belong to the poverty class; 99.5 percent are Negro; and about 70 percent of those over twenty-five have not graduated from high school.

Under the auspices of the University of Kansas, my colleagues and I are conducting two preschool programs with the children and parents from Juniper Gardens. One is for members of the "hard-core" poverty class, the other for members of the "upwardly mobile" poverty class. The chief difference between the two programs is that the first is for children only, whereas the second is for children and their mothers, and especially for the mothers.

Turner House

In the program for the hard-core group, the Turner House program, we teach the children skills that we hope will be useful to them in public school—to follow directions, to describe objects and events, and so forth. In the program for the upwardly mobile group, the Parent-Teacher Cooperative Preschool, we teach mothers how, in general, to communicate more effectively with their children and how, specifically, to teach them skills they will need in school. That is, the Turner House program supplements, while the Parent-Teacher Preschool attempts to modify, the home environment of the child.

For Turner House, we recruited four-year-olds from families characterized by multiple problems: absence of a father, many children, extreme poverty, ramshackle housing, child neglect, and histories of unemployment, poor health, criminal and deviant behavior, alcoholism, and the like. In some cases, it proved necessary to offer the mother a weekly cash fee for her "trouble" in getting the child ready for preschool; thus some of the twelve children in the program were, in effect, rented.

Most children arrived at school without breakfast. We therefore fed them supplementary meals, and we also experimented, very successfully, with the use of food as a reinforcement for behavior we wanted maintained. This is quite a departure from the usual teaching techniques of both public and nursery schools, which are based chiefly on positive social reinforcement. But with these children, warm praise rarely proved powerful enough to rapidly effect extensive changes in behavior.

The teachers carried about, in baskets and in their plastic-lined jumper pockets, sugar-coated cereals, grapes and pieces of apple, tiny sandwiches, M&M candies, and cookies. When the children worked at tables, teachers carried pitchers and poured small quantities of milk, juice, or warm soup into mugs for each child.

These snacks invariably were accompanied by smiling, warm-voiced statements of approval, appreciation, or affection, and these statements very often were offered without food. We hoped in this way to increase the effectiveness of social reinforcement with the children, and thus prepare them for the public-school classroom.

Some of the behavior we tried to teach the children at first may seem trivial. For example, we spent considerable time teaching them to say "good morning" to their teachers. This may not seem the stuff from which successful scholars are made. However, the child who says "good morning" cheerfully and consistently when he arrives at school will dispose most teachers quite favorably toward him—our own teachers testified to this during the experiment—and the credit he gains may survive a good deal of academic bumbling later in the day. This credit is useful, because it may make the teacher more likely to praise approximations of learning in the child. A similar rationale lay behind several other "social" projects, such as teaching the child to be quiet in some work situations and to converse in others, and to raise his hand and wait to be recognized before speaking in group discussions.

Rightly or wrongly, formal schooling is chiefly an exercise in language, so we gave considerable attention to developing the language skills of the children. We tried to improve their skill at imitation, so that they might make linguistic gains from any language community in which they found themselves. We also picked one especially inarticulate child—the author of the "poem" that opens this chapter—and taught him to describe, in logically connected, meaningfully elaborated, and even factually correct narratives, his own experiences.

These projects will serve to illustrate the kind of thing we tried to do and the way we tried to do it, but there were others, of course. For example, we trained the children in the use of color and number adjectives and studied the effect the training had on their spontaneous conversation. And we experimented with various kinds of reinforcement and reinforcement conditions. One, in addition to food, that proved especially powerful was the materials and equipment of the schoolroom. It seemed that, when a child wanted to ride a tricycle, nothing in his environment was as important to him as that tricycle. Teachers therefore made it available to the child only after he had performed some task, such as naming or describing it.

"Good Morning"

As each child entered the preschool in the morning, removed his coat, and proceeded to his seat, each of the three teachers (Nancy Reynolds, Dianetta Coates, and Betty Hart) smiled at him and said, "Good morning." At the beginning of the school year, only about 20 percent of the children answered any teacher appropriately. These the teachers would reinforce with social approval. Over the next three months, the average number of children answering the teachers' greetings rose from 20 percent to between 70 and 80 percent.

By mid-December, it was clear that no further improvement was likely. So, as a test of the durability of this new skill, the teachers discontinued the stimulus to which the children had responded. They stood at the door as usual, but they did not speak to the children as they entered. Although the children who continued to say "good morning" were answered and praised as usual, the number who did so fell immediately to 20 percent and fluctuated from 15 to 45 percent for six days. Then it collapsed to zero.

It appeared that behavior with social consequences would not be maintained unless supported at both ends, by a preceding stimulus as well as by subsequent approval. When the teachers began greeting the children with a smiling "good morning" again, 80 percent of the children promptly began replying.

However, our aim was to teach the children to say "good morning" whether greeted first by the teacher or not. Therefore we brought a more powerful reinforcer into play. Each teacher gave an M&M to each child who answered her greeting appropriately. The number of children replying rose at once to 100 percent and remained there for the last five days of this condition. Then the teachers again discontinued their initial greetings. As before, some children stopped saying "good morning" as they entered, but far fewer stopped than before. As long as the M&Ms were used, about 95 percent continued to greet the teachers despite the teachers' silence.

To make sure it was the candy that made the difference, we stationed all three preschool teachers at the door but supplied only one of them with M&Ms. We thought that over the weeks, when first one teacher and then another had the M&Ms, the children would speak most often to the teacher who distributed the candy. This turned out to be true (see Figure 1). However, we also expected the children to behave with a modicum of consistency toward the third teacher, who throughout the whole ten weeks of the experiment offered social reinforcement only, no candy.

Instead, most children spoke to the third teacher whenever they spoke to the first teacher. During the first seven weeks of the experiment, when the first teacher had M&Ms and the third did not, most children said "good morning" to both of them; during the last three weeks, when the first teacher had no candy, greetings to the third teacher fell off as well. I am sorry to report that this seemed to indicate racial discrimination in our children: the first and third teachers were white, and the second was Negro.

The public school, of course, does not offer M&Ms for desirable behavior. However, our results indicate the need for something more powerful than friendly approval to establish durable behavior in the children, especially if the behavior is to remain despite minimal stimulus support. Had we not run out of time, we would have begun shifting the behavior maintained by candy to the control of social approval only, a process that requires consistent social reinforcement combined with a gradual cutback on the distribution of candy.

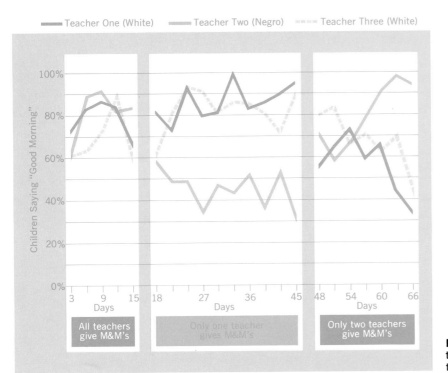

Figure 1. Effect of candy distribution on children's morning greeting to teacher.

Imitation

An ability to imitate the teacher, especially her use of language, is particularly valuable for the child from a culturally deprived background. Most culturally deprived children learn a different dialect at home from the one they will hear in school. Consequently they will have trouble understanding what they hear and being understood when they speak. It is unlikely that the child's dialect will be modified in school unless he undertakes the modification himself, a possible task— many a Midwesterner has done it at Harvard—but one that requires what is called a "good ear."

Therefore we set out to develop the children's ability to imitate. We did not begin by asking them to imitate verbal statements. We started with gross motor imitations, progressed to fine motor imitations, and then to facial responses, and only at the end added verbalizations. The program had two parts: training sessions that stressed each kind of imitation in turn, and nontraining sessions, or probes, that tested the effects of the training.

In the training sessions, three children worked with a model teacher. At first, the teacher did nothing more than sit down on a rug and take a bit of snack for herself from a bowl. The children were prompted by another teacher to do as the model teacher had done, including taking a bit of snack in their own cups.

Then the second teacher took charge of the snack bowl, and she provided food only when the child imitated the part of the model teacher's behavior that was the subject of training. In early sessions, the child was given a snack whenever he imitated the model teacher's gross motor behavior—raising the arms, leaning to one side, and the like. Later, training passed to more detailed motor imitations, and finally to speech.

Periodically, the model teacher tested each child's ability to imitate a complex performance. The tests consisted of four acts performed simultaneously: a gross motor act, a fine motor act, a facial expression, and a verbal statement. For example:

Probe I. Arms out to the side, palms of hands turned back, face frowning, statement: "This too shall pass away." During the test each child was reinforced if he imitated the teacher's gross motor act, whether he imitated the other components of her performance or not.

As it turned out, the children imitated all the teacher's actions with increasing accuracy. They imitated best the act that was the subject of training at the time, but they did not lose the skills they had learned earlier. So, when speech finally was added to the training, the children began to imitate it reliably, and they continued at the same time to imitate gross, fine motor, and facial acts. This apparently represented a growing ability to observe and imitate a complex performance, even when unreinforced, which was exactly the result we wanted.

It is always important in studies like this one to demonstrate that the outcome was indeed the result of the conditions applied. Otherwise one finds one's self clinging superstitiously to useless procedures. So, after the children were far into the program, we began giving bits of food to one child in each group of three when he did *not* imitate the model teacher. The procedure did greatly reduce the child's tendency to imitate. When snacks again were given for imitation, the child also began to imitate again, as well as or better than he had before (see Figure 2).

The ultimate intent of imitation training was to give the children the ability to listen to novel language performances and to repeat them. In one year, it was possible to develop training only to the point where the children consistently imitated fairly short sentences. To be useful, the program would have to increase the children's skill with longer and longer verbal performances. Whether that can be done remains to be seen; it is one subject of the current year's research. But the success of the program so far suggests that the extension of verbal imitative skills to complex statements is probably a practical goal.

Verbal Skill

Any child may have a much more elaborate verbal repertoire than he demonstrates in a spontaneous account of some happening. To find out whether we could bring that repertoire into use, and perhaps add to it as well, we chose a child who was probably the least articulate in the group.

We began by finding out just how inarticulate he was. The teacher asked, repeatedly over a period of thirteen days, five questions such as "Who do you like to play with?" In answer to these questions, the child usually answered with one word or two, yielding a grand average over repeated inquiries of one and one-half words per answer.

Then the teacher began training. She asked, "What did you see on the way to school?" When she prompted the boy's answers with "What else," he simply repeated one- and two-word answers, alternating between the two responses, "A doggie" and "TV," and repeating the pair over and over.

When it had become clear that this pattern was not likely to change by itself, the teacher provided a more logical prompt: "What kind of doggie?" The boy replied that it was a German shepherd, and the teacher praised him and gave him a bit of snack. Then she asked again what he saw on the way to school. He answered, "A doggie." At this point, the teacher raised her eyebrows, cocked her head, and waited. Presently the child amended his answer: "A German shepherd doggie," and was praised and fed.

When the original question was asked again, with the reply "A German shepherd doggie," the child was given a second prompt: the teacher asked what the doggie was doing. In this way the training proceeded, with the teacher prompting each logical step, waiting for all

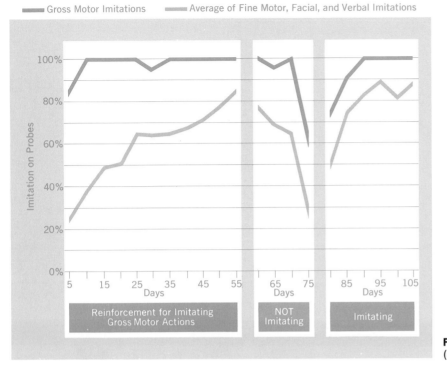

Figure 2. Effect of reinforcement (snacks) on imitating.

previous steps to be chained together in reasonable sequence, and reinforcing only increasingly long and meaningfully connected sequences. The child's average answer to this first question eventually rose to about 200 words per ten-minute sessions, which amounted to about fifty words per session if duplications were eliminated.

Then the teacher asked a new question, "What do you do when you go home from school?" The child's answer showed that he had profited from the training on the first question; therefore the teacher reduced her logical prompts and asked simply, "what else" or "what then," while continuing to dispense praise and snacks only for more and more elaborate phrases.

The child was trained on five questions in all (see Figure 3). After each of them, the teacher asked five other questions on which he had not been trained. The child answered them at length, in a meaningfully connected and understandable way. The average length of his answers to these questions was over five times greater than that of his answers to the questions that preceded training.

Although the boy's narrative skill developed admirably as the program progressed, it was thought that the accuracy of his stories was perhaps questionable. So the last training question was one that the teacher could check: "What have you been doing at school today?" The boy was reinforced only for accurate elaborations, and his answers to the question were not only longer and longer but more and more accurate.

We do not know yet whether this technique will work with other children, or whether it can be used with groups. But it is encouraging to discover that narrative ability can grow without step-by-step and word-by-word training. In many cases, the child seems to know the words and how to use them, so that virtually all he needs is an invitation.

How Turner House Is Different

Visitors to Turner House are sometimes surprised to find that it looks very much like any other nursery school, except that the children are somewhat better behaved. They enjoy the usual activities—playing house, painting pictures, "dancing" to piano music— and get along well with each other and with their teachers. It is true that every now and then a child receives a bit of food, and that observers with clipboards and stopwatches are scattered about the room, but the general atmosphere is warm, cheerful, and distinctly unmechanical.

Despite appearances, Turner House is in fact quite different from the traditional nursery school and from its stepchild, the "enrichment" preschool for the culturally deprived. It is unfortunate that enrichment nursery schools tend to be modeled on middle-class nursery schools, because middle-class nursery schools are for middle-class children. For example, they attempt to develop the child's ability to get along with other children, but skill at social interaction rarely is lacking in a child with a large family and many siblings near his own age. They try to enhance motor skills and uninhibited activity, but those skills are usually well developed in a child whose playground is the street. They try to stimu-

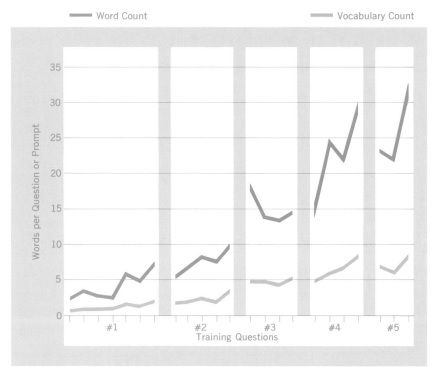

Figure 3. Effect of reinforcement (snacks) on one boy's vocabulary and sentence-making growth.

late intellectual development with puzzles, books, and manipulative toys, but the content of these items is as meaningless to the culturally deprived preschool child as to the culturally deprived kindergartner.

In addition, the methodology of the middle-class nursery school is inappropriate for the culturally deprived child. For example, fighting and "making trouble" are likely to be regarded as symptoms of insecurity, and therefore to be met by the teacher with understanding, acceptance, and love. In the culturally deprived child (and, indeed, in the middle-class child), aggressive and disruptive behavior may be nothing more sinister than a useful social tool—a tool that the child must replace if he is to get along well in public school. It is therefore more suitable to ignore the child when he behaves badly, and to reserve attention for behavior that one wants him to maintain.

Finally, though an atmosphere of warmth and approval is certainly helpful, its chances of success in effecting radical changes in the child's behavior are slim. For one thing, since responses to social reinforcement are usually weak and deficiencies in skills are unusually large in culturally deprived children, it may be necessary to begin with something to which they *do* respond, like food, in order to establish new skills rapidly. For another, if social reinforcement is to be effective at all, it must be specific. It must *immediately follow* the behavior to which it relates. Teachers who are not trained to praise a child's small achievements at once often fail to do so because without close attention and also considerable patience, it is easy to miss the brief and infrequent moments of desirable behavior that occur at first.

The Parent-Teacher Cooperative Preschool

It would be better, in the long run, to modify the home environment of the culturally deprived child than to try to make up for its deficiencies through a supplementary program. As a small step in this direction, the Juniper Gardens Parent-Teacher Cooperative Preschool provides daily lessons for mothers on how to teach their preschool children the skills that they will need for elementary-school work.

For this project we chose thirty four-year-olds and their mothers from upwardly mobile poverty families. The parents had a considerable amount of ambition for their children, and our aim was to channel that ambition into constructive behavior.

Compared to the children in the hard-core group, the upwardly mobile children had somewhat more motivation to achieve in school and somewhat stronger responses to social reinforcement. In addition, their mothers were willing to participate in the program. We did find, however, that it was useful to provide a bonus for attendance: we gave each mother a place setting of inexpensive china each week, at the rate of a dish a day, for coming to the preschool with her child.

The Parent-Teacher Preschool included many traditional preschool group activities, plus a carefully graded sequence of 150 daily lessons. The lesson series trained the mothers in teaching techniques and also showed them what their children should be learning—colors, numbers, rhymes, and so forth.

For the first six months of the program, each mother taught lessons to her own child. At a certain time during the day, she and the child would retire to one of several booths, each containing two chairs, a TV tray, and a shoebox of lesson materials such as crayons, toys, and pictures of various objects.

At first, the mothers were poor teachers. They used almost no praise or approval, and they showed very little grasp of the technique of attacking a complex problem by starting with its simplest form. Their usual pattern was to present a difficult problem and then to punish errors or silence with nagging or threats. They told the child to sit up, to pay attention; they informed him that they knew he knew the answer, so he had better say it.

Therefore we devised written instructions for the mothers to read before each lesson. Early instructions were very detailed. For example, Lesson One on naming objects began: "Hold up an object in front of the child. Say 'Can you tell me what this is?' Praise him by saying 'Good for you!' if he names it right." The same lesson ended with a general plea: "When he names something right, praise him."

Later in the lesson series, unless radically different materials or procedures were called for, the instructions were simple statements of what the child was to learn from the lesson.

Using these instructions, and with help from preschool teachers, the mothers' skill increased rapidly. But by the end of the year, though they praised their children's appropriate behavior much more often, they still did not praise it often enough. And the tendency to nag and threaten persisted.

So, at the start of the next school year, we made two changes in the program. First, we had each mother begin not with her own child, but with someone else's.

Second, we had the preschool teacher keep track of how often the mother dispensed praise, and flash a red light, mounted where the mother could see it, each time praise was recorded. We explained the purpose of the record and the light to the mothers, and we encouraged them to inspect the record after each lesson.

Under these revised conditions, all the mothers began to be much more liberal with praise (see Figure 4). At the same time, nagging and threats almost disappeared. Then we asked the mother to press a foot pedal whenever the child answered a question right. Her record of correct answers eventually corresponded to the preschool teacher's record of the mother's praise. At this point, except for covert reliability checks, we allowed each mother to record her own praise rate under the guise of recording the child's right answers.

After the mothers had learned to praise other people's children, we allowed them to begin teaching their own. In general, they continued to praise and to refrain from nagging. However, they did not teach their own children in quite the same way that they taught other children. When a mother taught her own child a lesson she already had taught to other children, she tended to praise him more than she had the others. When she taught him a lesson she had not taught before, she praised her child less than she later praised other children.

During the part of the day that was not taken up with lessons, the mothers supervised the children's group activities. As the rate at which they dispensed praise during the lessons rose, it also rose during play periods. However, it quickly became apparent that the

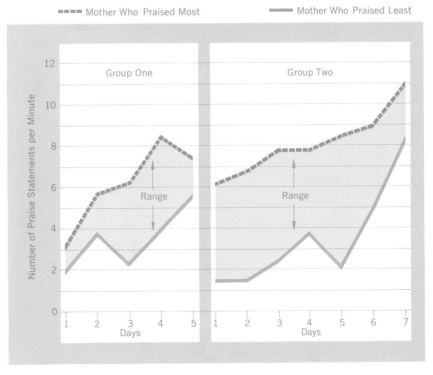

Figure 4. When mothers' praises in teaching their children were recorded, the number of praise statements dispensed grew considerably.

mothers had little skill in maintaining order. They responded to shouting and fighting by shouting back, shaking the children, and so forth. This was not only ineffective but directly contrary to the guiding principle of the program, which was to reinforce with attention only the behavior that they wanted the children to continue.

To remedy this situation, we developed a system for structuring the activities of the playroom. We defined the boundaries of each area—doll corner, block corner, and so forth—and then required the children to complete a "switching requirement" before moving from one area to another.

The switching requirement was a simple matching problem involving pegs on a pegboard. The child was told to go to the board, complete the problem, and raise his hand. At that point a mother would come over, approve of his work, and allow him to choose a ticket to a new play area.

We imposed the requirement more for immediate, practical reasons than for training in skills that mothers or children could use outside the preschool. It did, however, have some interesting results. Noting that a one-row problem increased the average time a child spent in one activity area from ten minutes to twenty-six, we decided to see what effect a four-row problem would have. In addition to reducing the switching rate still further, the four-row problem taught the children a good deal about matching. The first time one boy tried the problem, it took him half an hour; his eighth attempt took a mere nine minutes. In other words, moving from area to area served as an effective reinforcement for learning, just as did the use of equipment and materials at Turner House.

The Parent-Teacher Preschool was primarily a training program for mothers, but it did, of course, affect the children as well. Its benefits can be inferred from the marked change in their IQ scores. At the beginning of the program, the average child's score on the Peabody Picture Vocabulary Test was 69 and the range was from 48 to 81. At the end of the program, the average child's score on the same test was 87 and the range was 67 to 117.

As for the mothers, we found that they can learn to become fairly good teachers. However, they tend to teach other children better than they do their own, and they have trouble putting principles of positive reinforcement into practice in unstructured situations. These are problems that we are working on this year.

An important by-product of the project is that the mothers have participated in a community project, many of them for the first time. Indeed, we have tried to involve the community as closely as possible both at Turner House and at the Parent-Teacher Preschool. For example, one of the three full-time teachers at Turner House is a girl of nineteen from Juniper Gardens, who came to us from the neighborhood Youth Corps. The Parent-Teacher Preschool is supervised this year by one professional teacher instead of three; now the two assistant teachers are mothers who participated in the program last year.

In summary, it seems best simply to repeat the logic that led us to develop the Turner House program and the Parent-Teacher Preschool. One characteristic of culturally deprived children is that they have trouble in school, and in the United States we rely on the public schools to teach children the behavior that our society considers useful. The right kind of preschool might make it possible for culturally deprived children to learn what the public schools set out to teach.

Ideally, the schools will be teaching something meaningful, and teachers will see these particular children as valuable people for whom it is worth opening the doors to knowledge.

The Mentally Retarded Child

Sidney W. Bijou

The mentally retarded child is seen as an individual whose rate of development has been slowed down. Professor Bijou applies several principles from studies of operant conditioning to understanding this kind of handicap. He discusses four factors that may contribute to delays and failures in development and the ways in which they may occur. He points out that abnormalities in anatomical structure or physiological functioning may make it impossible for a child to make certain motor responses, or may severely restrict the range of stimuli with which he comes in contact. He discusses the effects of inadequate or indiscriminate reinforcement in slowing down the child's development, and he points out the consequences that may develop from insufficient discrimination training. He shows how reinforcing undesirable behavior may actually contribute to retarded development. And finally, he discusses how severe punishment, whether intentional or unintentional, may result in developmental retardation.

Tradition has it that mental retardation is a symptom of something deeper—of something called "defective intelligence," "clinically inferred brain damage" or "familial factors." This view has lost ground in recent years. The more modern one that is replacing it regards retardation not as a symptom but as a form of behavior: limited behavior that has been shaped by past events in a person's life. The new method does not assume that we can know what goes on inside a person. Instead, it concentrates on what can be scientifically observed.

No special theory is necessary to analyze the behavior of a mentally retarded person. The same principles apply to the development of all people—retarded, normal, and accelerated. Psychological development, according to behavior theory, consists of interactions between the behavior of the individual as a total functioning biological system and environmental events. It follows then that retardation is the result of conditions that prevent, reduce, or delay the development of effective ways of interacting with the environment.

In addition to being a total functioning biological system, an individual is a complex behaving system that changes his environment, and is also a source of stimuli that affect his own behavior and the behavior of others toward him. The second characteristic suggests that a person carries around with him part of his environment. This is indeed the case, as we shall see.

When I refer to environmental events, I mean the specific events that are actually related to a person's behavior. This is not the usual definition of environment. The dictionary defines environment as "an aggregate of surrounding things and influences," or as "external conditions." In this analysis, the environment, and synonymously, environmental events, refer only to those stimuli *that can be linked with the behavior of an individual*.

There is one other critical difference in the way behavior theory uses the term. Environment usually refers to the social, cultural, and physical conditions that influence a person's life. These conditions are part of the word *environment* as it is used in behavior theory, but so is another category—the biological. This biological environment, the one that a person carries with him all the time, is made up of stimuli that emanate from his own anatomical structure and physiological functioning.

As the so-called normal individual develops, opportunities become available to him for contact with a succession of environmental events. The rate at which the normal person takes advantage of these opportunities, and to what extent, is more or less typical of his culture. In addition, the normal person's biological structure and physiological functioning are adequate, and they mature at the usual rates. For the retarded person, on the other hand, the pace of successive social, physical and biological conditions is slowed down, and the effectiveness of many contacts is almost nil.

It is the quantity and quality of opportunities for contacts that determine a person's rate of development. The more extreme the restrictions on opportunities, the more extreme the retardation. The factors that contribute to delays and failures in development are therefore a major concern of scientists who hold the behavioral theory of retardation. I shall discuss these factors here in terms of (1) abnormal anatomical structure and physiological functioning, (2) insufficient reinforcement and discrimination histories, (3) the disadvantageous reinforcement of "undesirable" behavior, and (4) severe aversive stimulation.

The four categories will be presented separately for the sake of clarity; in reality, they interact with each other constantly, and in many complicated ways.

Anatomy and Physiology

A person who is biologically abnormal may well have altered response capabilities that affect the nature and progression of stimulating conditions. Since biological anomalies range from mild to severe, their effect on psychological development extends in turn from inconsequential to devastating.

Obviously, responses to stimuli are likely to be affected by impairments of the responding parts of the body and of internal coordinating systems such as the central nervous system. A child cannot possibly learn a response if it requires an anatomical part that the child does not possess or a physiological function of which he is incapable. A child with impaired vocal cords cannot be trained to make all the sounds necessary for normal speech. (He may, of course, be able to learn different responses that will serve the same purpose in the sense that they will affect the environment in the same way.)

Not so obviously, the stimulus that precedes a response may also be affected adversely by biological impairment. When skills in body management and locomotion are inadequately developed, the number and type of physical and social stimuli available for contacts are limited. Restricted mobility generates fixed behavioral repertoires. A child limited to lying on his back can only experience stimuli that are above his body or brought into his line of vision, while a child who can roll from side to side and sit up can interact with stimuli over a greatly extended range. Similarly, a child who can reach, grasp, and retrieve an object can have infinitely more experiences than a child who has yet to develop manual coordination and skill. The child who can move about can become involved in a great many novel situations compared to a physically handicapped child who must depend upon the good will of others for his locomotion. The biological impairment of some children makes certain stimuli forever inaccessible to them; for others, the stimuli will become available on a delayed time schedule.

The stimulation of the physically impaired child may also be restricted because of the way the child *looks* to others—because of his social stimulational characteristics. If the child's physical appearance is repugnant or unappealing, people may avoid him, leave him as quickly as possible, or ignore him. As Donald Zimmerman has commented, "These results superimpose social deprivation upon physical defect."

Because our society likes to think it demonstrates concern for the physically impaired, aloof behavior is often made to appear unavoidable. For example, a physically disabled youngster can be without positive social interactions for long periods because his parents are too "busy" looking after the other children, and his siblings are too "bogged down" with homework to engage in extended play with him. The children in the neighborhood exclude him from their games because he cannot "keep up with them." And the school principal bars him from school because he is not "ready."

Avoidant, abbreviated, and dutiful social relationships deprive any child, physically impaired or not, of the basic intellectual and social interactions that only people can provide. For example, complex behavior, such as thinking in abstract terms or solving problems, develops in later childhood and beyond only if people are available to arrange and rearrange stimuli (set up problems, bring dissimilar things together and point out similarities and differences), to stimulate responses (ask questions, offer hints and prompts), and to react appropriately to the responses given (confirm correct responses, assist in changing incorrect responses). Innumerable interactions of this sort, some very subtle, occur every day in the life of a normal child in the home, neighborhood, and preschool. For example, a mother on her way to the store may see a cow grazing in the pasture and say to her preschooler, "What is that over there?" To the response, "Doggie," she may say, "No, that's a cow," and describe the differences between the two animals. Similarly, the development of appropriate emotional behavior patterns seems to require, among other things, repeated experience with social contingencies such as attention, praise, approval, and affection for desirable behavior; with social support following adverse events, such as consolation after injury or frustration; and with corrective procedures that do not generate new emotional problems.

Structural and functional biological impairment is a fact of life, and many of the children it affects will always have limited behavioral repertoires: They will always be developmentally retarded. The important thing is that their development should progress as far as possible, and behavioral scientists will always be interested in ways of helping them accomplish this objective.

Reinforcement and Discrimination

Reinforcement is a difficult word to define to everyone's satisfaction. It is roughly synonymous with "reward," but only very roughly. As used here, reinforcement refers to a stimulus environmental event following a response that increases the probability of a similar response in a similar situation in the future. Behavior that is sensitive to such consequent stimulus events is called *operant behavior*. It includes verbal, motor, so-cial, and intellectual responses as well as much emo-tional behavior.

The stimulus following operant behavior is called a *stimulus event*, to emphasize that some identifiable change has occurred. The change may add something to the situation (giving a glass of orange juice to a child following his request, "Mother, may I have a glass of juice?") or remove something from it (taking off a child's sweater in response to, "My sweater itches"). Stimulus events that strengthen operant behavior are called *reinforcing stimuli*, and are said to have a reinforcing function.

Reinforcement does not take place in isolation. Other events occur at the same time, creating conditions that increase or decrease the probability that operant behav-ior will occur. Of particular interest here are stimulus events that occur immediately before the response that is likely to be reinforced. They are called *discriminative stimuli* (or cues) and are said to have a discriminative function because they provide the signal for behaving in a way that will probably produce reinforcement. Rein-forcing stimuli and discriminative stimuli are therefore interdependent.

One stimulus can serve *both* functions: it can be both a discriminative and a reinforcing stimulus. A smile from a parent in response to a child's good table manners may increase the probability of good table manners in the future (a reinforcing stimulus). A smile from the same parent in the living room may serve as a cue for the same child to climb onto the parent's lap (a discriminative stimulus). In the same way, receiving a sweet may be a reinforcing stimulus that strengthens the preceding behavior, which was the statement, "I want a cookie." The same cookie on a plate may be a discriminative stimulus for reaching, grasping, and bringing to the mouth. Because of the interlocking relationship between discriminating and reinforcing stimulus functions, we consider them together as condi-tions that retard or promote development.

In general, a child's progress in building a repertory of discriminations (as well as one of motor skills) depends on four things: the number and kind of opportunities made available to the child by the action of people (particularly parents); the properties of avail-able physical objects; the characteristics of the child's structure and physiological functioning; and his matura-tional and health condition. On the one hand, inter-actions that reinforce, discriminate, and interrelate cul-turally serviceable behavior are expected to produce people with large repertories of socially, intellectually, and vocationally valuable (highly reinforceable) behav-ior. Reports by Lewis Terman and his co-workers on the background and achievements of high IQ children and their offspring support this contention. On the other hand, environments with meager opportunities for rein-forcement, discrimination, and the development of

complex motor and verbal behavior are expected to produce children with limited repertories of socially serviceable behavior. With respect to the role of meager opportunities, Charles Ferster says:

Under this category belong individuals who are not making contact with important parts of their environment simply be-cause their history did not include a set of experiences (educa-tional) which could develop these performances during the normal maturation of the individual. Especially in the area of everyday social contacts, considerable skill is necessary for producing social reinforcements, and the absence of this skill either results in an individual without a social repertoire or one who achieves effects on his social environment by indirect means, as, for example, using aversive stimulation to gain at-tention.

On the basis of inferences from behavioral principles, there are at least three sets of circumstances under which inadequate behavior of this type may evolve: when reinforcements, particularly social reinforcements, are infrequent and weak; when reinforcements are lack-ing (extinction) or given indiscriminately; and when programs for the development of essential discrimina-tion and skills are lacking or ineptly arranged.

| INFREQUENT AND WEAK REINFORCEMENTS | Under-staffed child-care institutions may be responsible for one set of circumstances in which reinforcements are infre-quent and given in small amounts. For example, Wayne Dennis and Pergouchi Najarian observed children one to four years old in three Iranian institutions, each of which used different child-rearing practices. In two of the institutions, the children were markedly retarded in motor skills; in the other there was little evidence of such retardation. The investigators summarized their findings as follows:

The extreme retardation in Institutions I and II was probably due to the paucity of handling, including the failure of at-tendants to place the children in the sitting position and the prone position. The absence of experience in these positions is believed to have retarded the children in regard to sitting alone and also in regard to the onset of locomotion. The lack of experience in the prone position seems in most cases to have prevented children from learning to creep; instead of creeping, the majority of the children in Institutions I and II, prior to walking, locomoted by scooting. In Institution III, in which children were frequently handled, propped in the sitting posi-tion and placed prone, motor development resembled that of most home-reared children. The retardation of subjects in Institutions I and II is believed to be due to the restriction of specific kinds of learning opportunities.

In a later study of a similar institution in Beirut, Lebanon, Yvonne Sayegh and Wayne Dennis reported that additional stimulation given to infants could ac-celerate development. In their words, "appropriate sup-plementary experience can result in rapid increases in behavioral development on the part of environmentally retarded infants."

Inadequate reinforcement—and the retardation that

it leads to—may also occur in a home where, except for basic biological care, the child is left to his own resources because his parents are preoccupied with outside activities or have serious physical or mental health problems. Ferster has discussed how such child-rearing practices contribute to behavioral deficits in the early development of a severely disturbed child:

The most fundamental way to eliminate a kind of behavior from an organism's repertoire is to discontinue the effect the behavior has on the environment (extinction). A performance may also be weakened if its maintaining effect on the environment occurs intermittently (intermittent reinforcement). Behaviors occurring because of their effects on the parent are especially likely to be weakened by intermittent reinforcement and extinction, because the parental reinforcements are a function of other variables and behavioral processes usually not directly under the control of the child.

He went on to point out that speech and social behaviors are those most likely to be adversely affected by extinction (nonreinforcement) and intermittent reinforcement because at this early stage of a child's life the parents are the most important source of reinforcers for the development of those behaviors.

Note that I referred to parent-child interactions that create behavior deficits in severely *disturbed* young children. How does this relate to the task of analyzing retarded development? Simply this: there is good evidence that the conditions and processes contributing to severe behavioral disturbances in children also slow down development. Failure to perpetuate a behavior eliminates that particular behavior—one that the child has already established for dealing with current situations—from the child's repertory. It also puts him at a disadvantage in learning new behavior that requires a foundation of responses of the sort lost. Verbal development is a case in point. Because it is basic to so much other behavior, inadequate reinforcement of early verbal behavior can result in deficits in intellectual, social, emotional, and even motor development.

Many retarded children are also behaviorally disturbed, and practically all severely maladjusted children are also developmentally retarded. We distinguish between the behaviorally disturbed and the developmentally retarded only for practical purposes in grouping children for residential care and for educational and training programs.

There is another condition that may produce weak and rare social reinforcement: the physical appearance of a child considered repulsive by the social community. As I mentioned earlier, an atypical biological makeup can result in a shortage of adequate social contacts and experiences with physical objects. As a result, the markedly unattractive child does not have adequate opportunities to develop relationships with new reinforcing and discriminative stimuli.

| INDISCRIMINATE REINFORCEMENT, OR NONE | One of the ways behavior (particularly that supported by weak social and sensory stimulation) is eliminated is by withholding reinforcement. This process is called *extinction*. One might say that the extreme case of intermittent reinforcement is extinction.

There is a wide variety of behavior supported by scattered social interactions (a nod, a smile, a pat for showing commendable perseverance) and by the stimulation of physical things made available in interesting ways. When a family must struggle with poor health, adjustment difficulties, drug addiction, alcoholism, or the like, it may not provide the social interactions or physical objects necessary to reinforce behavior.

Behaviors may also be weakened or remain undeveloped if reinforcements are delivered indiscriminately, with no relevance to the response the parent wishes the child to learn. An example with which we are all familiar is the child who is chronically sick, disabled, or incapacitated. The parents, understandably concerned, react by maintaining close supervision and responding almost continuously, and without question, to each and every one of the child's needs or demands, reasonable or unreasonable. If the child screams for no obvious reason, the parent comes running, thus reinforcing the screaming; if the child spews out his food, the parent coaxes him to eat another mouthful; if the child demands constant companionship, someone is stationed nearby. This situation also tends to reduce the child's exploratory behavior, with consequences that will be discussed below.

| POOR DEVELOPMENT OF SKILLS | If there are few or no occasions for the child to interact with responsive people and interesting things, then there are few opportunities for him to acquire and retain serviceable behavior supported by reinforcement processes. Serviceable behavior includes skills in body management, manual dexterity, crawling, walking, running, jumping, skipping, climbing, and skating; the transformation of sounds into words, phrases, and sentences; and the relating of words, spoken or written, to things, symbols, and other words.

In a number of situations, severe restrictions on a child may retard his development. Here are a few.

1. *When a child is treated as though he were abnormal or chronically ill.* A study of a four-year-old girl in a laboratory nursery school showed that the infantilization practices of the parents resulted in the complete absence of speech, and in gross motor incoordination—to the point where she was unable to move about without stumbling and falling.

2. *When the parent engages in abnormal or idiosyncratic practices.* In a classic case, Kingsley Davis described an example of a deaf-mute mother who kept her illegitimate child in isolation. Mother and child spent most of the time together in a dark room, shut off from the rest of the family. The situation was discovered when the child was six and a half years old. She communicated with her mother by gestures and made

only "strange croaking sounds." Efforts to determine whether the child could hear were at first inconclusive; later it was established that her hearing was normal. She displayed fear and hostility toward others, particularly men. As one might expect, reactions to objects were unusual: when presented with a ball, she used it to stroke the interviewer's face. Psychological testing yielded a mental age on the Stanford-Binet of one year and seven months, and a social age on the Vineland Social Maturity Scale of two and a half years.

3. *When the environment is thinly populated with stimulating people and intriguing things.* A sparse social environment not only reduces the frequency of social reinforcing stimuli, it limits the opportunities for a child to engage in programmed activities that result in discriminations normally expected in his particular culture. People are necessary to arrange the environment so that the child can learn intellectual skills and develop a store of knowledge. People are necessary to create opportunities for the development of manners and morals. People are necessary to provide circumstances that establish values, interests, and attitudes appropriate for community life.

4. *When the necessary physical and cultural components of the environment are absent because of economic and social circumstances.* The detrimental effects on development of economic and cultural deprivation have now been recognized and are being stressed in programs designed to help children from underdeveloped areas and disadvantaged surroundings.

Reinforcement of "Undesirable" Behavior

In some situations, retardation may develop because "undesirable" behavior has been reinforced. Presumably no parent would *want* to develop bad behavior in a child, but it may evolve precisely because the parent dislikes it and finds that attending to it reduces or eliminates it. In the long run, though, this type of interaction strengthens both the bad behavior of the child and the attending behavior of the parent. The child is positively reinforced by the parent's action, and the parent is negatively reinforced by the action that has terminated the child's bad behavior. A familiar example is the child who gets what he wants by having a temper tantrum. Chances are that tantrum behavior was strengthened by the parent's compliance with the condition that instigated the tantrum. Chances are, also, that the parent "gave in" to terminate the distasteful or even alarming behavior displayed by the child. So the parent's response to the tantrum strengthened tantrum behavior on the part of the child, and the child's termination of the current tantrum strengthened "giving in" on the part of the parent.

This may be a plausible technical account of how a parent can strengthen undesirable behavior, but how does it relate to retarding development? First, undesirable behavior may become the child's main way of responding. If a child is constantly screaming or having tantrums, his learning of new socially and educationally desirable behavior will be slow or even static. Furthermore, the results of formal and informal tutorial interactions will be reduced; effective attention and work spans will be relatively short, and even minor nonreinforcement episodes such as correcting a color-naming error may set off strong and prolonged aversive behavior. A report by Montrose Wolf and his colleagues on the behavioral treatment and rehabilitation of a preschool boy diagnosed as autistic, retarded, and brain-injured described many instances in which strong aversive behavior had to be weakened considerably, or even totally eliminated, before the boy could be retrained. Second, unpleasant behavior may well make the child socially repugnant and so discourage people from approaching and participating in prolonged educational and social interactions with him. This, in turn, will limit his repertory of behavior. Children who display obnoxious behavior are often considered unteachable, or nearly so. They find themselves in a situation similar to that of a child who is avoided because he is physically repellent.

Severe Aversive Stimulation

Another kind of interaction that may retard development is called *contingent aversive stimulation.* This refers both to the practice of administering strong punishment to stop a particular behavior and to hurts and injuries that may occur, for example, during medical treatment or in a serious accident.

Aversive stimulation can have several consequences. First, it can stop ongoing behavior—it may suppress the behavior that preceded it. If the stimulation is moderate, the suppressed behavior is likely to reappear. A skinned knee slows down an active youngster only for minutes. If the stimulation is severe, however, suppressive effects may remain for some time. More than one clinical account has been given of a young child who stopped talking for weeks, months, or years following severe punishment by an intoxicated or disturbed parent.

Second, the setting in which aversive stimulation occurs may become aversive in itself: formerly neutral or positive situations can become distasteful or frightening. (After being thrown from his favorite horse, the youngster now reacts to the animal with fear.) The removal of such stimuli is negatively reinforcing. It strengthens the tendency to get away from the aversive situation or thing, to avoid it, or to become immobile when it arises. (If attempts to put the child back on the horse are discontinued because the youngster cries and hollers, then crying and hollering behavior is strengthened, and fear of the horse and of things associated with it remain.)

One cannot predict which classes of behavior will be strengthened by negative reinforcement, but it is certainly clear that excessive avoidant behavior can restrict

the range of interactions available to a child. In many instances the interactions that are terminated may be needed for further development (speaking, for example), and the situations that are avoided may be critical to a normal child-rearing environment (such as those involving the father) and may affect other similar aspects of the environment (all male adults). Thus, stimuli and responses that were not directly involved in the aversive interaction may come to have aversive properties in themselves.

Third, aversive stimuli may evoke physiological responses (such as gastric reactions to a fear-producing event) that affect biological functioning of the child and thereby reduce his potential for serviceable interactions.

While the consequences of strong aversive stimulation are most frequently discussed in the literature of child psychopathology under the heading of severe emotional disturbances (referred to as psychoneurotic, psychotic, and autistic), they are discussed here because aversive stimulation also retards development. Just as biological anomalies and social insufficiencies limit opportunities for development, so do strong avoidant reactions. All three foreclose many occasions for a child to make new adjustments.

I have singled out for discussion here the retarding effects of abnormal anatomical structure and functioning, inadequate reinforcement and discrimination histories, reinforcement of undesirable behavior, and severe aversive stimulation. There are, however, other processes. For example, there is the possibility that the termination (say, through death) of interactions with a mother-figure after a strong affection bond has been established can have strong retarding effects. It can weaken or even eliminate well-established behavior by removing the cues on which the behavior depended. It should be emphasized, however, that these other processes do *not* include assumed conditions such as "defective intelligence," "clinically inferred brain damage" and "familial factors."

Mimosa Cottage: Experiment in Hope

James R. Lent

The principles of operant conditioning (described in the preceding article) are applied to the training of mental retardates at Mimosa Cottage. Girls varying in age from eight to twenty-one are given intensive specialized training in personal hygiene, occupational skills, social behavior, and academic subjects. Through a series of simple steps, these retarded girls learn that appropriate behavior will be rewarded with tokens, that tokens, or coins, have exchange value, that desired articles may be purchased from a shopkeeper, and that social rewards are contingent on prior personal behavior.

Unlike normal children, retarded children show great difficulty in generalizing: a task that they have mastered in one setting may be too difficult in a new environment. Many retarded children have additional behavior problems of an idiosyncratic or even bizarre nature. These, too, are treated according to reinforcement theory, that is, by first identifying the reinforcing stimulus in the environment that perpetuates the behavior, and then removing it so that the child no longer is reinforced for the undesirable behavior. The author concludes by answering a number of questions typically raised about the Mimosa Cottage program.

Parsons, Kansas, is an unremarkable town inhabited, for the most part, by unremarkable people. One of them is a girl named Ellen, who helps care for the elderly patients in the community nursing home, where she works as a nurse's aide. At home, Ellen does her share of the housework; she prepares and serves the meals and babysits with the youngest member of the family, her six-year-old foster brother.

Today, Ellen's life is not very different from the lives of millions of unskilled and semiskilled workers in the United States, but that has not always been so. Five years ago, Ellen entered Mimosa Cottage at Parsons State Hospital and Training Center, a school for mentally retarded girls with measured IQs from 25 to 55. When she arrived, at the age of fourteen, Ellen was unable to tell time, count money, or find her way from the dormitory to the dining room alone. Now, at nineteen, she is almost a self-sufficient member of the community.

The Mimosa Cottage Demonstration Project, conducted since 1965 by the Parsons State Hospital and Training Center and the University of Kansas Bureau of Child Research, is a program designed to modify the behavior of mentally retarded girls between the ages of eight and twenty-one. Its overall goal is to train the Mimosa girls to behave as much like nonretarded members of the community as possible. Many girls, like Ellen, will eventually be able to live in the community. Others will continue to require care in an institution, but their adjustment to institutional life should be smoother as a result of the training they have received.

There are seventy-one "trainable" mentally retarded girls living in Mimosa Cottage. They are housed on three floors, according to age. On the bottom floor, Mimosa A, the girls are eight to twelve years old. Mimosa B, the middle floor, includes girls from twelve to sixteen. On the top floor, Mimosa C, are the older girls, aged sixteen to twenty-one. The overall goals are the same for all three groups. However, the reinforcement systems and the training programs differ in difficulty and complexity to reflect the different developmental levels of the three groups of children.

The basic method of the program is operant conditioning (see the preceding article), which is based on the premise that the receipt of a reward or reinforcer for specific behavior increases the probability that similar behavior will occur in the future. During the initial stages of the project, research assistants observed the dress and behavior of the people in the community, and the specific aims of the program were formulated from those observations.

The program includes four general training categories: personal appearance, occupational skills, social behavior, and functional academic subjects. Each of these is broken down into small and carefully defined behavioral components. These small components are the first objects of training. As the program proceeds, they are built into increasingly complex units of behavior.

As reinforcers to support the training, we use tokens

—generalized rewards that can be exchanged for items and privileges ranging from food and cosmetics to movies and dances. To serve its purpose, a reinforcer must have value for the person who receives it. Thus, our first task with each group of girls is to teach them that the tokens have value.

At first, we do not reinforce with tokens at all. Instead we offer such nontoken rewards as candy for desired behavior. Gradually, we substitute tokens for food. When the tokens are first used, we allow the girls to exchange them for food immediately. Then we increase the time between token exchanges. Eventually, we are even able to introduce saving by requiring several tokens for certain purchases.

Like the token system itself, the behavior for which tokens are given becomes more and more complex as training proceeds. It might be necessary at first, for example, to reward a girl for taking the smallest step toward painting a picture—for approaching the easel, say, or for touching the paintbrush. Later, the girl receives tokens only when she has painted for some time. Still later, the activity itself may become desirable and therefore reinforcing, and we can *require* tokens for the privilege of participating.

The tokens we give the younger girls (on Mimosa B) are coins—British half-pennies—which they keep in a bank attached to a wall of the cottage. They may spend the tokens for privileges, such as the use of a record player, or for items stocked at the cottage store. The cottage store, which resembles a small variety store, is an excellent place to teach the girls the behavior appropriate for shopping downtown. They must dress suitably, for instance, and they must communicate to the adult in charge what it is they want to buy. Depending on a girl's abilities, she is required to point to an item, to imitate its name after the adult in charge has said it, or to ask for it in a complete sentence.

The older girls on Mimosa C use a somewhat more abstract token-and-banking system. Their tokens take the form of marks on a gridded point card. The points on one side of the card can be redeemed for money; those on the reverse are "privilege points" that permit certain activities. Once a week, on Bank Day, the girls receive the amount of money shown on the financial side of their cards, money that they may keep themselves or, if they prefer, bank under lock and key. At the same time, their privilege points are recorded for use later on.

The money the older girls earn is spent in downtown Parsons—experience that helps shift the control of their behavior from extrinsic reinforcers to the normal reinforcers found in the community. To be eligible for a trip downtown, a girl must have privilege points, and to make purchases, she must use her own money. Thus she must have accumulated both kinds of tokens in order to "afford" an outing.

When a girl refuses to do a specific task or displays extremely deviant behavior, tokens may be taken away from her. Behavior that leads to the removal of tokens is called "costly behavior." One advantage of this system is that there is no need for emotionalism on the part of the staff. Without reprimands, nagging, or scolding, the adult simply removes the tokens.

It is important to keep the cost of goods and privileges realistic in comparison to community standards, and to accustom the girls to no more purchasing power for recreation than unskilled workers ordinarily have. Daily records of tokens received and spent allow us to make changes to meet the needs of individual children and, if necessary, to shift the level of the entire economy to offset depressions and inflations. This can be done by changing the quotas on token delivery, by changing the prices of articles stocked in the cottage store, and by changing the cost of activities.

The training itself includes personal skills such as cleanliness, grooming, and sitting and walking in ways that are appropriate to a noninstitutional community; domestic and occupational skills such as those needed to care for a house and to do simple repetitive work like that required in a sheltered workshop; social skills such as interpersonal relations and attitudes; and educational skills such as time-telling, arithmetic, vocabulary, and reading. A few examples will show how the training is done, and with what results.

Many of the Mimosa girls wear clothing that does not fit and is in poor condition. In part, the reason is the circumstances of institutional living—budget limitations, clothes sent by parents or issued by the institution without an opportunity for the girls to try them on. In addition, however, the girls do not know how to match colors and patterns or how to select styles that are appropriate for different occasions. These skills can be improved by training.

We begin by taking baseline data on each girl's level of skill without training. A test movie is shown of girls wearing various outfits. As each picture appears on the screen, the adult in charge describes the clothes ("This is a plain white blouse and a plaid skirt") and asks, "Do they match?" Then training begins. The staff member shows the girl different-colored cards and swatches of material and gives her a token when she matches them correctly. More complex matters follow, such as the proper use of checks and plaids and the choice of clothing appropriate to the season. At the end of the training, the test movie is shown again.

The results of the clothing program as a whole show some improvement in all areas. In three of the categories, color matching, type matching, and appropriateness to the occasion, our test showed significantly fewer errors after training than before. In the categories of figure matching and proper fit, however, the distribution of scores indicates that the program needs improvement. It is being revised this year.

Another fairly obvious deficiency in the personal

appearance of the Mimosa girls is their hair, which is often poorly combed, inappropriately styled, and dirty. Part of the problem is poor habits, but almost all the girls also lack skill in setting and combing, and they cannot identify hair styles that are suitable for them or for different social occasions.

One evening a week, a beautician from the community comes to the cottage and shows the girls how to style, set, and care for their hair. At first, the girls receive tokens each time they groom their own hair. Once they learn to do this regularly, the tokens are faded out and replaced with more natural consequences, such as beauty contests, Polaroid pictures, and praise from an adult or from another girl.

Townspeople from Parsons can often tell the Mimosa children from other children in the community simply by the way they walk. So we devised specific corrective programs for each small motor movement involved in walking. Many of the girls, for example, walk with their heads forward and down. To correct this, we use the following procedure. A piece of tape is attached to the wall at the exact height of the girl's chin, and the girl is asked to walk toward the spot from twenty feet away, keeping her eyes focused on it and pointing her chin at it. If necessary, the instructor places the girl's head in the proper position manually. Later, the girl walks toward the instructor instead of the spot of tape, maintaining eye contact and aiming her chin at the instructor's. When the girl holds her chin too low, the instructor signals that fact by raising his own chin. At the same time, an audio signal sounds. Finally, the girl walks twenty feet toward a mirror, maintaining eye contact with her own reflection and using the mirror to determine whether she needs to raise her chin. If her self-evaluation is faulty, the audio signal is used.

In addition to head position, the walking training includes five other components. Data taken at the end of 1966 showed considerable improvement in all six areas.

Not too surprisingly, good results obtained in training sessions do not always generalize to other life settings. Currently, we conduct the sessions on walking with a background auditory stimulus presented at a tempo of 116 beats per minute. Later, outside the training sessions, the auditory stimulus will be presented intermittently for short periods of time in the hope that the walking patterns established in training will be evoked. In the meantime, we have received a bonus: Performance during training has improved simply because the girls must always walk at the selected tempo; 116 beats per minute is an average walking speed, and walking and posture errors apparently are exaggerated when the pace is noticeably slower or faster.

Domestic skills such as sewing, ironing, housekeeping, and cooking are built up in the same gradual way as motor skills like walking. Sewing, for instance, begins with needle threading and button sewing and progresses through straight-line sewing to, for many girls, machine sewing. Several girls have been able with little help to make shifts, dresses, jumpers, and slacks. They choose and buy their own patterns, lay them out, cut the material, and sew the garments on the machine.

In the writing of all such training programs, the most useful rule we have discovered is: Do not assume that the subject will be able to generalize. This means that training programs must be written in far greater detail and much more explicitly than teaching plans for children of higher mental ability. It also means that what the girls learn to do in the cottage they may not do outside the cottage—in a home, in a job, or in a community store. Some problems with generalization can be foreseen and prevented. For example, housekeeping training begins in the model living area at the cottage and continues in more intensive and more complex form in homes in the community.

Other problems with generalization must be taken up individually as they occur, which may not be until after the girl has left Mimosa Cottage to live in the community. A girl who has been trained to recognize stewed tomatoes in a certain kind of can and to read prices marked in a certain numbering style may have trouble when she confronts the array of tomato products stocked by the usual grocery store. If she cannot generalize, she must be retrained—not only on tomatoes, but on beans, corn, and a variety of other products.

Like most institutionalized retarded persons, the girls at Mimosa have limitations, often severe, in such behavior as speech, social attitudes, and heterosexual interaction. For this reason, training in social skills is an important concern of the cottage program.

Leisure-time activities, some individual and some group, show the children how to entertain themselves and teach them to get along with one another. The games and activities must have absolute carry-over value, that is, they must be the same things many people in the community do to occupy their time—puzzles, card games such as canasta and solitaire, dominoes and checkers, jacks.

Dances are organized for the girls from Mimosa Cottage and retarded boys from a nearby cottage. The dances offer an opportunity for instruction in social manners and in posture. Many of the girls show poor posture when sitting or standing, and they do not really know how to begin or end a dance. Training includes nine steps, beginning when the girl is asked to dance and ending when she tells her partner she enjoyed the dance. The instructor tells the children the behavior expected of them and uses marks on their reinforcer cards to indicate that they have performed satisfactorily. At the end of the dance session, the children can use the marks they have earned to attend a special party, where cookies and punch are served.

Our experience with this program taught us something about the selection of target behavior. All the children in the first two classes attained criterion behavior, and we were pleased that the program was serving its purpose. However, in reviewing a movie of a training session, we suddenly noticed that the session did not look like a teen-age dance. The children's manners and movements were more similar to those of middle-class, middle-aged persons. At this point, the middle-aged author designed a new program on the basis of actual observations of teen-age dances held in the community.

Instruction in heterosexual association and sex hygiene is a regular part of the social training. It is frank and to the point. An illustrated program covers the fundamentals of reproduction; in addition, again with boys from another cottage, the girls are taught what is proper and what is not and what is proper in some places but improper in others.

Although the measured IQs of the Mimosa girls classify them as trainable rather than educable, many of them are able to acquire basic academic skills. Instruction in arithmetic, time-telling, phonics and reading has been initiated with individuals and small groups, and the procedures are being analyzed and improved as we gain experience.

All programs, with one exception, have been developed by the project staff, since published materials have not proved useful with trainable (as opposed to educable) children. The Rainier Reading Program developed by Sidney W. Bijou and his colleagues is the one available program that we have been able to use with the Mimosa girls.

The development of speech and language skills in the Mimosa girls is one of our most important goals. The articulation improvement program carried out with ten girls on Mimosa C for the past year will illustrate.

The method of therapy was such that learning was acquired gradually and surely. A set of ten words was presented to each girl by means of picture cards. Her verbal responses to the cards were our baseline data. Then we evoked responses by means of simple, concrete stimuli and gradually shifted to more abstract, more natural means of evoking responses. The sequence was (1) auditory-visual (word and picture); (2) visual stimuli (picture card); (3) grapheme (printed word); (4) intraverbal stimuli (a sentence with a missing word to be supplied by the girl). As a final test, we presented words that contained the same sound elements as those used in training, but had not themselves been used. This was a partial measure of generalization.

Nine of the ten girls did significantly better on the post-test than on the pre-test for each set of ten words and were able to generalize the effects of training to new words with considerable success. The tenth girl made few errors to begin with, and therefore did not make significant gains.

One final type of training that should be mentioned is that used to remedy the specific behavioral problems of individual girls. For instance, one fourteen-year-old

resident of Mimosa Cottage made a practice of placing rocks, beads, and other small objects in her ear canal. She did so with such force that the objects could not be removed except by medical specialists. We tried to find out just what circumstances preceded and followed the girl's behavior, but it was not possible to identify a pattern. We did discover, though, that the doctors and nurses at the hospital where she was taken for treatment took care of her almost immediately and expressed great sympathy and concern. It seemed that this process might well be maintaining the behavior.

Since irreparable damage had already been done to the child's eardrum and ear canal, the hospital agreed to try anything that might reduce further damage. The next time the child placed an object in her ear, the cottage aide said, "All right, see me about it tomorrow. I'm busy now." The next day the child was sent by herself to the outpatient clinic, where the only attention paid to her was that her name was taken down by a nurse. Three hours later she was seen by the doctor, who treated her in a very matter-of-fact manner and assigned her to a recovery room. She stayed there for two weeks, by herself; her only contact with the staff was at meals, bed change, and clean-up time, and these encounters were brief.

After the behavior modification procedure began, there was one further incident and then an abrupt cessation for eight months. At that time, the child was called for a hearing examination. She prepared herself for the occasion by placing a bead in her ear. Since then there have been no further incidents.

Using the same principles of behavior modification and similar techniques, several other individual behavior problems have been successfully modified. Many of these problems are quite ordinary, such as tantruming and loud talking. Others are more bizarre—a girl who smeared butter over her face and clothing at meal time; a girl who stole food from other children's trays; a girl who tore her shoes at the seams; a girl who talked incessantly and incoherently to herself and to others. In many instances it was possible to discover events that typically followed the child's behavior and maintained it. Modification then involved manipulating the environment in such a way that reinforcement was no longer provided. In addition, we tried to arrange for the child to develop an alternative—a desirable response that was incompatible with the undesirable one. For instance, there are children who only get attention from adults when they are screaming or yelling. Training adults to ignore the tantrum is half the job; training the child to get attention in desirable ways is the other half.

People who hear about the Mimosa project often have questions to ask, some about its design and some about its "ethics." Here are a few of the ones we hear most often, and the answers we give.

"Couldn't time rather than training be responsible

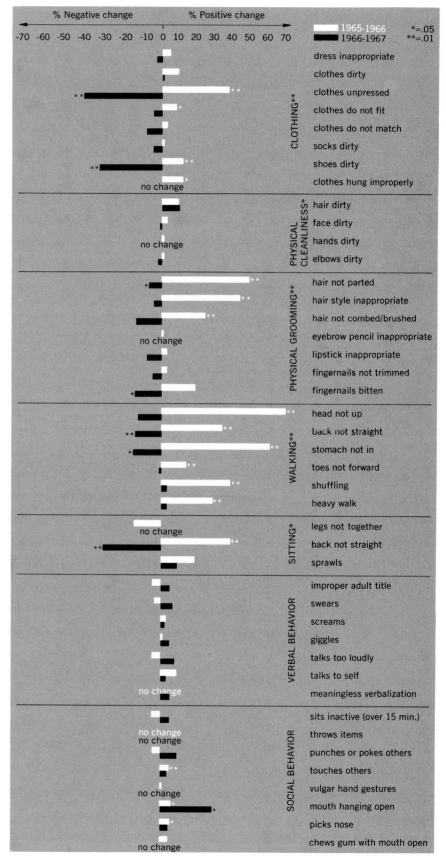

Figure 1. Behavior modification as a result of the girls' training. Note that in 1965–1966, improvement in personal skills was stressed, with noticeable improvement, whereas their verbal and social behavior had not improved. In 1966–1967, training in verbal and social skills was stressed, and these areas showed improvement.

for changes in the girls' behavior?" Several studies, conducted in this country and abroad, have shown that institutionalization has a crippling effect on the behavior of retarded children. Their behavior tends to deteriorate with time, not to improve. For example, L. F. Cain and S. Levine of San Francisco State College gave a social competency test to trainable retarded children living in institutions and to similar children living at home. They found that the scores of the children living at home rose with the passage of time, while those of the institutionalized children decreased significantly.

"Isn't it hard for aides to act natural, spontaneous, and 'happy' with the children when so much behavior is prescribed?" When aides first start reinforcing on a schedule, their behavior is somewhat mechanistic and stilted. However, they soon become accustomed to giving reinforcement and they are, after all, pleased when a child behaves appropriately. As the training takes effect, the children behave appropriately more and more often, which reinforces the staff and makes them "happy." The children, in turn, are reinforced by the quiet, predictable, pleasant behavior of the adults in charge.

"Doesn't it seem *wrong* to pay a girl to do something she should do for nothing, like comb her hair?" Well, the alternative is to *punish* the girl when she does *not* comb her hair, which seems wronger and is also less effective. Positive reinforcement is the best way we have to establish new forms of behavior. Once the behavior is established, tokens can be phased out and natural reinforcers substituted.

"Are you sure you chose the right goals for the girls?" Behavioral principles themselves are amoral. They can be used to prepare a child to vegetate in an institution, or to prepare him for life in the community. What we do is use them to reach goals on which most members of the community agree. For example, most people in Parsons agree that it is better for an adolescent girl to know how to cook and sew than not to know how to cook and sew. Most agree that it is better for a girl to say "please" when she requests something than not to say "please."

"Isn't the program terribly expensive?" Yes, the program is expensive. It costs about $35,000 per year more

than regular hospital treatment. However, if it trains a girl to support herself outside an institution for the rest of her life, it will save the taxpayer about $100,000.

The final question, of course, is "How well does the program work?" The answer is that it works fairly well, and we keep trying to make it work better. During 1965–1966, the girls improved considerably in such personal skills as care of clothing, physical cleanliness, physical grooming, walking and sitting. However, there was no overall improvement in verbal or social behavior. This meant that the training procedures, or the reinforcement system, or perhaps both, needed revision.

In 1966–1967, we shifted the emphasis of training away from personal skills and toward verbal and social ones. The space for verbal and social tokens on reinforcement cards was more than tripled, and aides were told to give more points for appropriate responses in these areas than they had the last year. In addition, aides and research assistants received supplementary training to develop their sensitivity to social behavior.

The change in emphasis worked almost too well: the pattern for 1965–1966 reversed itself in 1966–1967. Social and verbal behavior improved significantly, while personal skills held steady and even, in some cases, declined. The decline suggested that we had overreacted to the preceding year's results—although, since personal skills had already reached a high level, the decrease was not as serious as it might have been (see Figure 1).

Twelve of the Mimosa girls have now returned to the community. Five are too young to work and are living with their natural families. Seven are older and they are all working, full- or part-time. These older girls range from 20 to 69 in IQ and from seventeen to twenty-two in age. They have spent between four and one-half and twelve years in institutions.

Some of these girls have rejoined their natural families; others have been placed in foster homes. They are not fully independent, but they are able to take care of most of their personal needs and to move about the community alone. One of them is Ellen and, like Ellen, all of them lead simple but productive lives. Those around them may even forget, at times, that they were ever labeled "mentally retarded."

The Autistic Child

C. B. Ferster

Entirely different from the mentally retarded child (described in the preceding two articles) is the autistic child, whose behavior is highly disturbed and often destructive. The author points out that such primitive behaviors are also seen in normal children, but they occur less often and with less intensity.

Although not all experts in the field of psychopathology would agree with the author's environmental explanation of childhood autism, he focuses on postnatal experiences to account for the development of the disorder. He suggests ways in which the responses, or nonresponses, of parents may encourage a child to remain at a simple level of development, or may even promote regression to primitive behavior. Even though such experiences occur in the lives of all children, the author suggests that their frequency and the intensity of their occurrence in the life of the autistic child are responsible for the extreme behavioral disorders. He discusses some of the problems involved in the treatment of autistic children and concludes by describing in detail an initial therapy session between a gifted child therapist and an autistic girl; he analyzes the events of that session in terms of behavioral principles derived from the experimental laboratory.

The autistic child lives in a world apart from others. He cannot reach out, and no one can reach in. A good part of the time the child does nothing but sit quietly in a chair, or sleep, or lie huddled in a corner. At other times he is active, sometimes violently so, but his activity affects only himself. He may spend hours compulsively rubbing a rough spot on the floor, moving his fingers in front of his face, babbling to himself, licking his body like a cat, or flipping sand to produce a visual pattern. He may beat his head against the wall, hit himself until he is covered with bruises, or use his fingernails and teeth to tear his own flesh.

Some autistic children are mute. Others make inarticulate sounds or echo bits of the speech they hear around them. But they do not talk to or with other people. When an autistic child does try to communicate, it is by biting, kicking, screaming, having tantrums —primitive forms of behavior, called *atavisms*, which create a situation others will go to almost any lengths to eliminate.

If one were to watch an autistic child for a day and then watch a normal child for a month, one would see much of the autistic child's behavior reproduced by the normal child. Almost any child, on occasion, will gaze out the window for an hour or more, make bizarre faces, or have severe tantrums. Any child may run sticks over picket fences, step on (or over) all the cracks in the sidewalk, or chew a piece of rubber balloon to shreds.

But normal children are only out of touch with their surroundings once in a while, and primitivisms are not their only form of behavior. They interact with their physical and social environment in many different ways. The autistic child's behavior is far more restricted. He has very few ways of changing and being changed by the world around him.

Since his behavioral repertoire is so small, what there is of it is used over and over again. It is the *frequency* of withdrawn, self-stimulatory, or atavistic behavior, not simply the fact that it occurs, that distinguishes the autistic child from the normal one.

Autism is a very rare disorder, affecting only one child out of 50,000 or 100,000. We need to know how autism comes about and how it may be treated not only because these few children desperately need help but because the study of autism contributes to our understanding of other forms of behavior. There are parallels, for example, between the development of autism in young children and the development of schizophrenia in adolescents. In addition, the past experiences of the autistic child, like his present behavior, differ from those of the normal child not so much in *kind* as in *intensity* and *frequency*.

We do not know yet whether the causes of autism are biological or environmental, or both. Parents of autistic children sometimes report that the child seemed "different" from birth, that he stiffened each time he was picked up. Some autistic children have shown neurological anomalies such as abnormal EEG patterns. So far, however, the evidence for an inborn biological deficiency is meager.

A child's environment can have very dramatic effects on his behavioral development. This has been shown repeatedly. There have been infants who spent most of their early lives locked in closets and became primitive, animallike children. There also have been primitive, animallike children who have learned new forms of behavior when a new environment was arranged for them. Thus, it makes sense to examine the surroundings of the autistic child for circumstances that might explain the gross deficiencies in his behavior.

The major processes by which behavior is acquired and lost are *reinforcement* and *extinction*. If a rat receives a pellet of food when it presses a bar, the rat will press the bar more and more often. When the pellets are no longer delivered, bar pressing decreases in frequency and finally stops. Similarly, a person's ordinary speech usually is reinforced by the reply it gets, and a speaker who gets no reply soon stops talking. Behavioral processes are harder to observe in a natural social environment than in an experimental laboratory, but they operate similarly.

Lack of Reinforcement

The very limited repertoire of the autistic child may come about because his behavior is not successful. Ted is an example of an autistic child whose behavioral development was thwarted because little of his behavior was reinforced. At first this was hard to see because Ted's mother did not seem unresponsive. She was a very active woman who moved busily around the house, accomplishing many tasks and talking a great deal.

The child, however, was prevented from completing any action he happened to begin. When he reached for a lamp, his mother appeared as if by magic to seize his hand and hold it back. When he reached for the doorknob, again she intercepted him. When he approached his brothers and sisters, his mother separated them. When he held out a receipt he had gotten from the newsboy, she walked past and left him standing with the slip of paper in his hand.

Even the mother's speech did not make contact with the boy. While the boy was in the living room, his mother called him from the kitchen. "Ted, come over here," she said. "I want to read you a story. Ted, Ted, don't you want to read a story? Ted, come over here and read a story, TED, where are you?"

Ted paid no attention. After five minutes of calling, the mother came into the living room and picked up the book. She continued to call, "TED, TED, TED. . . . Come on and read your book." When he happened to wander near enough, she took hold of him, sat him down next to her, and began to read.

The boy did not object and seemed happy to sit with his head against his mother's shoulder. But it was obvious that the physical contact was what kept him there. The reading was irrelevant, as was most of the mother's speech.

In short, only a tiny part of the mother's behavior had a reinforcing effect on the child. Furthermore, by interrupting or ignoring his attempts to do things for himself she was preventing him from successfully completing an action—any action—of his own.

Sometimes a child's behavior succeeds only under very specific conditions—with one particular person, for example. If the circumstances suddenly change, a great deal of behavior can be lost. This happened to a little girl of four who spent a year in the care of a teen-age baby-sitter.

The girl's mother was a very disturbed, nearly psychotic, woman. She remained in the home while the baby-sitter was there, but she had nothing whatever to do with the child. If the child said, "Mom, can I have a cookie?" there was no answer. If she said, "Janet, can I have a cookie?" Janet said yes and gave her a cookie. If the girl said, "Let's go out," the mother did not answer. Janet might reply and take the child outside.

This situation might be compared to that of a laboratory pigeon being trained to peck a green key instead of a red key. If the pigeon pecks the green key, a piece of grain appears, but if it pecks the red key, nothing happens. After a while the pigeon doesn't bother pecking the red key at all.

When the baby-sitter left at the end of the year, this child lost almost her whole behavioral repertoire. She became incontinent, she talked less and less, she could not be kept in nursery school. Eventually she needed chronic care at a state home for the retarded. The reason for this massive loss of behavior was not just the sudden switch in caretakers but the fact that the mother had been present at the *same time* as the baby-sitter. If the mother had been away for the year and had been able to respond normally to the child when she returned, there probably would have been only a slight, temporary break in behavior. If the mother had been away but had *not* been able to treat the child normally when she came back, the same severe loss probably would have occurred, much more slowly.

Punishment and Primitive Behavior

Parents and children constantly influence each other's behavior. Even punishment is usually more productive than no reaction to the child at all.

This is not to say that punishment is a desirable form of behavioral control. Although its main effect is to *strengthen* behavior that avoids or ends the punishment, punishment can weaken behavior if all positive reinforcement is withdrawn. If a parent not only spanks a child but refuses to speak to him for the rest of the day, he may reduce the frequency of parts of the child's repertoire that he did not intend to affect.

In addition, punishment can promote less advanced forms of behavior. Punishment is most likely to be dispensed when a child is doing something fairly active, such as finger-painting on the wall or trying to drive his parents' car. A child who sits on the kitchen floor studying his fingers will probably be left alone. If a child is consistently punished when he tries to have a strong effect on the environment, such attempts will begin to produce considerable anxiety. So the child may substitute simpler activities, such as rubbing a spot on the floor.

He may also resort to primitive controlling behavior, like screaming and tantrums. If he finds that he *can* affect his environment in this way, he is likely to keep on using atavisms in preference to other behavior.

When one sees the amount of control some autistic children exert over their parents by means of tantrums and other atavisms, it is hardly surprising that the behavior is so durable. One child's parents told us that they took turns standing guard all night at the door of his room because a tantrum started if they left and ceased only when they moved back. Another mother slept with her arm over her child every night for five months, so that she could stop him when he woke and clawed at his face.

Possible Causes of Autism

Everything described so far—lack of reinforcement, sudden changes in its source, the withdrawal of approval, and practices that encourage primitive behavior—also occurs in the lives of children who do not become autistic. Accounting for the autistic child's massive failure of development therefore presents a problem. The explanation seems to be that the autistic child has faced more severely damaging situations more often than the normal or nearly normal child. Most of the evidence that this is true is anecdotal, but compelling.

One often finds, for instance, that autistic children have parents who are completely unable to respond to the child's behavior. A parent who is a drug addict, an alcoholic, chronically ill, or severely depressed may not even acknowledge the child's existence for days on end. One also finds parents who have beaten, tortured, starved, or incarcerated their children for long periods of time. One woman kept her child in a dog run.

When we look at the child rather than at the parents, we often discover a history of serious or chronic illness during infancy. In such cases, the child's standard way of communicating with the parents usually has been to cry and fret. After the child recovers, the crying may persist, and the parents may very well keep on reacting. So the child deals with the parents through primitive behavior, and the parent responds in order to end the behavior. The child's development, already retarded by his illness, may progress no farther.

A child is not usually identified as autistic until some complex form of behavior (such as speech) fails to develop—that is, until the child is two, three, or even four years old. Although this does not prove that autism was not present earlier (indeed, parents occasionally report deviant behavior in very young infants), it does suggest a careful examination of that period in the child's life when the disorder may express itself.

A two-year-old is at a stage of development when his behavior is especially vulnerable to disruption. For one thing, he is more likely than a younger child to provoke a negative reaction from his parents. The activities of a baby are simple and relatively unobtrusive. But when a child begins to crawl, walk, reach for ashtrays and lamps, and cry loudly when crossed, he may also begin to frighten and upset his parents and thus to invite the kind of treatment that weakens behavior.

Furthermore, the child's new behavior is not at all firmly established. New behavior develops fastest when it has a consistent, reliable effect on the environment. Since the child can only approximate what he is trying to do at first, his efforts succeed only part of the time. If an enthusiastic parental response is lacking too, the child may very well abandon the behavior.

Sometimes a parent will praise the child's first nonsense syllables but become angry a month later when the child still cannot speak in complete, intelligible sentences. This sudden shift in the performance required for reinforcement can have the same effect on the child as suddenly requiring a laboratory pigeon to peck 300 times instead of 25 for a piece of grain: the behavior stops.

Adolescence

However, sudden changes in the kind and amount of behavior required for reinforcement are more likely to occur in adolescence than in early childhood. A ten-year-old may need do no more than hold out his hand for his allowance or run next door to find a playmate. A sixteen-year-old is expected to work for his money and to master an elaborate courtship ritual. At school, where assignments used to be frequent and short, the teen-age student may have to work for weeks or months before he finds out from the teacher how he is doing. In general, the adolescent must perform a substantial number of specific acts before his behavior is reinforced, often without benefit of a complete series of intermediate, transitional experiences.

If the change in kind or amount of behavior an adolescent must deliver is too sudden or too large, the effect on his development can be disastrous. One cannot build the Empire State Building if there is only a toothpick holding up the twentieth floor. One schizophrenic boy had a job as a truck driver before he was hospitalized; he would not stop at the restaurant where the other drivers ate because he did not know how to order food from the waitress. Another young man in the ward had frequent and violent temper tantrums; their source turned out to be his inability to tie his shoelaces.

Treatment

Autistic children are very difficult to treat. Until recently, they were considered virtually hopeless. So much of the normal repertoire is missing; a long history of experiences must be re-created; dealing with a six-year-old child as if he were one or two years old presents innumerable problems. Some therapists have succeeded with prolonged residential treatment. In addition, recent experimental attempts have sometimes produced dramatic changes in the children's behavior. Even when these experiments are not entirely successful from a therapeutic point of view—when, for example, the changes do not last—they represent progress because they show the child's potential for development.

One promising approach to rehabilitation is illustrated by a project that I am participating in at the Linwood Children's Center for autistic children, located between Washington, D.C., and Baltimore. The Director of the Center, Jeanne Simons, is chiefly a clinician, and I am chiefly an experimentalist. What we are trying to do is produce a kind of model for cooperative work between the two fields.

During our collaboration we found that our methods are a great deal alike. I tend to approach an experiment, even in the animal laboratory, from a clinical point of view; Miss Simons manipulates the environment in her clinic much as I do in the laboratory. I might be called a sheep in wolf's clothing, and she a wolf in sheep's clothing.

Miss Simons is an unusually gifted therapist. Like many gifted therapists, she has trouble explaining to other workers how she gets her results. Her metaphors —"Walk behind the child so that you can see where he is going"—describe the principles of operant reinforcement very well, but they helped the staff little in everyday dealings with the children.

Here was an area where an experimentalist could help. A functional analysis of Miss Simons' methods, in objective language, would make it easier for the staff to understand and evaluate them. It would also give Miss Simons a new perspective on her own work.

As I watched Miss Simons deal with the children, I saw the application of every principle of behavior that I know. But I did not always recognize them at first. There was one boy who teased Miss Simons by pulling her hair. When she continued to give him her full attention, I wondered why. It seemed clear that her attention was reinforcing the annoying behavior. But when I looked more closely, I saw that Miss Simons was holding the boy's wrist close to her hair so that he couldn't pull it. She released her grip only when he made a move toward some more desirable kind of behavior.

To illustrate the kind of thing Miss Simons does (and the way behavioral language can clarify it), I will describe an encounter she had with an autistic girl named Karen. Karen was mute and had very little contact with her environment. She cried continuously and softly, and she had a doll that she always carried with her.

The encounter took place only a short time after Karen arrived at Linwood, and it was the child's first sustained interaction with another person. It lasted for about half an hour. During that time, there were perhaps 200 instances in which Miss Simons' behavior was clearly contingent on that of the child. The general therapeutic goals were to diminish Karen's crying, weaken the compulsive control of the doll, and begin developing more constructive forms of behavior that Karen could use to manipulate the environment herself. The third goal was the most important, and during the encounter it became clear that the extinction of the crying and the weakened control of the doll were byproducts of the reinforcement of other behavior.

Miss Simons placed Karen on a rocking horse in the playroom and began to rock her and sing to her. The rocking and singing stopped the child's crying. Then, for brief periods, Miss Simons kept on singing but stopped rocking. She sensed very accurately how long the pause could be without the child's beginning to cry again.

After a few minutes of this, the therapist took the doll from the child and placed it on a table. But she moved the table very close to Karen so that the child could easily take the doll back again. When she leaned over to do so, Karen rocked *herself* slightly. From then on, Miss Simons sang only when Karen rocked herself, which Karen did more and more frequently.

Miss Simons placed the doll on the table several times and the child calmly took it back. Then Karen *herself* put the doll on the table. Miss Simons began to rock the horse vigorously. The intensity of her voice as she sang kept pace with the rocking.

Up to this time, Miss Simons sang whenever the child rocked herself, but now she occasionally did not sing even though the child rocked. As this new situation began, Karen took the doll back off the table—having been without it for more than a full minute for the first time since her arrival at Linwood.

As she picked up the doll, it accidentally dropped to the floor. Karen began to cry. "Do you want to pick it up?" Miss Simons asked. "I'll help you." She lifted Karen off the horse and the *child* picked up the doll. When Miss Simons asked if she wanted to get up again, Karen raised her hands and Miss Simons helped her climb back into the saddle.

Karen dropped the doll again, and again Miss Simons helped her pick it up and get back on the horse. This time Karen came closer to mounting by herself, though Miss Simons still provided some support. The therapist rocked the horse vigorously and moved the doll to a couch, not far away but out of reach, and she stopped the rocking for a moment. Karen glanced at the doll and then withdrew her attention. Miss Simons picked up the doll and tapped it rhythmically; Karen looked at her, made a sound, and began to rock in time with the tapping. Miss Simons gave her the doll.

The next time the therapist took the doll away, Karen cried but kept on rocking. Miss Simons began to sing, which stopped the crying. Then she took the child off the horse so that Karen could get the doll from the couch. They sat together on the couch for a few moments, the child on the therapist's lap. When Karen tried to persuade Miss Simons to go back to the horse by pulling her arm in that direction, Miss Simons smiled and picked the child up but carried her in another direction.

Here there seemed to be a deliberate switch in contingencies. Miss Simons had developed a repertoire of performances in Karen that involved the rocking horse. Now she had shifted to a new set of reinforcers, picking Karen up and interacting with her through body contact and singing. She did not reinforce any attempts to go back to the horse. I don't know what Miss Simons would have done if Karen had struggled in her arms and continued gesturing toward the horse, but I suspect she knew this was improbable before she made the shift.

Even though the behavioral processes that operated here were the same ones I knew from laboratory experience, I would not have been able to put them into practice as Miss Simons did. For example, I might have kept Karen on the horse, without the doll, until her crying stopped. What Miss Simons did instead was wait until Karen's behavior was strongly controlled by rocking and singing before she took the doll away. Later, when Karen dropped the doll and began to cry, Miss Simons reacted at once and used the doll itself to reward the girl for picking it up.

Observation of Jeanne Simons' therapy has taught me many new ways in which the behavior of autistic children can be developed. As for her, she says she is more aware of her own actions. She sees more clearly the individual elements in her complex interchange with a child and has a better understanding of the specific effect of each small act. This helps her refine and modify her procedures and also allows her to describe them more clearly for the staff.

"I think I can explain little step-by-step procedures now so that people don't just look blindly at me with awe," she says. "I'm not even sure intuition is so mysterious. I think it's having eyes all over the place and seeing the tiny little things that children are doing. . . . And I am able to see the tiny little steps and explain much better what I am doing with the children. So the magic is out of Linwood—which I think is wonderful!"

Biographies

ATKINSON   BERNSTEIN   BESDINE   BESSELL   BIJOU   BRUNER

RICHARD C. ATKINSON ("The Computer as a Tutor") joined the faculty of Stanford University in 1956, after receiving his Ph.B. from the University of Chicago and his doctorate from Indiana University. He is a professor of psychology and holds courtesy appointments in the Schools of Education and Engineering. Dr. Atkinson is coauthor of the fourth edition of Ernest Hilgard's textbook, *Introduction to Psychology* (1967), and a frequent contributor to scholarly and professional journals. His chief research interest is learning theory, particulary the formation and testing of mathematical models for human learning and memory.

EMMANUEL BERNSTEIN ("What Does a Summerhill Old School Tie Look Like?") entered the doctoral program in counseling psychology at the University of Oregon after completing his undergraduate work at the University of Pennsylvania. He decided to work with children of every age in order to know them as fully as possible. He has been a nursery-school teacher, a recreation worker, a children's receptionist at a child guidance clinic, a psychological interviewer, an elementary-school teacher, a high-school counselor, and a college instructor.

It was while he taught emotionally disturbed children with reading problems at the Kingsley School in Boston that he became interested in Summerhill. Since that time he has used modified Summerhill techniques. In 1967, along with the faculty of the Johnston, Rhode Island, public schools, Bernstein wrote a Summerhill summer reading program for underachievers about to enter junior high school.

He is currently in the process of writing a book, to be titled "Living with Freedom."

MATTHEW BESDINE ("Mrs. Oedipus") considers himself basically a Freudian psychoanalyst in private practice. Having taken on teaching duties as a clinical professor at Adelphi University's post-doctoral program in psychotherapy and psychoanalysis, at the National Psychological Association for Psychoanalysis, and at the Institute for Practicing Psychotherapists, Dr. Besdine has in a sense come full cycle, since he started out as a graduate of the City College of New York in 1926, prepared to teach history in the New York City schools.

The late Clara Thompson invited him to study at the William Alanson White Institute, and he was among a group of students who later arranged a series of private seminars with Theodore Reik to complete their training. This nucleus became the charter membership of the NPAP in 1948. At about the same time, Dr. Besdine completed his residence credits in the doctoral program in clinical psychology at New York University.

Dr. Besdine has been president of NPAP, co-chairman of the Joint Council for Mental Health Services and a fellow of the Center of Human Development at the Hebrew University in Jerusalem, among other things. He is presently doing a psychoanalytic study of Isadora Duncan and other female geniuses.

HAROLD BESSELL ("The Content Is the Medium: The Confidence Is the Message"), a clinical psychologist in private practice, was born in New York City, attended college in Florida, and did his doctoral studies at Purdue University in Indiana. His professional experience has taken him from Kansas, where he was chief clinical psychologist at the Wichita Veterans' Administration Mental Hygiene Clinic, to California, where his offices are located in La Jolla.

His concern for young children is longstanding, and his doctoral dissertation was written on the relation of parental attitudes to the behavior of preschool children. Bessell's major interest at present is the Human Development Program.

SIDNEY W. BIJOU ("The Mentally Retarded Child") is a professor of psychology and director of the Child Behavior Laboratory at the University of Illinois. Before joining the Illinois faculty, he taught psychology and served as director of the Developmental Psychology Laboratory at the University of Washington for almost 20 years.

Bijou received his B.S. from the University of Florida, his M.A. from Columbia, and his Ph.D. from the University of Iowa. He has been editor of the *Journal of Experimental Child Psychology*, associate editor of the *International Review of Research in Mental Retardation*, and a frequent contributor to professional journals. He is a member of the Research Advisory Board for the National Association for Retarded Children, the American Psychological Association, and the Society for Research in Child Development.

JEROME BRUNER ("Up from Helplessness"), who helped found Harvard's Center for Cognitive Studies in 1960, is a graduate of Duke University. Bruner received his Ph.D. from Harvard in 1941, joined the Harvard faculty in 1945, and has been a professor of psychology there since 1952. He has published many books and articles on the nature of cognitive processes, including *On Knowing: Essays for the Left Hand* and *Toward a Theory of Instruction*.

Dr. Bruner has served on committees advising the White House, the State Department, the United Nations, the Department of Defense, the National Science Foundation, and the National Institutes of Health; he is a founding member of the National Academy of Education and a past president of the

M. COLE   S. COLE   CRAMER   FERSTER   FLACKS   GOLDIAMOND   THE HARLOWS

American Psychological Association. In 1962, the APA awarded him its Distinguished Scientific Award.

MICHAEL COLE (coauthor, "Russian Nursery Schools") is taking part in a new interdisciplinary program for the study of language and development at the Irvine campus of the University of California. In this program anthropologists, linguists, psychologists, and other social scientists bring their skills to bear on the problem of cultural change and development.

Dr. Cole began his research on human learning during his doctoral program at Indiana University. Then, as a postdoctoral fellow in the Soviet-American Exchange Program, he studied at Moscow University under Alexander Luria. There he was introduced to cross-cultural research on the development of cognitive processes.

While at Stanford University, he became interested in a mathematics-learning project in Africa and now commutes regularly between California and Liberia.

SHEILA COLE (coauthor, "Russian Nursery Schools") with her husband, Michael, spent the summer of 1966 in the Soviet Union, helping with preparations for the 18th International Congress of Psychologists and gathering material on Soviet nursery schools.

Mrs. Cole received her B.A. from Indiana University and her M.S. from the Columbia Graduate School of Journalism. She has worked on several newspapers, usually as an education writer, and is now a free-lance journalist.

PHEBE CRAMER, contributing editor, wrote the overviews for this collection. She has taught developmental psychology at Barnard College, Columbia University,

where she was assistant professor of psychology, and at the University of California, Berkeley. Currently, she is research associate at the Institute of Human Learning at Berkeley.

Dr. Cramer obtained her B.A. in psychology from the University of California, Berkeley, and her Ph.D., in clinical psychology, from New York University in 1962. In addition to working as a clinical psychologist in hospitals and clinics, she has maintained a strong interest in research, particularly in the areas of verbal behavior and cognition. Recently, she has been investigating the role of associative processes in thinking. Last year she published a book, *Word Association*, that reviewed this area of study.

C. B. FERSTER ("The Autistic Child") is a professor of psychology at Georgetown University in Washington, D.C. For several years before joining the Georgetown faculty, he served as a director and as senior research associate at the Institute for Behavioral Research in Silver Spring, Maryland, working under a research career development award from the National Institutes of Health.

Dr. Ferster did his undergraduate work at Rutgers University and received his M.A. and Ph.D. from Columbia. After leaving Columbia, he spent five years as a research fellow at Harvard, and then moved on for more research and teaching at the Yerkes Laboratory of Primate Biology in Florida, the Institute of Psychiatric Research at Indiana University, and the University of Maryland.

He is coauthor of *Behavior Principles* (with M. C. Perrott, 1968) and of *Schedules of Reinforcement* (with B. F. Skinner, 1957) and has written more than 50 articles for professional journals.

RICHARD FLACKS ("Student Activists: Result, Not Revolt"), a former national officer of Students for a Democratic

Society, is now assistant professor of sociology at the University of Chicago. His Ph.D. work, done with Theodore Newcomb, was a study of Bennington College, its alumnae and students, published as *Persistence and Change* (Wiley, 1967).

ISRAEL GOLDIAMOND ("Moral Behavior: A Functional Analysis") is a professor in the Department of Psychology and Psychiatry at the University of Chicago, where he received his Ph.D. in experimental psychology with an additional major in clinical psychology.

Until recently he was executive director of the Institute for Behavioral Research and a professor at Johns Hopkins University School of Medicine.

He has been actively engaged in the experimental analysis of perception and signal detection and of problems of clinical, social, and educational relevance. His research has included the development of specific programs to alter the behaviors studied.

HARRY and MARGARET HARLOW ("The Young Monkeys") are famous for their work with surrogate mothers, both wire and cloth. During the last ten years the Harlows have discovered a variety of affection ties in monkeys. They have experimentally produced social and asocial monkeys, good and bad mothers, as well as sexually adjusted and maladjusted monkeys.

Dr. Harlow, a past president of the American Psychological Association, received his Ph.D. from Stanford and went to the University of Wisconsin in 1930 to "enrich the literature on rodents." When he arrived, he found that the university had demolished its animal laboratory to make room for a building finally erected thirty years later. In desperation, he turned to the Madison Zoo—and to the monkeys. "For better or worse," he says, "I became forever a monkey man."

HESS   KAGAN   KAVANAUGH   KELLOGG   KOHLBERG   LENT   NEILL   RISLEY

Mrs. Harlow came to the university as a specialist in human development but soon broadened her interests to include other primates.

ROBERT D. HESS ("Political Attitudes in Children") did his undergraduate work at the University of California, Berkeley, then spent almost 20 years at the University of Chicago. In 1966 he went to Stanford as a fellow at the Center for Advanced Study in the Behavioral Sciences and is now Lee Jacks Professor of Child Education and professor of psychology at Stanford.

Hess received his Ph.D. in human development from Chicago in 1950. He was chairman of the Committee on Human Development from 1959 to 1964, then professor of human development and education, and, during his last few years on the Chicago faculty, director of the Urban Child Center and the Early Education Research Center.

JEROME KAGAN ("The Many Faces of Response" and "Sex-Role Identity") is a professor of developmental psychology at Harvard. Doctoral studies at Yale and a position at Ohio State University preceded his Army service, during which Kagan did a research study on attrition at West Point. He found that the poor risks were youths who were aware of a bad or hostile relationship with their fathers.

Later research at the Fels Research Institute, Antioch College, resulted in *Birth to Maturity*, 1963 winner of the Hofheimer Prize for research by the American Psychiatric Association.

ROBERT E. KAVANAUGH ("The Grim Generation") is Revelle College Counselor, University of California, San Diego. In his work with students, he concentrates on the solution of problems that interfere with academic achievement or personal growth. Kavanaugh has been

a management consultant, a child-welfare worker, and a member of the faculty at Michigan State University. He has been involved in marriage, family- and sex-education clinics and programs. His fields are both philosophy and the social sciences.

RHODA KELLOGG ("Understanding Children's Art") is the executive director of San Francisco's 80-year-old Golden Gate Kindergarten Association and administrator of the Phoebe A. Hearst Preschool Learning Center, a model kindergarten operated by the Association. With more than 40 years' experience in working with and observing children, Miss Kellogg has received widespread recognition for her work in preschool education. She is perhaps better known, however, as an international authority on preschool art. She hopes to show that certain children's reading difficulties can be prevented by analyzing the way they draw as preschoolers.

LAWRENCE KOHLBERG ("The Child as a Moral Philosopher") received his Ph.D. in psychology at the University of Chicago. A postdoctoral residence at Children's Hospital, Boston, "confirmed my opinion that psychoanalysis had little to offer the systematic study of the development of moral ideals and feelings." Dr. Kohlberg then spent two years at Yale, studying psychosexual development and identification in early and mid-childhood. A year at the Center for Advanced Study in the Behavioral Sciences was followed by five years at the University of Chicago. Dr. Kohlberg then spent a year at the Harvard Human Development Laboratory and has now settled at Harvard as professor of education and social psychology.

JAMES R. LENT ("Mimosa Cottage: Experiment in Hope") specializes in applying the principles of operant conditioning

to the problems of handicapped children. He is particularly interested in programs that allow the placement of mentally retarded children in the community.

After receiving his doctorate in special education from Syracuse University, Lent worked with handicapped children in several states. He joined the staff of the Parsons Research Center in 1964. The Mimosa Cottage Project, financed by a National Institute of Mental Health grant, is conducted by the Research Center under the joint auspices of Parsons State Hospital and Training Center and the Bureau of Child Research at the University of Kansas.

ALEXANDER SUTHERLAND NEILL ("Can I Come to Summerhill?"), headmaster of Summerhill School, was born 86 years ago in Scotland. His ideas remain as controversial today as when they caused his resignation from the staff of King Alfred School in 1920. The forerunner of Summerhill was founded in 1921, when Neill set up an international school in Dresden, Germany. He moved this school first to the Austrian Tyrol and then, after seven months of harassment by the local peasants and the Austrian government, to England.

Neill, who holds the M.A. degree, is a graduate of Edinburgh University, where his major subject was English. He has written a number of books on education and child psychology.

TODD RISLEY ("Learning and Lollipops") began his professional career by studying the uses of operant conditioning with autistic and severely retarded children. Now, at preschools for culturally deprived four-year-olds, he is trying to apply behavioral analysis to the problems of more normal children.

Dr. Risley was born in Alaska, graduated from San Diego State College, and

ROSENTHAL   TRABASSO   WOHLWILL

received his M.S. and Ph.D. degrees in psychology from the University of Washington. Before joining the University of Kansas faculty, he taught psychology at Florida State University. In addition to his preschool research, Risley conducts laboratory research on basic questions of animal behavior.

ROBERT ROSENTHAL ("Self-fulfilling Prophecy") is a professor of social psychology at Harvard University. Born in Germany, which he left in 1938, Rosenthal received his Ph.D. from the University of California, Los Angeles, in 1956. He has extensive training and experience in the field of clinical psychology. In 1960 he was awarded the AAAS Socio-Psychological Prize (with Kermit Fode) for research on experimenter expectancy effects, and in 1967 he received with Lenore Jacobson the American Psychological Association's Cattell Fund Award for work on teacher expectancy effects in the classroom.

Dr. Rosenthal is the author of many articles and several books. His most recently published book is *Pygmalion in the Classroom*, coauthored by Lenore Jacobson. His current research interests include methods to control experimenter effects, differences in the responses of volunteers and nonvolunteers in behavioral research, and expectancy effects in everyday life.

TOM TRABASSO ("Pay Attention") is a professor of psychology at Princeton University. At the time his article was written, he was at the University of California, Los Angeles. He teaches courses in general and quantitative psychology, learning, and cognitive processes. Prior to going to UCLA he did postdoctoral work at Stanford University. Dr. Trabasso did his undergraduate work at Union College, where he majored in psychology, and went on to receive his M.A. and Ph.D. degrees from Michigan State University. His research interests have centered on human conceptual behavior and the application of mathematical models to these problems. His recent book with Gordon Bower, *Attention in Learning* (Wiley, 1968), represents a synthesis of these methods and interests.

JOACHIM F. WOHLWILL ("The Mystery of the Prelogical Child") is a professor of psychology and director of the Graduate Training Program in Developmental Psychology at Clark University. Dr. Wohlwill worked with Jean Piaget at the Institut Rousseau in Geneva. He was graduated from Harvard in 1947 and received his Ph.D. in 1957 from the University of California, Berkeley. His main present interests are the development of perception and thinking in the child and formal instruction as opposed to spontaneous activity. This has led him to a related interest—people's responses to their physical environments, both natural and man made.

Bibliographies

I The Development of Cognitive Abilities in Early Childhood

Up from Helplessness

THE AUTOMATIC GRASPING RESPONSES OF INFANTS. T. E. Twitchell in *Journal of Neurophysiologia*, Vol. 3, pp. 247–259, 1965.

THE DEVELOPMENT OF LANGUAGE. D. McNeill in *Carmichael's Manual of Child Psychology*. P. H. Mussen, ed. Wiley (in press).

PROCESSES OF GROWTH IN INFANCY. J. S. Bruner. Clark University Press and Barre Publishers, 1968.

STRUCTURAL ANTHROPOLOGY. C. Lévi-Strauss. Basic Books, 1963.

The Many Faces of Response

BIRTH TO MATURITY: A STUDY IN PSYCHOLOGICAL DEVELOPMENT. J. Kagan, H. A. Moss. Wiley, 1962.

IMPULSIVE AND REFLECTIVE CHILDREN: SIGNIFICANCE OF CONCEPTUAL TEMPO. J. Kagan in *Learning and the Educational Process*. J. D. Krumboltz, ed. Rand McNally, 1965.

INFANTS' DIFFERENTIAL REACTIONS TO FAMILIAR AND DISTORTED FACES. J. Kagan, B. A. Henker, A. Hen-Tov, J. Levine, M. Lewis in *Child Development*, Vol. 37, pp. 519–532, 1966.

ON THE NEED FOR RELATIVISM. J. Kagan in *American Psychologist*, Vol. 22, pp. 131–142, 1967.

PERSONALITY AND THE LEARNING PROCESS. J. Kagan in *Daedalus*, Vol. 94, pp. 553–563, 1965.

PERSONALITY, BEHAVIOR, AND TEMPERAMENT. J. Kagan in *Human Development*. Frank Falkner, ed. Saunders, 1966.

STIMULUS-SCHEMA DISCREPANCY AND ATTENTION IN THE INFANT. R. B. McCall, J. Kagan in *Journal of Experimental Child Psychology*, Vol. 5, pp. 381–390, 1967.

The Mystery of the Prelogical Child

THE CHILD'S CONCEPTION OF GEOMETRY. J. Piaget, B. Inhelder, A. Szaminska. Basic Books, 1960.

THE CHILD'S CONCEPTION OF NUMBER. J. Piaget. Norton, 1965.

CONCEPT GROWTH AND THE EDUCATION OF THE CHILD. J. G. Wallace. National Foundation for Educational Research in England and Wales, 1966.

COUNTING AND MEASURING. E. M. Churchill. University of Toronto Press, 1961.

THE DEVELOPMENTAL PSYCHOLOGY OF JEAN PIAGET. J. H. Flavell. Van Nostrand, 1963.

THE GROWTH OF BASIC MATHEMATICAL AND SCIENTIFIC CONCEPTS IN CHILDREN. K. Lovell. University of London Press, 1962.

INTELLIGENCE AND EXPERIENCE. McV. J. Hunt. Ronald Press, 1961.

Pay Attention

ATTENTION IN DISCRIMINATION LEARNING. E. Lovejoy. Holden-Day, 1968.

ATTENTION IN LEARNING. T. Trabasso, G. H. Bower. Wiley, 1968.

THE DISCRIMINATION PROCESS AND DEVELOPMENT. B. J. Fellows. Pergamon Press, 1968.

THE ROLE OF ATTENTION IN RETARDATE DISCRIMINATION LEARNING. D. Zeaman, B. J. House in *Handbook of Mental Deficiency*. N. R. Ellis, ed. McGraw-Hill, 1963.

SELECTIVE ATTENTION IN ANIMAL DISCRIMINATION LEARNING. N. J. MacKintosh in *Psychological Bulletin*, Vol. 64, pp. 124–140, 1965.

Understanding Children's Art

ANALYZING CHILDREN'S ART. R. Kellogg. National Press, 1969.

CHILDREN'S DRAWINGS AS MEASURES OF INTELLECTUAL MATURITY. A REVISION AND EXTENSION OF THE GOODENOUGH DRAW-A-MAN TEST. D. B. Harris. Harcourt, Brace & World, 1963.

THE ETERNAL PRESENT. S. Giedion. Pantheon Books, 1962.

EYE AND BRAIN. R. L. Gregory. McGraw-Hill, 1966.

FORM SIMILARITY BETWEEN PHOSPHENES OF ADULTS AND PRE-SCHOOL CHILDREN'S SCRIBBLING. R. Kellogg, M. Knoll, J. Kugler in *Nature*, Vol. 208, No. 5015, p. 1129, 1965.

RHODA KELLOGG CHILD ART COLLECTION. R. Kellogg. Microfiche cards showing 7500 drawings of children aged 24–40 months. Microcard Editions, Inc., 1967.

II Education and the Development of the Child

Self-fulfilling Prophecy

CLEVER HANS, THE HORSE OF MR. VON OSTEN. O. Pfungst. C. L. Rahn, tr. Holt, Rinehart and Winston, 1965.

EFFECT OF EXPERIMENTER'S EXPECTANCIES (THE "ROSENTHAL EFFECT") ON CHILDREN'S ABILITY TO LEARN TO SWIM. J. R. Burnham, D. M. Hartsough. Paper presented at the meeting of the Midwestern Psychological Association. Chicago, May 1968.

EXPERIMENTER EFFECTS IN BEHAVIORAL RESEARCH. R. Rosenthal. Appleton-Century-Crofts, 1966.

INFLUENCE OF BIASED PSYCHOLOGICAL REPORTS ON TEACHER BEHAVIOR AND PUPIL PERFORMANCE. W. V. Beez in *Proceedings of the 76th Annual Convention of the American Psychological Association*, 1968.

PYGMALION IN THE CLASSROOM: TEACHER EXPECTATION AND PUPILS' INTELLECTUAL DEVELOPMENT. R. Rosenthal, L. Jacobson. Holt, Rinehart and Winston, 1968.

Russian Nursery Schools

A HANDBOOK OF CONTEMPORARY SOVIET PSYCHOLOGY. M. Cole, I. Maltzman, eds. Basic Books, 1968.

PROGRAMMA VOSPITANIIA V DETSKOM SADU [The Program of Education in Nursery School]. M. V. Zaluzhskaia, ed. Gosidarstvennoe Uchebno-Pedagogicheskoe Izdatel'stvo Ministerstua Prosveshcheniia [Ministry of Education, RSFSR]. Moscow, 1962.

TEORIIA I PRAKTIKA SENSORNOVOV VOCPITANIIA V DETSKOM SADU [The Theory and Practice of Sensory Training in Nursery School]. A. P. Usovoi, N. P. Sakulinoi, eds. Proveshcheniia, Moscow, 1965.

The Content Is the Medium: The Confidence Is the Message

CLIENT-CENTERED THERAPY. C. Rogers. Houghton Mifflin, 1959.

THE INTERPERSONAL THEORY OF PSYCHIATRY. H. S. Sullivan. Norton, 1953.

METHODS IN HUMAN DEVELOPMENT. H. Bessell, U. Palomares. 1967. Available from the author.

NEUROSIS AND HUMAN GROWTH. K. Horney. Norton, 1950.

SOCIAL AND EMOTIONAL DEVELOPMENT OF THE PRESCHOOL CHILD. K. Bridges. Kegan Paul, 1931.

STABILITY AND CHANGE IN HUMAN CHARACTERISTICS. B. Bloom. Wiley, 1964.

A THREE-DIMENSIONAL THEORY OF INTERPERSONAL BEHAVIOR. W. Schutz. Holt, Rinehart and Winston, 1960.

Can I Come to Summerhill?

FREEDOM, NOT LICENSE! A. S. Neill. Hart, 1966.

SUMMERHILL: A RADICAL APPROACH TO CHILD REARING. A. S. Neill. Hart, 1960.

What Does a Summerhill Old School Tie Look Like?

EDUCATION AND ECSTASY. G. B. Leonard. Delacorte, 1968.

THE FREE SCHOOLS OF LEICESTERSHIRE COUNTY. *Christian Science Monitor*, May 14, 1966.

FREEDOM, NOT LICENSE! A. S. Neill. Hart, 1966.

SUMMERHILL. A. S. Neill. Hart, 1960.

SUMMERHILL: A FOLLOW-UP STUDY OF ITS STUDENTS. E. Bernstein in *Journal of Humanistic Psychology*, Vol. 8, No. 2, Fall, 1968.

SUMMERHILL AFTER 50 YEARS. E. Bernstein in *The New Era*, Vol. 48, No. 2, pp. 30–31, 1967.

TEACHING CHILDREN TO THINK; SCHOOLS FOR CHILDREN. J. Featherstone in *New Republic*, August 19, September 2, September 9, 1967.

THIRTY SCHOOLS TELL THEIR STORY. Wilfred Aiken in *Adventure in American Education*, Harper & Row, 1943, Vol. 5.

Political Attitudes in Children

CHILDREN AND THE DEATH OF A PRESIDENT: MULTI-DISCIPLINARY STUDIES. M. Wolfenstein, G. Kliman. Doubleday, 1965.

CHILDREN AND POLITICS. F. Greenstein. Yale University Press, 1965.

DEVELOPMENT OF POLITICAL ATTITUDES IN CHILDREN. R. D. Hess, J. V. Torney. Aldine, 1967.

POLITICAL LIFE: WHY PEOPLE GET INVOLVED IN POLITICS. R. Lane. Free Press, 1959.

POLITICAL SOCIALIZATION: A STUDY IN THE PSYCHOLOGY OF POLITICAL BEHAVIOR. H. Hyman. Free Press, 1959.

The Computer as a Tutor

COMPUTER-ASSISTED INSTRUCTIONS IN INITIAL READING. R. C. Atkinson, D. N. Hansen in *Reading Research Quarterly*. Vol. 2, pp. 5–25, 1966.

COMPUTER-BASED INSTRUCTION IN INITIAL READING: A PROGRESS REPORT ON THE STANFORD PROJECT. H. A. Wilson, R. C. Atkinson in Technical Report 119, Institute for Mathematical Studies in the Social Sciences, Stanford University, 1967. (To be published in *Basic Studies in Reading*, H. Levin, J. Williams, eds. Harper & Row.)

HUMAN MEMORY: A PROPOSED SYSTEM AND ITS CONTRACT PROCESSES. R. C. Atkinson, R. M. Shiffrin in *The Psychology of Learning and Motivation: Advances in Research and Theory*, Vol. 2. K. W. Spence, J. T. Spence, eds. Academic Press, 1968.

III The Development of the Individual

The Young Monkeys

AFFECTION IN PRIMATES. M. K. Harlow, H. F. Harlow in *Discovery*, Vol. 27, pp. 11–17, 1966.

BEHAVIORAL ASPECTS OF REPRODUCTION IN PRIMATES. H. F. Harlow, W. Danforth Joslyn, M. G. Senko, A. Dopp in *Journal of Animal Science*, Vol. 25, pp. 49–67, 1966.

LEARNING TO LOVE. H. F. Harlow, M. K. Harlow in *American Scientist*, Vol. 54, pp. 244–272, 1966.

LOVE IN INFANT MONKEYS. H. F. Harlow in *Scientific American*, June, 1959.

MATERNAL BEHAVIOR OF RHESUS MONKEYS DEPRIVED OF MOTHERING AND PEER ASSOCIATION IN INFANCY. H. F. Harlow, M. K. Harlow, R. O. Dodsworth, G. L. Arling, in *Proceedings of the American Philosophical Society*, Vol. 110, pp. 329–335, 1967.

Sex-Role Identity

BIRTH TO MATURITY. J. Kagan, H. Moss. Wiley, 1962.

THE CHILD'S SEX ROLE CLASSIFICATION OF SCHOOL OBJECTS. J. Kagan in *Child Development*, Vol. 35, pp. 1051–1056, 1964.

CHILD'S SYMBOLIC CONCEPTUALIZATION OF PARENTS. J. Kagan, B. Hosken, S. Watson in *Child Development*, Vol. 32, pp. 625–636, 1961.

THE CROSS-CULTURAL GENERALITY OF VISUAL-VERBAL SYNESTHETIC TENDENCIES. C. E. Osgood in *Behavioral Science*, Vol. 5, pp. 146–169, 1960.

MEN AND WOMEN: PERSONALITY PATTERNS AND CONTRAST. E. M. Bennett, L. R. Cohen in *Genetic Psychology Monographs*, Vol. 60, pp. 101–153, 1959.

PERSONALITY: DYNAMICS, DEVELOPMENT AND ASSESSMENT. I. L. Janis, J. Kagan, G. Mahl, R. Holt, eds. Harcourt, Brace & World, 1969.

Mrs. Oedipus

THE CREATIVE IMAGINATION. H. M. Ruitenbeek, ed. Quadrangle, 1965.

THE DEVELOPMENTAL PSYCHOLOGY OF JEAN PIAGET. J. H. Flavell. Van Nostrand, 1963.

THE FIRST YEAR OF LIFE. R. A. Spitz. International Universities Press, 1965.

JOCASTA AND OEDIPUS: ANOTHER LOOK. M. Besdine in *Pathways in Child Guidance*. Bureau of Child Guidance, New York City Board of Education, March 1968.

THE JOCASTA COMPLEX, MOTHERING AND GENIUS. M. Besdine in *The Psychoanalytic Review*, Vol. 55, No. 2, 1968.

THE MAN BEHIND THE ARTIST: A PSYCHOANALYTIC STUDY OF MICHELANGELO BUONARROTTI. M. Besdine (in press).

THE MATURATIONAL PROCESSES AND THE FACILITATING ENVIRONMENT: STUDIES IN THE THEORY OF EMOTIONAL DEVELOPMENT. D. W. Winnicott. International Universities Press, 1965.

PATTERNS OF MOTHERING: MATERNAL INFLUENCE DURING INFANCY. S. Brody. International Universities Press, 1956.

The Child as a Moral Philosopher

THE DEVELOPMENT OF CHILDREN'S ORIENTATIONS TOWARD A MORAL ORDER: 1. SEQUENCE IN THE DEVELOPMENT OF MORAL THOUGHT. L. Kohlberg in *Vita Humana*, Vol. 6, pp. 11–33(b), 1963.

DEVELOPMENT OF MORAL CHARACTER AND IDEOLOGY. L. Kohlberg in *Review of Child Development Research*. M. L. Hoffman, ed. Russell Sage, 1964.

EQUALITY. J. Wilson. Hutchison, 1966.

THE LANGUAGE OF MORALS. R. M. Hare. Oxford University Press, 1952.

MORAL EDUCATION IN THE SCHOOLS: A DEVELOPMENTAL VIEW. L. Kohlberg in *School Review*, Vol. 74, pp. 1–30, 1966.

MORALS IN EVOLUTION: A STUDY OF COMPARATIVE ETHICS. L. T. Hobhouse. London, 1951.

THE PSYCHOLOGY OF CHARACTER DEVELOPMENT. R. F. Peck, R. J. Havighurst. Wiley, 1960.

STAGES IN THE DEVELOPMENT OF MORAL THOUGHT AND ACTION. L. Kohlberg. Holt, Rinehart & Winston (in preparation).

Moral Behavior: A Functional Analysis

DISCRIMINATIVE PROPERTIES OF PUNISHMENT. W. Holz, N. Azrin in *Journal of the Experimental Analysis of Behavior*, Vol. 4, pp. 225–232, 1961.

A FUNCTIONAL ANALYSIS OF BEHAVIOR. I. Goldiamond, D. M. Thompson (in preparation).

MOTIVATIONAL ASPECTS OF ESCAPE FROM PUNISHMENT. N. Azrin, et al., in *Journal of the Experimental Analysis of Behavior*, Vol. 8, pp. 31–44, 1965.

REINFORCEMENT THEORY. D. Premack in *Nebraska Symposium on Motivation: 1965*. M. Jones, ed. University of Nebraska Press, 1965.

STIMULUS CONTROL. H. S. Terrace in *Operant Behavior: Areas of Research and Application*. W. Honig, ed. Appleton-Century-Crofts, 1966.

THE WISDOM OF THE BEHAVIOR: LEARNING, CONDITIONING, AND PSYCHOPATHOLOGY. I. Goldiamond in *Neurobiological Aspects of Psychopathology*. J. Zubin, C. Shagass, eds. Grune and Stratton, 1968.

All over the country today students are taking an active role in the quality of their education. They're telling administrators what they like and what they don't like about their campus communities. They're telling teachers what they like and what they don't like about their courses.

This response card offers you a unique opportunity as a student to tell a publisher what you like and what you don't like about his book.

FIRST CLASS
PERMIT NO. 59
DEL MAR, CALIF.

BUSINESS REPLY MAIL
No Postage Stamp Necessary if Mailed in the United States.

Postage will be paid by

CRM BOOKS

Del Mar, California | 92014

EVALUATION QUESTIONNAIRE

1. **Your school:**_____

   _____

2. **Your year:** ☐ Freshman ☐ Sophomore ☐ Junior ☐ Senior
   ☐ Graduate student

3. **Title of course in which READINGS was assigned:**_____

   _____

4. **Course level:** ☐ First year ☐ Second year ☐ Third year
   ☐ Fourth year ☐ Graduate

5. **Length of course:** ☐ Quarter ☐ Trimester ☐ Semester ☐ Year

6. **How many articles were you assigned to read?**_____

7. **How many articles did you read that weren't assigned?**_____

8. **Did you find the majority of the articles:**
   ☐ Very interesting ☐ Fairly interesting ☐ Not interesting

9. **If you think there's a gap between what you're studying and
   what's going on in the world today, did you find that the articles
   in READINGS helped bridge that gap?** ☐ Yes ☐ No

   If yes, how?
   ☐ Shed light on events in
   the news.
   ☐ Offered insight into personal problems and gave me
   ideas about solving them.
   ☐ Discussed the problems of
   individuals in ways that
   helped explain people I know.
   ☐ Offered insight into social
   problems and gave me ideas
   about solving them.
   ☐ Gave me information and
   arguments for attacking ideas
   I disagree with.
   ☐ Presented information and
   arguments that changed my
   own ideas.
   ☐ Other:_____

   _____

   _____

   If no, why?
   ☐ Seemed irrelevant to
   events in the news.
   ☐ Didn't identify personal
   problems important to me or
   suggest ways to solve them.
   ☐ Didn't make discussion of
   individual problems relevant
   to people I know.
   ☐ Didn't identify social
   problems important to me or
   suggest ways to solve them.
   ☐ Discussed individual and
   social problems but didn't
   make them important to me
   personally or show ways
   to deal with them.
   ☐ Didn't cause me to
   change my ideas about any
   important topic.
   ☐ Other:_____

10. **How interesting were the materials used in your course?
    How do you rate them?**
    Rating: 1 = Most interesting   7 = Least interesting
    Materials used:

Materials used:	1	2	3	4	5	6	7
☐ **READINGS**	☐ 1	☐ 2	☐ 3	☐ 4	☐ 5	☐ 6	☐ 7
☐ Textbook	☐ 1	☐ 2	☐ 3	☐ 4	☐ 5	☐ 6	☐ 7
☐ Lectures	☐ 1	☐ 2	☐ 3	☐ 4	☐ 5	☐ 6	☐ 7
☐ Films	☐ 1	☐ 2	☐ 3	☐ 4	☐ 5	☐ 6	☐ 7
☐ Laboratory work	☐ 1	☐ 2	☐ 3	☐ 4	☐ 5	☐ 6	☐ 7
☐ Paperbacks	☐ 1	☐ 2	☐ 3	☐ 4	☐ 5	☐ 6	☐ 7
☐ Other_____	☐ 1	☐ 2	☐ 3	☐ 4	☐ 5	☐ 6	☐ 7

11. **How helpful were the introductions to each article?**
    ☐ Very helpful   ☐ Sometimes helpful
    ☐ Not helpful   ☐ Did not read them

12. **Would additional materials printed with each article have
    been helpful?** ☐ Yes ☐ No
    If yes, what kind?
    ☐ Marginal outlines of key points.
    ☐ Review questions.
    ☐ Glossaries of themes and concepts.
    ☐ Other:_____

13. **What textbook did you use?**
    Author(s):_____

      Title:_____
    How would you rate it?

Content:	Level:	Illustrations:
☐ Covered each area fully.	☐ Easy to read and generally interesting.	☐ Easy to understand, attractive, informative.
☐ Too much on some topics, not enough on others.	☐ Hard to read: explanations too complicated.	☐ Inadequate: hard to understand.
☐ Seemed up to date.	☐ Quality of writing not interesting.	☐ Unclear, unattractive.
☐ Seemed out of date.		☐ Didn't help in understanding.
☐ Other: _____	☐ Other: _____	☐ Other: _____

14. **Are laboratory experiments part of your course work?**
    ☐ Yes ☐ No
    If no, would you have liked to have had the equipment and
    opportunity to do psychological experiments as part of your
    course work? ☐ Yes ☐ No

15. **Comments on course, text materials, etc.:** _____

    _____

    _____

    _____

    _____

    _____

16. **What do you think of this questionnaire?**_____

    _____

    _____

    _____

    _____

IV Contemporary Problems for Youth

The Grim Generation

THE AMERICAN COLLEGE. N. Sanford. Wiley, 1962.

NO TIME FOR YOUTH: GROWTH AND CONSTRAINT IN COLLEGE STUDENTS. J. Katz, *et al.* Jossey-Bass, 1968.

THE STUDENT AND HIS STUDIES. E. Raushenbush. Wesleyan University Press, 1964.

THE STUDENT IN HIGHER EDUCATION. J. Kaufmann, *et al.* Hazen Foundation, 1968.

THE UNCOMMITTED. K. Keniston. Harcourt, Brace & World, 1965.

YOUNG RADICALS: NOTES ON COMMITTED YOUTH. K. Keniston. Harcourt, Brace & World, 1968.

Student Activists: Result, Not Revolt

ACTIVISM AND APATHY IN CONTEMPORARY ADOLESCENTS. J. H. Block, N. Haan, M. Smith in *Contributions to the Understanding of Adolescents.* J. F. Adams, ed. Allyn & Bacon, 1967.

FROM GENERATION TO GENERATION. S. N. Eisenstadt. Free Press, 1956.

THE LIBERATED GENERATION. R. Flacks in *Journal of Social Issues* (in press).

THE PORT HURON STATEMENT. Students for a Democratic Society, 1962.

A PROPHETIC MINORITY. J. Newfield. New American Library, 1967.

STUDENT POLITICS. S. M. Lipset, ed. 1967.

THE UNCOMMITTED. K. Keniston. Harcourt, Brace & World, 1965.

V Children with Handicaps

Learning and Lollipops

CHILD DEVELOPMENT. S. W. Bijou, D. M. Baer. Appleton-Century-Crofts, 1961, 1965. Vols. 1 and 2.

CONTROL OF HUMAN BEHAVIOR. R. Ulrich, T. Stachnik, J. Mabry. Scott, Foresman, 1966.

EFFECTS OF ADULT SOCIAL REINFORCEMENT ON CHILD BEHAVIOR. F. Harris, M. M. Wolf, D. Baer in *Young Child*, Vol. 20, pp. 8–17, 1964.

ESTABLISHING FUNCTIONAL SPEECH IN ECHOLALIC CHILDREN. T. R. Risley, M. M. Wolf in *Behaviour Research and Therapy*, Vol. 5, pp. 73–88, 1967.

SCIENCE AND HUMAN BEHAVIOR. B. F. Skinner. Macmillan, 1953.

The Mentally Retarded Child

APPLICATION OF OPERANT CONDITIONING PROCEDURES TO THE BEHAVIOR PROBLEMS OF AN AUTISTIC CHILD. M. M. Wolf, T. R. Risley, H. L. Mees in *Behavior Research and Therapy*, Vol. 1, pp. 305–312, 1964.

CHILD DEVELOPMENT. S. W. Bijou, D. M. Baer. Appleton-Century-Crofts, 1961, 1965. Vols. 1 and 2.

A CONCEPTUAL APPROACH TO SOME PROBLEMS IN MENTAL RETARDATION. D. W. Zimmerman in *Psychological Record*, Vol. 15, pp. 175–183, 1965.

THE EFFECT OF SUPPLEMENTARY EXPERIENCES UPON THE BEHAVIORAL DEVELOPMENT OF INFANTS IN INSTITUTIONS. Y. Sayegh, W. Dennis in *Child Development*, Vol. 36, pp. 81–90, 1965.

FINAL NOTE ON A CASE OF EXTREME ISOLATION. K. Davis in *American Journal of Sociology*, Vol. 57, pp. 432–457, 1947.

INFANT DEVELOPMENT UNDER ENVIRONMENTAL HANDICAP. W. Dennis, P. Najarian in *Psychological Monographs General and Applied*, Vol. 71, No. 7, Whole No. 436, 1957.

POSITIVE REINFORCEMENT AND BEHAVIOR DEFICITS OF AUTISTIC CHILDREN. C. B. Ferster in *Child Development*, Vol. 32, pp. 437–456, 1961.

REINFORCEMENT AND PUNISHMENT IN THE CONTROL OF HUMAN BEHAVIOR BY SOCIAL AGENCIES. C. B. Ferster in *Psychiatric Research Reports*, Vol. 10, pp. 101–118, 1958.

Mimosa Cottage: Experiment in Hope

THE EFFECT OF AN INSTITUTION ENVIRONMENT UPON THE VERBAL DEVELOPMENT OF IMBECILE CHILDREN. J. G. Lyle in *Journal of Mental Deficiency Research*, Vol. 3, pp. 122–128, 1959.

ENVIRONMENTAL INFLUENCE ON VERBAL OUTPUT OF MENTALLY RETARDED CHILDREN. B. B. Schlanger in *Journal of Speech and Hearing Disorders*, Vol. 19, pp. 339–345, 1954.

PROGRAMMED INSTRUCTION AS AN APPROACH TO TEACHING OF READING, WRITING, AND ARITHMETIC TO RETARDED CHILDREN. S. W. Bijou *et al.* in *Psychological Record*, Vol. 16, pp. 505–552, 1966.

RESIDENTIAL CARE OF MENTALLY HANDICAPPED CHILDREN. J. Tizzard in *British Medical Journal*, Vol. 1, pp. 1041–1046, 1960.

SHIFTING STIMULUS CONTROL OF ARTICULATION RESPONSES BY OPERANT TECHNIQUES. J. McLean. Unpublished doctoral dissertation, University of Kansas, 1965.

A STUDY OF THE EFFECTS OF COMMUNITY AND INSTITUTIONAL SCHOOL CLASSES FOR TRAINABLE MENTALLY RETARDED CHILDREN. L. F. Cain, S. Levine. San Francisco State College, 1961.

The Autistic Child

ARBITRARY AND NATURAL REINFORCEMENT. C. B. Ferster in *The Psychological Record*, Vol. 17, No. 3, pp. 341–347, 1967.

AN EVALUATION OF BEHAVIOR THERAPY WITH CHILDREN. C. B. Ferster, J. Simons in *The Psychological Record*, Vol. 16, No. 1, pp. 65–71, 1966.

INFANTILE AUTISM. B. Rimland. Appleton-Century-Crofts, 1964.

OPERANT REINFORCEMENT OF INFANTILE AUTISM. C. B. Ferster in *An Evaluation of the Results of the Psychotherapies.* S. Lesse, ed. Charles C Thomas, 1968.

PERSPECTIVES IN PSYCHOLOGY: XXV, TRANSITION FROM ANIMAL LABORATORY TO CLINIC. C. B. Ferster in *The Psychological Record*, Vol. 17, No. 2, pp. 145–150, 1967.

POSITIVE REINFORCEMENT AND BEHAVIORAL DEFICITS OF AUTISTIC CHILDREN. C. B. Ferster in *Child Development*, Vol. 32, No. 3, pp. 437–456, 1961.

Index

Cover photograph by John Oldenkamp

Photographs by
Steve McCarroll: pages 8, 16, 24, 42, 48, 80, 92, 98, 102,
    128, 130, 146, 148, 154, 164
William G. Mac Donald: pages 2, 5
John Oldenkamp: pages 11, 12, 18, 27, 54, 58, 59, 60, 65,
    68, 74, 105, 108, 116, 138, 156, 161
Tom Suzuki: page 124

Illustrations by
George Price: pages 171–174

Photography courtesy Richard C. Atkinson: page 83

Illustrations courtesy Rhoda Kellogg: pages 30, 31, 33–39

CRM BOOKS
David A. Dushkin, *President and Publisher*, CRM BOOKS

Richard L. Roe, *Vice-President, CRM BOOKS, and Director, College Department*
Sales Manager, College Department: Richard M. Connelly
Fulfillment Manager, College Department: Nancy Le Clere
College Department Staff: Elaine Kleiss, Carol Walnum, La Delle Willett

Jean Smith, *Vice-President and Managing Editor*, CRM BOOKS
Senior Editor: Arlyne Lazerson
Editors: Gloria Joyce, Cecie Starr, Betsy H. Wyckoff
Editorial Assistants: Jacquelyn Estrada, Cynthia MacDonald, Johanna Price,
    Ann Scales
Rights and Permissions: Donna L. Taylor

Jo Ann Gilberg, *Vice-President, CRM BOOKS, and Director, Manufacturing and
    Production*
Production Manager: Eugene G. Schwartz
Production Supervisors: Barbara Blum, E. Cecile Mayer, P. Douglas Armstrong
Production Assistants: Georgene Martina, Patricia Perkins, Toini Jaffee
Production Staff: Mona F. Drury, Margaret M. Mesec

Tom Suzuki, *Vice-President, CRM BOOKS, and Director of Design*

Art Director: Leon Bolognese
Promotion Art Director: John Isely
Designer: George Price
Associate Designers: Catherine Flanders, Reynold Hernandez
Assistant Designers: Robert Fountain, Pamela Morehouse
Assistant Promotion Designer: John Madison Hix
Art Staff: Jacqueline McLoughlin, Kurt Kolbe.

Paul Lapolla, *Vice-President, CRM BOOKS, and Director, Psychology Today
    Book Club*
Assistant: Karen De Laria

Controller: Robert Geiserman
Assistant: Maryann Errichetti

Office Manager: Lynn D. Crosby
Assistant: Janie Fredericks

Officers of Communications/Research/Machines, Inc.
John J. Veronis, *President*; Nicolas H. Charney, *Chairman of the Board*;
David A. Dushkin, *Vice-President*; James B. Horton, *Vice-President*

This book was composed by American Book–Stratford Press, Inc., New York,
    New York
The book was printed and bound by Kingsport Press, Inc., Kingsport, Tennessee.